Gated Grief

*The Daughter of a GI
Concentration Camp Liberator
Discovers a Legacy of Trauma*

Gated Grief

*The Daughter of a GI
Concentration Camp Liberator
Discovers a Legacy of Trauma*

by

Leila Levinson

CABLE PUBLISHING

Brule, Wisconsin

GATED GRIEF
The Daughter of a GI Liberator Discovers a Legacy of Trauma

First Edition

Published by: Cable Publishing
14090 E Keinenen Rd
Brule, WI 54820

Website: www.cablepublishing.com
E-mail: nan@cablepublishing.com

Hardcover: ISBN 13: 978-1-934980-54-5
              ISBN 10: 1-934980-54-4

Soft cover: ISBN 13: 978-1-934980-55-2
              ISBN 10: 1-934980-55-2

Library of Congress Control Number: 2010933481

FRONT COVER: Prisoners and US army soldiers stand behind the gate of Buchenwald Concentration Camp on which is written *Jedem das seine*, the translation of which is "To each his just desserts." The photograph was taken shortly after US troops liberated Buchenwald, April 15, 1945. ERIC SCHWAB/AFP/Getty Images

Unless otherwise indicated, the photographs in this book were taken by the U.S. Signal Corps and were supplied by the National Archives and Records Administration.

Printed in the United States of America

To the blessed memory of my father
Reuben Levinson, M.D.

Reuben Levinson on beach at Cannes, April 1945, after two weeks of
treating survivors of Nordhausen Concentration Camp

We are not used to associating our private lives with public events.
Yet the history of families cannot be separated from the histories of
nations. To divide them is part of our denial.

—Susan Griffin, *A Chorus of Stones*

Table of Contents

Prologue

Part One - The Aftermath

Part Two - Scenes of the Crimes

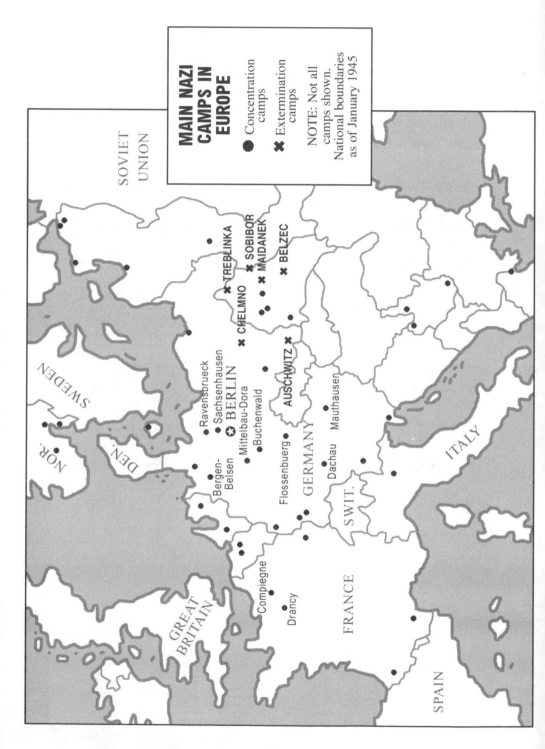

MAIN NAZI
CAMPS IN
EUROPE

● Concentration camps

✖ Extermination camps

NOTE: Not all
camps shown.
National boundaries
as of January 1945

SOVIET UNION

SWEDEN

NOR.

DEN.

GREAT BRITAIN

FRANCE

SPAIN

GERMANY

SWIT.

ITALY

✖ TREBLINKA
✖ SOBIBOR
✖ MAIDANEK
✖ BELZEC
✖ CHELMNO
✖ AUSCHWITZ

Ravensbrueck
Sachsenhausen
☆ BERLIN
Mittelbau-Dora
Buchenwald
Bergen-Belsen
Flossenburg
Dachau
Mauthausen

Compiegne
Drancy

i

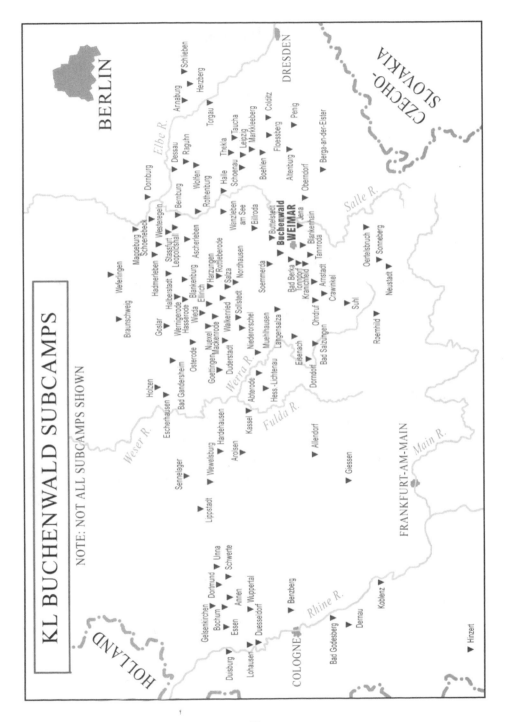

KL BUCHENWALD SUBCAMPS

NOTE: NOT ALL SUBCAMPS SHOWN

Prologue

Perth Amboy, New Jersey, 1980

It is still April 1945, and you are speeding through the heart of Germany—with its immaculate farms, its lush and manicured fields. The roofs are freshly thatched, the streets swept clean. The evident community pride echoes what you left behind in Kansas, Missouri, Virginia. In the towns, white sheets fly from every window, signaling the residents' acceptance, even welcoming, of the Allied victory. Pretty girls with pink cheeks and golden blonde hair emerge from the homes, blushing as they offer cheese, smoked ham, apples and eggs. The village mayor, sporting a clean suit and broad smile, appears and declares the Americans to be honored guests. The townspeople invite you into homes with downy beds and crisp white linens. The Army issues orders not to fraternize, because the GIs find everyone so agreeable and pleasant. But the orders do not keep you and your comrades from strolling with giggling girls who have not seen a man under seventy-years-old in months, or from accepting a home-cooked meal from the farmer, the lonely mother, the school teacher.

Then, during patrol, on the outskirts of town, the pleasant air gives way to a stench that turns the stomach and assaults the nose. Then the trees turn gray. Gray? A swipe of the finger removes what feels like ash...but from what? The answer rises in the distance, in the middle of the woods, like a vision from a Grimm's fairytale: a smokestack, belching out coal-black smoke. A few steps closer, wooden guard stations and barbed wire become visible. It is some kind of compound.

Is this one of those concentration camps like the ones in the U.S. for the Japanese? Is this where they keep their Jews, their Communists, their political prisoners?

But the smell....

There is no resistance. There are no guards. The gates swing open. Your mind somersaults, freezes. What is this? *What in God's name is this?* The eyes take in more than the mind can allow itself to know. More than the tongue is able to speak. More than the world will ever admit. Because this cannot be of our world.

The order to fall in and move on brings relief. *Thank God, let's get out of here.*

But if you are a doctor, you cannot leave. You must stay and sort through the living and the dead and decide which of the living have any chance to stay alive. There is not enough medicine or plasma for even the ones who might live. You must make impossible choices.

Which ones are still living?

The virtuous townspeople say, "We did not know. We had no idea." Yet the odor clings to your clothes all the way back to New York Harbor. Though there is no getting rid of it, back home, no one seems to notice. So you do not say where you have been, what you have seen, because there are no words—and besides, who wants to hear them? So you say nothing. You get on with life, make up for the lost time, pick yourself up by your bootstraps. You immerse yourself in creating security for your family, whom you now want to protect more than ever.

But even from their exile in your mind's furthermost recesses, the bodies will not let you forget. They creep in during the night, bringing with them the scent of death.

And though you do not tell a soul, though you convince yourself it is only a nightmare, the dreams linger in the silence that permeates the household, filling every corner with their essence of melancholy—a disease made more potent by its invisibility.

The images coalesce into a locked gate that separates you from your children. If they asked, you might open it—a crack—and share your memories. But in their eyes, you see no such interest, and they, peering through the bars, see no inclination in you to answer.

Part One

The Aftermath

What cannot be talked about cannot be put to rest. And if it is not, the wounds will fester from generation to generation.

—Bruno Bettelheim, *Surviving and Other Essays*

Opening the Trunk

Harrowing photographs do not inevitably lose their power to shock. But they are not much help in the task to understand. Narratives can make us understand. Photographs do something else: they haunt us.

—Susan Sontag, *Regarding the Pain of Others*

My brother and I pulled into the driveway of my father's medical office in Perth Amboy, New Jersey—the flat-roofed, one-story brick building looking as crisp as new. The precisely pruned box shrubs, the crystal-clear porch light, the raked grass—everything looking as if my father had just stepped out for lunch and a patient might walk up, ready for an appointment. As I opened the storm door, I read the sign to its left: Reuben Levinson, M.D., General Surgeon. Throughout my childhood I wondered: *How could Dad be a general if he wasn't in the army?* Not until I was in junior high school did he first mention World War II—his having been present at D-Day, the Battle of the Bulge—but by then I understood that "general" described his surgical expertise, not his rank.

Alan's hand trembled as he turned the key in the lock. I shared his tension. We were walking for the first time into our father's sanctuary without him being there. The smells of PHisoHex and rubbing alcohol cut through me. A sob sucked out my breath. The squeaking of our shoes on the sparkling linoleum echoed through the empty rooms. More than the words over the telephone, more than seeing the body that bore only the slightest resemblance to my father, more than the funeral and burial, the silence of the office convinced me he was gone.

Alan and I began appraising our job of going through the thirty years of our father's possessions. In the throne room of the castle, as my stepmother and I called the office, shelves of books covered the walls. Photographs bordered the window: a studio portrait of Alan as a toddler; Alan and our older brother Robert as a five-year-old, the two of them in matching plaid jackets; our school portraits; my father's Yale undergraduate and University of Edinburgh Medical School class photos. (Edinburgh had turned him into an anglophile, taking him in when the anti-Semitic quotas for Jews during the 1920s and '30s kept him out of American medical schools. "We don't want those Jews taking over," the dean of Harvard said in the mid-1930s.)

On the bookshelf stood a portrait of my grandfather, ramrod straight and holding an umbrella, his sculpted mustache as dark as his eyes. From the snapshot next to it, my grandmother's sad eyes emerged as the only clear feature in a face defeated by fatigue. It had been taken, my father once told me, not long before she fell ill to a virulent cancer. By the time he returned home from Scotland, she had been dead a week. Her photograph sat alongside what I considered my father's most precious belonging—her 18th century leather-bound *siddur*, the Jewish prayer book she carried from what was then Russia and is now Lithuania to Ellis Island. One Sunday afternoon, when we stopped by his office to pick up some forms, I saw him caress the *siddur* as if it were his mother's hand. Using only my fingertips, I lifted the cover half an inch so as not to deepen the binding's cracks. Fragments of yellowed paper fell out—orphaned Hebrew letters.

The space in which we stood had been our father's true home. Even on weekends he had found some reason to drive the seven miles from our house to the office. It was from here that he called me, once I went off to college, every Saturday at 9:15 am, wanting to know how I was doing, how my studies were going, and how the weather was behaving. No conversation lasted more than ten minutes. Whenever I wanted to broach a difficult subject, I went to the office during his lunch break, always hoping that this time he would open up.

Still hanging on the study's wall was a piece of paper, so old the yellow had turned brown, on which I had, as a second-grader, written the first stanza of Emily Dickinson's poem, "Autumn." "The morns are meeker than they were...." I turned toward the desk where there were photographs tucked under the protective glass covering the mahogany: Alan and I holding our schnauzer, Corky; me in a camp sweater with a huge gap-toothed smile; Dad holding one of the babies he delivered when he was still doing obstetrics, his face lit with delight.

A paperweight sat next to my father's old-fashioned check register—right where he had placed it twenty-six years before. A mosaic of colored shards—half-inch slices of glass—sat under a crystal dome, still attached to the cardboard base with yellowed surgical tape. I cupped my hand around the paperweight, picked it up, turned toward the window and drew back my arm, relishing the prospect of glass shattering and coating the room in shards. Then the shame poured in. *I* had given this to him.

"Leila?"

I slipped the paperweight into my purse as Alan walked into the room.

We continued to the back of the office, into the kitchen where I had once sat with my father at the small table, eating peanut butter-and-jelly sandwiches and sipping tea. No matter what my reason for being there (but hadn't the reason always been the same?) he had brought out the black-and-white composition notebook in which he had listed the stocks he had bought in my name. "You will always have a safety net under you, so you can pursue the work you want. Because you know, Leila, you always have your work." That phrase was his mantra, but it was only that afternoon after his death that I began realizing why he needed his work to be a refuge.

As Alan and I approached the basement door, I began smelling the mildew of damp cinderblock, books and cardboard boxes. As I looked down the stairs, an image appeared in my mind: a pea-green army trunk with "Reuben Levinson" stenciled on it in white letters and a Nazi helmet sitting on top. Sunday afternoons when Dad needed to go by the office to do some paperwork, Alan and I would sneak down there, the light bulb at the top of the staircase casting spindly shadows on the cement floor and walls.

The first time I saw the helmet, Alan educated me.

"This belonged to a Nazi," he had said, pointing to the helmet. Dull gray, it was cut severely low and straight across the brow, and I wondered how a soldier could see out of it. An eagle in flight decorated the sides, its wings spread wide, its talons holding a strange X, the lines bent at each end.

"And this," Alan's hand moved to the X, "is a swastika. The Nazi symbol."

"What's Nazi?" I asked.

"German Jew killers. They hated us, killed everyone they could get their hands on. That's why Dad fought in the war, to get back at the Nazis."

Alan's knowledge usually awed me, but that time his words turned me around and propelled me up the basement stairs. Though I tried to reassure myself that my father had beaten them, that night Nazi faces leered at me from the roses on the wallpaper.

Peering down the steps now, I wavered like a pin caught between magnets. "Do you think we should look down there?"

"Well, we're going to have to, eventually," Alan said as he switched on the light. Letting him go first, I gripped the railing. The trunk sat in the far corner, the helmet still standing watch on top.

I walked over and circled it, the air around it heavy. I felt as if I was underwater, drifting close to an artifact that held some ancient secret. I squatted and held my breath. I gripped the surprisingly cold helmet and set it on the floor, then unlatched the trunk's brackets and raised the lid. On top lay the army jacket my father wore in the portrait hanging in the family den, its dark green wool softer than I had imagined. Alan held it up, and I saw mysterious emblems: a Roman numeral VII within the shape of a seven-point star, an odd pyramid-shaped gold form surrounded by blue. Four gold bars bordered the cuff of one sleeve. No moth holes, no mildew. The trunk had preserved the jacket well.

Inside the trunk sat a Florsheim shoebox big enough to hold boots. When I took off the lid, photographs spilled out. There were hundreds inside. One showed endless ocean, faint ripples the only clue that the empty expanse was water, illuminated by a cloud-shrouded moon. My father's seismographic handwriting noted on the back: *The English Channel, June 2, 1944. Prelude to the Invasion.*

Crossing the English Channel
en route to Utah Beach,
June 4, 1944
(Reuben Levinson collection)

The Clearing Station on Utah Beach
(Reuben Levinson collection)

The First Area- Luther Lewis,
Vince Sciullo, Bill Chaikin and myself.
The First Platoon, Le Grand Chemin,
Normandy, June 8, 1944, just after coming
off the beach. *(Reuben Levinson collection)*

Combat exhaustion
(Reuben Levinson collection)

Our nurses
(Reuben Levinson collection)

Charley Beck, the obstetrician,
Chef-du-pont, July 1944
(Reuben Levinson collection)

On the Egg Route, drinking the
famous Normandy Fire-calvados
(Reuben Levinson collection)

42nd Field Hospital
(Reuben Levinson collection)

Doughnut truck
(Reuben Levinson collection)

The remains of Julich, Roer River Crossing
(Reuben Levinson collection)

GI cemetery
(Reuben Levinson collection)

Henri Chapelle
cemetery in
Belgium
Some of the boys who
died in the ARDENNES
and Rhineland Battles
Cano was a lad
from our Battalion

Notation on back of
"GI cemetery"

Returning home
(Reuben Levinson collection)

Other photos were of GIs lying on the ground—white bandages on their crowns, arms, and thighs. Of soldiers wearing Red Cross armbands, notations like *The Clearing Station on "Utah" Beach, Normandy, June 8, '44.* Of huge circus-sized tents, emblazoned with enormous Red Crosses. Lines of GIs holding plates and cups. Mountains of rubble next to the remains of churches and homes. Expanses of snow, of tanks and bodies covered in snow. Fields covered with white crosses and an occasional Star of David. *The boys who died in the Ardennes. A lad in our battalion.*

I flipped through the photos, repetitive records of war's destruction until, at the bottom of the box, different types of images seized my eyes. Rows and rows of blurred stripes that cascaded into a wave. A foot emerged from the chaos, a leg. Many legs. Grotesquely frozen faces. My fingers pinched the top corner and turned the photo over. *Nordhausen, Germany.*

(Reuben Levinson collection)

11

(Reuben Levinson collection)

Nordhausen. What was Nordhausen? Another photo, more focused: a long canal-shaped ditch filled with bodies. An endless row of bodies. *The burial of the concentration camp victims. April 15, 1945.*

When I tell my friends about this moment, they want to know: What did you feel when you discovered that your father had witnessed a Nazi concentration camp? For the longest time I searched for the word. Fear? Anguish? None felt true, yet how could I not have felt anything at what has come to be one of the defining moments of my adult life?

I tell them the basement went white around me. My lungs pressed against my ribs and I felt desperate to breathe. That I dumped the photos back into the box and ran up the stairs, up and out into the hallway, the smell of rubbing alcohol relaxing my lungs.

Only now have I found the word. Shock. I went into shock.

Moments after I ran up the basement staircase, Alan stood next to me, shutting off the basement light.

"Those photographs were intense," he said.

I nodded, pain in my temples squeezing my head like a clamp. As we drove back to our family's home in nearby Metuchen, I placed my purse on my lap and felt the weight of the glass paperweight against my thigh. I closed my eyes and leaned my head against the cold window. Morbid stripes undulated under my eyelids. What, what were those photos doing among my father's photographs? Why had he made notes on the back of them—as if he had been there—as if he had seen a concentration camp? It wasn't possible. There was no way he could have seen one of the camps and not have told us.

"Unless you want it, I'll ship the trunk back to my place along with the other things I'm taking," Alan said.

"Fine, sure," I replied. "You can have them."

My father never talked about the Holocaust. Until I was sixteen, the only reason I knew about concentration camps was because our cantor was missing half of his right hand. "He survived Auschwitz," my stepmother answered when I asked one evening at dinner. Seeing my forehead wrinkle, she added, "A concentration camp." Having gone off to a camp every summer since I was six, I could not imagine how he lost his hand at a camp, but the curtness of her explanation—along with my father's pursed lips—conveyed that I should not delve further.

Four years later, out of boredom one Saturday night, I went to the Jewish Community Center to see a movie with the strange title—*Night and Fog*—by Alain Resnais. As I ran home after the movie, the film's images of boxcars and ovens and endless lines of kerchiefed people carrying bundles and children sat like putrid meat in my throat. I poured out my anguish to my parents.

"Don't think it can't happen here," was my father's response. He wagged a finger at me before walking up the stairs and closing his bedroom door.

L' dor va dor

L'dor va dor nagged golecha
From generation to generation we will declare your greatness

—from the *Amidah*, the prayer Jews say every day

I married the year after my father died, and during the next four years I had two children. Ray's and David's needs and challenges pruned away all but my most immediate concerns. Even at six months, David woke up every two hours to nurse—turning me into a sleep-deprived zombie. He behaved as if he were going to lose me forever. If I left the room, he cried. When I sat him down, he cried. When I left him with a babysitter, he screamed. There was no quelling his fear of separation. He wanted to consume me.

Each morning the day loomed like a 12,000-foot peak, and I longed to sink into the bed and burrow under the quilt.

"You're depressed," my husband, Burke, said. "You need help. Hire a babysitter—some college girl who can spare a couple of hours a week."

I hated him, hated his opinion, hated his going off to an office every day and especially hated, upon his return from work in the evening, his asking "So, how did your day go?" with a big smile on his face.

Then came my recurring nightmare of a submerged woman trying to strangle me. Again and again I woke up, soaked in sweat, yelling, "No, no!" I became frightened to go to sleep and doubly exhausted by the prospect of facing another day of crying and tantrums.

"You need to see a therapist," Burke advised. So I did.

It was easy telling the therapist about my childhood. But when she began to suggest that I was repressing anger towards my father for neglecting my emotions and ignoring the "trauma" of losing my mother, I told myself it was just like a shrink to make a mountain out of a molehill. Anyone raising a child with separation anxiety and intense moodiness like David's would be depressed. And I knew many people who had lost their mothers during their childhoods. I didn't see how my childhood qualified as traumatic. All I needed to do was soldier my way through, just like I had done ever since I could remember.

I would simply *will* the nightmare away.

But my will proved weaker than the nightmare, and for the next few years, depression became my adversary, threatening to encroach on the happy childhoods I had vowed to create for my children. Every day was a battle to prove myself strong. And happiness seemed like a silly Hollywood fantasy.

One afternoon, when Ray was eleven and David seven, they came running into the house shouting, "Mom, the UPS man is bringing us a trunk!" I looked out the window to see my father's pea-green army trunk riding up my front walk on a dolly. My brother was moving and had decided to divest himself of it.

Once I directed the UPS man to deposit the trunk in the middle of my living room, my sons hung over it as if it were a pirate's treasure chest. Thinking of the photographs I had seen in it twelve years before, I held my breath as I raised the lid...and exhaled when I saw my father's army jacket spread out on top of the trunk's contents.

"Wow! Look at those buttons!"

As Ray reached for the jacket, the shoebox became visible amongst the yellowed ledgers and magazines. I slipped it out of the trunk and under the couch while in my mind I gave my brother a good kick in the shins for sending me this ominous piece of our history.

Whether by uncanny coincidence or providential design, Ray was studying World War II in his social studies class.

"I can't believe your dad fought the Nazis!" he said to me at dinner.

"He was a surgeon for the army."

"Where did he fight? What did he see?"

My husband turned and looked at me, waiting to see how I would answer. My tongue lay cemented to my jaw.

"I, I'm not sure," I finally managed to say.

Burke shifted in his chair. "You need to understand what those photographs mean for you, for our family," he pronounced. "This is important."

"What photographs?" Ray asked.

"Photos your grandfather took in the war, in Germany," Burke said.

"You mean of the Holocaust? Of concentration camps?"

His question whipped my head around. "How do you know about the concentration camps?"

"That's our next unit in social studies, and Mr. Knowles told us a little about it last week. The Nazis killed a lot of Jews."

"In sixth grade you're studying the Holocaust? How come we parents don't know about this?"

"It's okay, Leila," Burke interrupted. "I think Ray can handle it. How do you feel about studying it, Ray?"

"I guess okay. But it's weird being the only Jewish kid in the class. Everyone expects me to know about this stuff. So I feel kind of stupid."

"I'm sorry, honey," I said. "I just thought eleven was a little young to hear about such awful history."

"Can I see those photographs? I'll show them to the class!"

"Ah, I don't think so." Seeing his face sink, I added, "I'll think about it," although I knew there was nothing to reconsider.

After dinner Burke told me that as much as I wanted to—as much as we both wanted to—I couldn't protect Ray. "You're going to have to decide whether you want to bring those photographs out of the trunk. They're important, whether you want them to be or not."

"Okay, okay."

I turned away, irritated at him for pronouncing what was important for the family—and for me. I did not want those hideous photographs to be important.

Later that night I opened the shoebox and spread the contents over my bed. The photographs of Nordhausen, of endless skeletal bodies, were staggering. The blurred focus and distorted angles told me my father's hands had been quivering when he took them. He had been overwhelmed. He had seen the worst.

I gathered the photographs together and shoved them back in the box. No, Ray could not see these.

For the previous three years I had been teaching composition

An American soldier views a child and an infant in an open grave in
Nordhausen concentration camp upon liberation in 1945.

to freshmen at a small Catholic university, and for reasons I did
not stop to analyze, I proposed a Holocaust literature course to
the university for the following fall after noticing that the school
did not offer any courses on the Holocaust. One evening while I
was at the public library finding a book I was thinking of assigning, a title caught my attention: *Children with a Star* by Deborah
Dwork. I pulled it out and, flipping through the pages, saw its
subject was the fate of Jewish children during the Holocaust. On
the next-to-the-last page, a photograph startled me. It showed a
pit in the ground with two children at the bottom: a boy, five or
six years old, with a Star of David on his coat, and a baby, half
naked, her arms spread out on either side of her small body.
Alongside the pit stood a GI gazing down into it.

I closed the book, returned it to the shelf and left the library.

I fled past the stacks, through the revolving front door. I somehow drove home without noticing the traffic lights or intersections. And when my husband and children greeted me at home, I nodded my head and went to bed, where I stayed for over twelve hours.

"Why," my husband asked, "is that photograph affecting you in the same way that seeing your father's photographs did?"

I didn't see a resemblance in the behaviors, and I told myself that he just hated it when I got depressed. After all, the photograph of the two murdered children would affect anyone.

The curriculum for my literature course focused on memoirs and poetry written by witnesses to the Nazi concentration camps. They included GIs who liberated the camps as well as survivors of the camps and their children. Elie Wiesel's *Night* and Charlotte Delbo's *Auschwitz and After* reveal how the psychological and physical brutality, and the constant presence of death in the camps, claimed the spirits of all their prisoners—the survivors as well as the dead. "None of us should have returned," Delbo observes, because the price of their survival was their "deep memory" of the horrors that no amount of time could erase. In *Days and Memory*, Delbo describes that a membrane-thin wall encapsulated the annihilating memories of the camp, memories that seeped out unpredictably, hurling the survivors back through time into the hell of the camps.

And so, despite the intentions of the survivors, their children were exposed to their parents' traumatic memories. Much of the literature by the children expresses how the single most defining moment of their lives occurred before they were born, because the Holocaust—Auschwitz, in many instances—imprisoned their own lives. Even if the parents never broke their silence about what they had witnessed, melancholy and anger permeated the children. So as well as feeling deep compassion and love for their parents, the children, often named for loved ones lost in the Holocaust, felt resentment and rage in addition to guilt and inadequacy—for not living up to their parents' expectations and not having suffered like their parents did.

"Wow!' my students said, every semester I taught the course. "Trauma lives on like that?"

While I had a wealth of literature by children of survivors to include in my course, I found only one book that explored the experiences of GIs who witnessed the camps. *In Evidence* by Barbara Helfgott Hyett resulted from an oral history project that the Boston University Hillel did in the early 1980s. Hyett, one of the interviewers, arranged portions of the liberators' words into poetic form.

You know, the funny thing is
the memories I have—
I'm not sure that I could say where I was, what I was doing.
The only thing I have is the picture that I know
I took. I took the picture.
I had the camera. I had to
have been there. Otherwise
I wouldn't have known.

Our men cried.
We were a
combat unit.
We'd been to Anzio, to
southern France,
Sicily, Salerno,
the Battle of
the Bulge, and
we'd never, ever
seen anything
like this.

My students asked, "How did the GIs deal with the horror of what they saw? Did their trauma affect their children like it did those of the survivors?"

Facing their curious faces, their eyes creasing at the corners as they moved to the edge of insight, my body tilted into the space these questions opened before me.

Over the next few days, the wavy lines of my father's photographs kept appearing in my mind, insisting on my attention. I went up to the attic, opened the trunk, took out the photographs and spread them out on my bed. My head kept turning away from the images of twisted corpses that looked like parts of mannequins. *Look*, I told myself. I forced my eyes onto them, forced myself to see what lay before me.

I needed to learn what Nordhausen was and what my father witnessed.

First, I turned to *Inside the Vicious Heart* by Robert Abzug. A history of the American GIs' liberation of the Nazi concentration camps, it was published in 1985, three years before my father died. This is what Abzug writes about Nordhausen:

> Even as the small hell of Ohrdruf was registering in the minds of the commanding officers, other U.S. Army units were uncovering new and more awful conditions due north of Ohrdruf, near the town of Nordhausen. The Nordhausen-Dora complex of labor camps had been built in 1943 to supply labor for building V-2 factories in man-made caves dug out of the Harz Mountains.... [The Timberwolf Division] came upon 3,000 corpses and more than seven hundred barely surviving inmates. The vast majority of both the living and dead lay in two double-decker barracks, piled three to a bunk or half-hidden in mounds of excelsior and straw on the floor. Many were too

weak to move, and the rooms reeked of death and excrement. "Only a handful could stand on rickety, pipestem legs," wrote a *Newsweek* reporter on the scene. "...their eyes were sunk deeply into their skulls and their skins under thick dirt were a ghastly yellow. Some sobbed great dry sobs to see the Americans. Others merely wailed pitifully, and one poor, semiconscious Jew...kept crying *"Ey yaah."*

The entrance to the tunnel at Mittelbau-Dora
(Reuben Levinson collection)

Abzug quotes a soldier, C.W. Doughty of the 49th Engineers Combat Battalion, attached to the Third Armored Division, who was also there at Nordhausen in April of 1945: "Many of the boys I am talking about now—these were tough soldiers, there were combat men who had been all the way through on the invasion— were ill and vomiting, throwing up, just the sight of this...." Doughty goes on to describe men as having undergone a "psychic closing off," a partial numbing of their senses and feelings.

I learned through Web sites and books that Nordhausen was a subcamp of Buchenwald situated three miles outside of the town of Nordhausen. Its purpose was to produce the V-1 "buzz bombs" and V-2 long-range missiles after the Allies discovered the testing facility at Peenemunde. Nazis transferred prisoners from Buchenwald and Dachau to Mittelbau-Dora, forcing them to carve tunnels through the Harz Mountains with hand chisels and dynamite. Then the prisoners had to live within the dank caverns and assemble the rockets. When they could no longer work, the Nazis shot and burned them in a crematorium built at the camp once the bodies became too numerous to transport to Buchenwald.

On April 11, 1945, the liberators of Nordhausen discovered the nature of their enemy. My father saw the death throes of his people's genocide. Was it possible he had been immune to such horror? Perhaps his silence had been a firewall to keep out the ghosts of his memories. Perhaps his set jaw evidenced his effort to compartmentalize the horrors he had witnessed in Nordhausen: the countless rows of disfigured, unrecognizably human bodies; the walking corpses covered with lice begging for a cigarette or drop of water; the barracks saturated in excrement, the tunnels in the mountains from which walking dead emerged, after having excavated tunnels with no more than pickaxes. These were images that even the medieval surrealist Flemish painter Hieronymus Bosch could not have imagined.

From the little I knew about trauma, I understood that, unless tended to and resolved, part of the personality splits off, taking with it the awful memories and intolerable emotions so that the individual can continue to function. But the repression of memories and emotions from the traumatic experience also suppresses joy, delight, and ebullience.

"Oh, yes," my Aunt Joan told me, "Your father had the bad luck of being assigned to take care of survivors at a camp. It affected him terribly. He didn't ever talk about it once he was back."

Joan was a British "war bride" who met one of my father's brothers, Leon, in London during the war. Perhaps, I thought, Dad had talked more to one of his siblings. I asked his sister what she knew about his time at Nordhausen.

"He had a nervous breakdown after seeing that place," she said. "He spent two weeks there taking care of survivors. Can you imagine? When he lost it, the Army sent him to the Riviera for some R&R. That's why it took him so long to return to the States. We couldn't understand why, six months after all the other boys were back, Reuben was still over there."

Remembering the photos in the shoebox of Dad on a beach in Cannes, I was too stunned to ask more. My father, the bulwark of my life, had suffered a nervous breakdown? But could I trust my aunt's words? They did not speak in the two years before my father died after she accused him of embezzling their father's trust account, the sole contents of which was meager rental income from their decrepit childhood home in Perth Amboy.

There seemed to be no way of knowing with any certainty how Nordhausen affected my father. His only other surviving sibling suffered from dementia and even in lucid moments disliked talking about unhappy memories. But then, at the end of my literature class one day, I opened *In Evidence* from the back and saw on the last few pages the names of the veterans who gave their oral histories—and even the towns where they had resided in 1981, the time of the interviews. Now I could contact the veterans and learn how witnessing the concentration camps had affected their lives since the war ended.

I wrote a grant proposal to cover the cost of traveling around the country to meet veteran liberators and then through telephone directories on the Internet, I found addresses for forty-two

Cannes - April 1945 *(Reuben Levinson collection)*

men. I wrote them letters explaining that I was a daughter of a late, reticent veteran who had also liberated a camp. I explained that I hoped to gain an understanding of my father and to write a book about what the consequences had been for military witnesses of Hitler's death camps. (Every single concentration camp became a death camp. Those like Nordhausen and Mauthausen, created to extract labor, those like Dachau and Buchenwald created to imprison, those like Auschwitz and Majdanek—all in Poland—created to exterminate, all produced, in the end, the same result: an all but certain death.)

Minutes passed like hours over the next few days until one evening, right before dinner, the phone rang.

Untold War Stories

The Holocaust is obsessed with us; its stories follow us.

—Robert Kraft, *Memory Perceived: Recalling the Holocaust*

Joseph Guttman, age 19, a survivor of
Buchenwald, and Sgt. William Best

"Hello," a man's faint voice said with a strong southern Massachusetts accent, "This is Eli Heimberg, calling for Leila Levinson. Yes, yes, I'd be glad to talk with you." The call unnerved me at first. The man's voice sounded so much like my father's— filled with warmth and kindness. Clearly, he had also grown up in a Jewish home with immigrant Yiddish-speaking parents.

After I explained my project, Heimberg was ready with his response. "Well, you know, I went into Dachau with the chaplain of the 42nd Infantry, Rabbi Bohnen," he said. "And as horrible as it was to discover what had happened to our fellow Jews, what I like to focus on is the work I did *after* liberation with displaced persons. So, yes, I'd love to share that with you, because people need to remember what happened in the Holocaust."

We made plans to meet at his home in southeastern Massachusetts six weeks later, after my family's vacation in the Adirondacks. When I got off the phone, my heart raced with excitement, but I also tasted a familiar metallic sadness. Evoking those countless Saturday morning phone calls with my father, the tenor of Mr. Heimberg's voice pulled the scab off my grief.

"You're the age of his own daughters," Burke pointed out. "Maybe that's why he and these other veterans are willing to speak with you."

Indeed, four more veterans called, each generously agreeing to meet with me, each expressing the same motive as Mr. Heimberg: They did not want people to forget. ("Those crazy Holocaust deniers are not going to tell me what I did or did not see; so I must put my words into the record," said one.) I was to be their amanuensis, their medium to record what they witnessed. Perhaps that I was a liberator's daughter also created some trust.

But not all of the veterans wanted to speak.

"I think it's grand what you're doing," one man said in a shaking voice, "but, I'm sorry, I just can't revisit those memories."

As I realized he was crying, I wished I could reach through the phone to embrace him and take back my request.

I suddenly doubted my project. Speaking with the veterans would likely trigger intense emotion in them, pain they had managed to avoid for years. Who was I to bring up painful memories? The prospect of placing myself in a minefield where any possible question might trigger tears filled me with anxiety. But when I got news from the foundation to which I had applied for a travel grant that my proposal was successful, my confidence revived.

A friend familiar with oral histories suggested I read some transcripts of interviews other people had done. Another friend believed the Holocaust Museum Houston might have interviewed liberators, so I called to see.

"Yes," the librarian told me. "In the late 1990s the museum interviewed and taped over two hundred veterans who witnessed the camps."

Over two hundred!

The next week I drove the three hours to downtown Houston. At the small museum, which opened in 1996, the director and librarian introduced me to their archives. Their work in gathering testimonies was impressive. Within minutes I was watching a tape of an interview with Dr. Ed Zebrowski, who served with the 71st Infantry Division. I stepped into his dream, his nightmare.

It was a beautiful, sunny, warm spring day in Austria, just outside of Wels, where we entered this very dense pine forest. At first, the smell of pine was beautiful, and it seemed so peaceful and quiet in the woods, but then this horrible stench came, and we immediately recognized it was the stench of death mixed with human excrement and rotting bodies, and then we saw what looked like piles of discarded clothes scattered throughout the pines, and they suddenly began to move, vaporous apparitions, lifting themselves off the ground. They were people, as if they were lifting themselves off their own dead bodies, and they seemed to float up off the ground. And they came towards us.

We first reacted with dread, because the skin of these people was grimy and ulcerated, crawling with vermin. They were gaunt. The facial skin was just a thin membrane, pasted up against their bones, and we drew back. But they were speaking to us with a sort of incoherent babble, but their tone, as they came closer and began touching

*us, patting us and caressing us, their tone was so gentle as they said
brot and wasser [bread and water] that we knew instinctively,
without knowing the meaning of the words, that we were forming a
relationship, and we couldn't believe that anyone could cause
human beings to come to this point in their lives.*

*These people had escaped from Gunskirchen, a death camp a lit-
tle further down the road, where 15,000 human beings lay dead and
rotting. And another 3,000 were like those we met in the forest.
There was a railroad siding with boxcars as far as you could see, in
front of each one a tremendous pile of corpses. It was a total shock,
because no one had prepared us for what we were going to see.*

The language of Dr. Zebrowski, a bearded man with a long
thin face, glasses, and deep voice, transformed his memory into
poetry, the apparitions in the forest imprinting themselves on my
mind. But then the poetry vanished: "This has been with me ever
since. Last October, when Wolf Finkelman told us his experiences
during our army reunion in San Antonio, everybody was crying,
and we all felt: *Please stop. We can't stand this torture anymore.*"

He lowered his head, placing a handkerchief between his glasses and his eyes to absorb his tears.

Johnnie Marino encountered the evil of Nazism when his battalion, part of the 12th Armored, walked into Hadamar,
Germany.

*We couldn't believe what we were seeing—people stacked like cord
wood, others in railroad cars, thousands had been thrown into a
huge ravine. This wasn't a camp where people had been held prisoner; they were brought in from other places and murdered here. There
were gas showers and ovens here; everybody was dead. There was no
life whatsoever. It didn't seem real. Thousands of people just laying
there, their eyes open, staring up at the sky. I thought I had seen war,
death, Omaha Beach, Battle of the Bulge, but I never, never was*

prepared to witness something like Hadamar. I believe all of us there will never forget it; I know I haven't. I have asked my Lord to take it from my mind, but I see them today as I saw them then, especially the children.

Survivors of Mauthausen
Concentration Camp
(Donald Dean, Army)

He broke his narrative, placing his face in his hands, unable to continue speaking.

Calvin Massey, also with the 12th Armored, despite having promised himself that he would not, began crying a few minutes into his interview.

This is going to be hard, and I'm liable to break up. This bit at Landsberg was the worst part of the whole war for me. I think a lot about my mama calling me "Skinny." My mama would tell me I was skin and bones, you know. But you don't know what skin and bones are until you see some of these people. I don't know how in the world they could walk or move because it was literally skin and bone. First thing I saw was these train cars full of dead people. I started crying. I just cried and walked and cried, like a zombie. At first it was fear, nail-biting fear covering my whole body, and that fear turned to hatred. I just hated the German people for what they had done. But then my attitude changed to compassion for these people the Germans had been so cruel to. Excuse me, my whole body's just...

The grief surrounding me sucked the room of its air. I rushed out to breathe.

31

A GI liberator with a survivor of Dachau
(Eli Heimberg collection)

Only as I drove home that evening did I realize that the inter-viewers hadn't asked any of the men how the pain from witness-ing the camps had affected their lives since the war. While Dr. Zebrowski said that seeing Gunskirchen caused him to become a doctor rather than a journalist, no one asked him if and how he had healed.

I needed to ask this question. I needed to become a detective, identifying and locating eyewitnesses, gathering clues, like pieces of torn paper from all corners of the country into one frame, so I might solve the mystery of how this unprecedented, unimaginable experience altered the liberators.

The librarian at the Holocaust Museum Houston told me about a 1988 exhibition that the Jewish War Veterans Museum in

Washington, D.C., had organized: "GIs Remember" focused on the role of Jewish GIs in liberating the camps, and the museum published a book to accompany the exhibition. I ordered one as soon as I got home and requested the museum ship it priority mail. When it arrived, I hurried into the kitchen for scissors to open the packaging. Out slipped a softbound magazine-sized book with a gray-and-white photograph on the cover. It showed two men. One wore the striped pajama-like uniform of the inmates and a striped beret sitting tightly over his bare forehead. His thin lips were pressed together, but his light-colored eyes, tentative and guarded, stared right through the camera. The broad smile of the other man—a young, dark-haired GI—reminded me of my older brother when he was a teenager.

My gaze moved down and saw that the GI held an unopened mess kit while the survivor extended towards the camera a metal bowl full of food, as if he wanted to make sure the photographer included it in the picture.

Each page of the book featured a veteran and included photographs he or she took at the camp they liberated along with a short statement about his or her experience. "David Cohen – Ohrdruf; Sol Tanenbaum – Ohrdruf; Charlotte Chaney – Dachau; Seymour Mermelstein – Buchenwald; Alvin Ungerleider – Nordhausen; Albert Schwartz – Nordhausen."

Nordhausen, the camp my father had witnessed! Schwartz wrote:

Although there had been rumors about concentration camps, which we dismissed as exaggerations, we were stunned by what we found—an absolute abomination. When I got there I just couldn't believe my eyes. I got sick to my stomach because of what I saw and smelled. That traumatic experience is forever imprinted on my memory.

Our Division medics were there, and later on, units from the

Corps [that would have included Reuben Levinson]. *Our medics did everything they could to make the few survivors more comfortable but* most of them died. [author's emphasis] *We made German civilians help us clean up and bury the victims in mass graves.*

Many of my friends still don't feel as deeply about being Jewish as I have since this experience. It affected me deeply.

I ran over to the computer and looked up their names on an Internet telephone directory, my heart racing as addresses came up. Ungerleider and Schwartz were still alive! I sent letters requesting to talk with them.

The next week crept by until an email appeared in my inbox. "Yes, I would be glad to meet with you," wrote Colonel Al Ungerleider. Now I would learn from an eyewitness about the liberation of Nordhausen—what it was like for the doctors, what they did, how long they were there, and how many GIs seemed to suffer shock. Col. Ungerleider would be the eyes and ears to recall my father's experience.

Albert Schwartz called, too, but quickly explained that he had just had serious surgery and would not be able to offer much help. My hopes rested with the colonel, with whom I arranged a visit at the end of my interviews in August.

Memorializing

Only through acknowledgement and incorporation of this erasure and void of Jewish life in Berlin can the history of Berlin and Europe have a human future.

—Daniel Libeskin, architect, Berlin's Jewish Museum

Gunskirchen Concentration Camp,
the day of its liberation

Certain that the World War II Memorial Dedication in Washington, D.C., would be a great opportunity to meet other liberators, I made plans to fly to the nation's capital for Memorial Day weekend in May 2004.

"Don't go, Mommy, I don't want you to go," David pleaded with me when I told them at dinner one evening of my plans.

"She needs to go," Ray told him. "She's writing a book."

The morning Burke drove me to the airport, Ray wished me good luck, his bright eyes shining. I reached up to hug him, as he stood a good six inches taller than I.

"Mom will be fine," Burke assured David. "And so will we."

While the official events of the dedication began on Friday of that weekend, on Thursday the United States Holocaust Museum (USHMM) honored the GI liberators of the camps with an hour-long ceremony. It received little publicity other than an advertisement in *The Washington Post* the day before, and I only knew about it through a conversation with a staff member at the museum two weeks earlier.

The ceremony began at noon in the museum atrium, the three-story-high brick walls of which created the ambience of a prison yard. As an audience gathered, anticipation charged the air. Five people walked up a set of stairs connecting the atrium's ground floor to a small platform about twelve feet above us; only one—a woman—looked under seventy-five years old.

A pattern became apparent around me: Everyone was either a veteran, made clear by words and pins on his hat, or a member of his family, including people my age. The veterans in front of me began exchanging names.

"Don Robbins, 4th Infantry..."

"Bill Wood, 89th Infantry..."

"89th?" a third man exclaimed. "I was in the 89th. John Peterson."

"Peterson? My God! I know you. Don't you remember? I took a bullet in the thigh at Utah but made them send me back in time for the Bulge. I'm Robert Thompson."

"Bobby!"

They embraced like long-lost brothers as the woman in the seated group, who would identify herself as the director of the USHMM, approached the microphone. She stated how important it was during the dedication weekend to honor the GIs for liberating the prisoners of the Third Reich. "I want to assure each of you that the museum will preserve the memory of the Holocaust in our great republic's collective memory."

Then Col. William Scudder, retired from the 89th Infantry, stepped forward and began speaking in his eighty-eight-year-old frail voice.

"It was early April in 1945, and we knew we had the Nazis beat, that what was left before us was merely the clearing out of any pockets of resistance and getting the official decree of surrender. We were just outside of Gotha in southern Germany when a horrible stench hit us, the stench of burning bodies. And then we came upon an area completely enclosed by barbed wire. And what we discovered inside..." his voice broke, "was a hell worse than any of us could have imagined: bodies—hundreds of bodies—pieces of bodies...." His words began breaking apart, as though his tongue resisted forming them. "Bodies only partly burned on top of railroad ties, soaked in creosote...."

He took a large white handkerchief from his pants pocket and wiped his eyes. The atrium was silent, the men around me also wiping their eyes and then placing their arms around one another's shoulders.

"I apologize," Col. Scudder continued. "It is still so hard to speak of this." He shifted from remembering the liberation of Ohrdruf Concentration Camp to the importance of not letting the world forget what happened in Nazi Germany and what the Nazis proved was within human capability. When he finished, the audience gave him rousing applause.

I asked a woman nearby if her husband had witnessed a camp. She nodded yes. "But he doesn't talk much."

I turned to a man wearing a dark blue cap decorated with pins. His shoulders rose up, his palms open to the air, his eyelids holding back tears. He told me his battalion had liberated a small satellite camp of Dachau, in the middle of a forest outside of Munich, that held about two hundred prisoners. "My name's Herman Zeitchik," he said, handing me a card. "I served with the 4th Infantry, and sure, come by my house tomorrow."

The next day's *The Washington Post* printed a photograph of Mr. Zeitchik embracing Col. Scudder. During my two hours of conversation with Mr. Zeitchik that afternoon, he told me about landing on Utah Beach on D-Day, the treacherous fog of Huertgen Forest, and the deadly cold at the Bulge, but he did not mention Dachau. When I asked about it, he said he gave one of the prisoners his government-issued Jewish prayer book. "It had my name written on the inside cover, and all these years I've wondered if that man would ever get in touch with me."

I could not find words to ask him what he had done with his grief, which was visible in the weight of his eyes.

Col. Scudder's words were the only official ones I heard from any veteran about the Holocaust during the entire WWII Memorial dedication weekend. Even though I heard many veterans share memories of key moments in the war, the words "concentration camp," "Jews," or "Holocaust" only appeared during President Bush's address when he mentioned the discovery of the camps at the war's end. This puzzled me. A list created by the USHMM included thirty-nine camps and subcamps. So if a division had a few hundred soldiers and one, if not two, divisions liberated each of those camps, at a minimum some 13,000 GIs witnessed the death camps.

In 2007, researchers discovered Nazi documents in what had been the Eastern bloc that establish the existence of hundreds of subcamps for each of the camps listed by the USHMM (Buchenwald had some 150 subcamps, see page ii). Once we factor in subcamps, the total number of camps increases to 20,000, placing the number of GIs who witnessed a camp at a minimum of 300,000. The larger figure becomes probable if it includes auxiliary troops like the medical battalion of my father, brought in by

the various Corps to help survivors. In addition, presciently antic-
ipating Holocaust deniers, General Eisenhower ordered every
battalion within fifty miles of a discovered camp to send soldiers
so they would become witnesses.

Yet none of the dedication weekend's events referred to the
Holocaust, as if the sacrifices of the GIs did not have a purpose
beyond ending Nazi occupation and aggression. I remembered a
passage in *In Evidence*, the book from my Holocaust literature
course, in which a veteran remembers his reaction to discovering
Dachau: "If we had known, this war would have ended six
months ago." Upon seeing Ohrdruf, General Eisenhower said,
"We are told that the American soldier does not know what he is
fighting for. Now, at least, he will know what he is fighting
against."

I approached many men either sitting on chairs lining the Mall
or walking around the various tents and asked if their battalion
had helped to liberate a camp. More than half of these nodded or
said yes, but when I went on to ask if they would mind sharing
what they witnessed, they either shook their heads or looked
down at their hands. The common response was: "I don't think so."

One veteran's affable nature at a panel discussion encouraged
me to approach him afterward. I asked Joseph DeLuca if he had
witnessed a camp.

"Oh, yes. I saw more than my share of what the Nazis did to
Jews and other people." With the 101st Airborne Division,
DeLuca went to Landsberg, where he saw a screaming mob beat
an SS guard to a bloody pulp.

"We didn't know any better yet and took him from them. As
we're about to drive away, I see a small smile come on the guy's
face, and then a Frenchman who spoke English came over and
said to follow him. We're entering the woods, and I'm thinking,
what's going on here? And I take the safety off my rifle, but then
I could smell it. You can't believe the smell. I could hardly eat for

General Eisenhower at Ohrdruf, the first concentration camp in Germany liberated by American GIs. Before him are burned remains of victims.

weeks, and when I see photographs today I can still smell it. In this huge ravine there must have been 5,000 bodies. The Frenchman told us that when they couldn't work anymore, they took them out here and shot them. To tell you the truth, I felt like shooting that SS guy myself after that. I should have let the people finish him off."

A week later, Mr. DeLuca's battalion came to Dachau, which had been liberated three days before. "If I had seen Dachau first," he told me, "I would have responded differently to that mob. After Dachau, we fought harder. I guess that's what the brass wanted, because they sent a lot of us to go see it to get our adrenaline going and get the war over with."

After he returned stateside, he told his father a little bit about what he had seen but he never said a word about it to his mother. "As it was, she said she didn't get the same boy back, and I thought, *if* she only knew. I look back on it now and think that was someone else who went through that. I can't believe it was me. I wonder if people even believe me when I tell them about it. But these kinds of stories—you can't make them up." After witnessing Landsberg and then Dachau, a part of Mr. DeLuca split off, making it possible to suppress the memories, senses, and most of all, the emotions that followed the experience.

Remembering a similar reaction from Mr. Zeitchik, who had not been able to talk about what he saw at the subcamp of Dachau, I began to wonder how common this disassociation from the memories of the camps was among the liberators. I sensed I was glimpsing how witnessing the camps might have affected these men long after the war. Clues about my father seemed within reach, and I became impatient for August to arrive.

What the GIs found in woods outside of Landsberg

The following month my family spent three days on the road driving to the Adirondacks. I insisted that our motel have Internet connection and rushed to the room to check my emails. The second evening a note arrived from Col. Ungerleider's wife. "We have decided to go to Vermont for our wedding anniversary and are sorry we won't be here after all during that time." My stomach lurched, my hands gripped the edge of the desk.

"What's wrong?" my husband asked.

"The wife wrote that her husband won't be able to meet with me."

"Well, maybe he's had a downturn."

"Then why isn't she being forthright? I don't think she wants me talking to him."

"Well," said Burke as he stretched out on the bed alongside David, watching *Sponge Bob, Squarepants* on the television. "That's her prerogative."

I squeezed my hands into fists, my frustration with Col. Ungerleider's wife about to boil over onto my husband. She wanted to keep me from talking to the one man I most wanted to talk to, the one who could provide specific information about my father's experience.

That night I stared at the ceiling. I turned over and over, got up, drank two sips of awful-tasting motel water. I had to talk with Col. Ungerleider. His narrative in *GIs Remember* included a remark that, for many years, he had had bad dreams—dreams that his wife most likely didn't want getting stirred up again. Had she even told him, I wondered, that she was fending me off?

I emailed her back that next morning to ask if I could rearrange my time of visit. She became more candid in her response, admitting that he wasn't doing too well and she thought an interview would overtax him. She suggested that perhaps she could fill me in herself, as she knew the story as well as he did. The idea did not appeal to me.

The next day, as we passed Ohio's cornfields, our car rolling over the gentle hills, disappointment flooded me. I focused on my knitting project, forcing stitches off the needles as though they were adversaries. Breaking more than an hour of silence, Burke asked for my thoughts.

"I don't have any," I said.

My husband glanced over at me as he drove.

"Try not to lose sight of what your project is about. You seem to be blurring the objective of learning how that experience affected these men with your yearning to dissect your father. That's doing a disservice to everyone involved, including yourself."

Three stitches dropped off my needle. I tossed the knitting at my feet and stared out the window. The endless, meticulously aligned rows of corn increased my agitation. I took up the copy of *GIs Remember* and began flipping through the pages, my husband mercifully not saying more. I looked at the enigmatic eyes of the liberated man on the cover. Those eyes still saw the place he left. He was still in passage from a place I prayed I would never be able to imagine.

I thought of my talk a week before we left for our vacation with Dr. Harry Wilmer, an eighty-five-year-old Jungian psychiatrist who lived forty miles north of my home in Austin. Dr. Wilmer was one of the first psychiatrists to work with Vietnam veterans' psychological wounds. Recognizing that the horrors of the battlefield psychologically altered the soldiers, Wilmer helped to gain clinical recognition of the phenomenon of post-traumatic stress. I had discussed with him whether GIs might have suffered post-traumatic stress disorder after liberating the camps.

"There's no question about it," he said. "The eyes, the nose, the ears took in more than the mind could integrate. The totality of it, the implications especially, overwhelmed these men, because they were thrown into a well of human evil. But what *you* most stand to gain from is the story of Lot's wife. Do you remember what happened to her when she turned to look back at the destruction of the city where her own brothers still were with their families?"

"She turned to salt."

"Not a desirable fate, eh?"

As I stared at those rows of Ohio corn, I wondered if I was asking the veterans to do what Lot's wife (and why does she not have a name?) had done. Would my questions cause them to look back at memories and emotions they'd suppressed for sixty years? But the GIs had not left behind family members, I assured myself; God had not forced them to abandon loved ones. I pushed a CD into the car stereo and picked up my knitting.

Nine days later I sat on a wooden dock on Lake Pleasant in the Adirondacks as Ray and David fished out on the lake from a rowboat. Ray had convinced David they would be safe and catch some big sunnies. When they pushed the rowboat from the dock, their fishing poles raised like super-sized toothpicks, delight and satisfaction blossomed within me. Despite my melancholic childhood, Burke and I had managed to raise happy children. The air in perfect harmony with my skin assured me that we would be all right.

I turned my face up to the sun and closed my eyes. In that moment I fully understood with my heart, not just my head, that looking back undoes us. Grief can unravel our reconstituted lives.

This is what I was going to stir in the veterans out of my desire to understand my father. I lay down on the dock and pressed my forehead against the wood and cried for the pain they had carried for sixty years, cried for my own standing on another shore, cried for my arrogance.

"You know," Robert Powers had told interviewers at the Holocaust Museum in Houston, "I didn't say a word for over forty years, and then these Holocaust deniers started up with their crap, and I knew I had to talk, I had to tell the world I had seen it. This was no make-believe." The men who had answered my letter had chosen to talk for reasons far beyond my own personal concerns. Yes, my underlying motivation was my desire to know more about my father, but I could not allow the interviews to have that as the only goal; otherwise, I would never hear what these people had to tell me. I had to honor each of them compassionately as a distinct individual with his own experience of events. My project provided the veterans a rare opportunity to speak their truths to future generations of what they saw—and what they have lived since.

Leila Levinson

George Kaiser:
After Shock Comes Devastation

My mind froze. The shock was complete and total. Especially when we saw the crematorium.

—George Kaiser

George Kaiser in front of a bombed
German train
(George Kaiser collection)

To get to Winthrop, Massachusetts, where I would interview a veteran named George Kaiser, we turned east off of Route 1 north of Boston and soon found ourselves in a congested, densely populated area. An overcast day accentuated the grayness of the buildings, the dilapidation of the empty warehouses, the cracked asphalt lots outlined with eviscerated chain-link fencing. As we passed Victorian houses nestled around a bay, I reminded myself I wasn't driving into Perth Amboy, but the echo between the two northeastern industrial towns was eerie. They both had once known natural grandeur that they both had lost many decades before. I could easily have been driving to my father's office, what with the shop windows full of *quincinera* dresses and the sagging corner liquor stores with their lottery ticket signs in English and Spanish, just like those on Convery Boulevard back home.

"How long will this take?" David asked.

"I don't know, maybe two hours," I answered.

"Two hours?"

Why, I began wondering, did I think it would work to piggy-back the interviews onto our family vacation? I needed to focus, not worry about David's boredom and possible meltdowns.

"You and Ray and I will walk along the beach," Burke assured David. "The veteran's house is right near the beach. We can look for shells."

Ray was listening to his iPod as he looked out the window, his hands drumming on his thighs.

"You're really going to take two hours?" David asked again.

I nodded.

"You nervous?" Burke asked.

I nodded again.

"You'll do fine," he said, words my father had often said to me.

I asked Burke to drop me off a block from Mr. Kaiser's so I'd have time to take some breaths before knocking on the front door. I walked by well-maintained, modest, century-old colonials. My heart was beating fast. In Mr. Kaiser's yard an American flag flew from a flagpole; a man with darker hair than I expected answered the door. Except for his slightly stooped shoulders, Mr. Kaiser looked much younger than his eighty-one years.

"Come in, come in," he said, welcoming me into a brightly lit living room. I sat down on a couch covered with yellow and gold mums under an oil painting of sailboats skimming over the water, their sails puffed out like inflated balloons. Photographs of a boy and girl from their toddler years through their young adult years, including the boy's wedding, filled two shelves of a bookcase. I thanked Mr. Kaiser for his willingness to talk with me.

Settling into an armchair, Mr. Kaiser urged me to call him George. "Any time I can in some way ensure that the world remembers the Holocaust and what happened to the Jews, I'm glad to do so." His words poured forth quietly and steadily. As his pain began to surface in wrinkles on his face, I reminded myself to keep my own face neutral. I did not want to add to his discomfort by revealing my own pain.

Mr. Kaiser told me that for decades after the war he had not been able to talk about seeing Dachau. Seeing an advertisement in the Boston newspaper for an oral history project for GI liberators at Hillel at Boston University in 1981 was a turning point. Because after he told his story to the interviewer, he suddenly found himself able to talk about it. He said, "My wife, Cyma, had no idea until then. I hadn't told anyone." He did not answer my question why he thought he hadn't told her sooner—the first of several questions he skipped over as if he had not heard them.

Instead, he explained why he enlisted in the army. It was "clear as hell" to Mr. Kaiser that the rest of the world was not doing anything to help Europe's Jews. To enlist, he lied about his age (he was only seventeen) and left behind a wife and new baby, whom he saw as his constant source of determination and support. When he returned, his wife was "gone, just vanished, no letter, nothing." She had gone off with another man. The betrayal consumed his thoughts, prevented him from going to college like most of his veteran buddies, as he could not focus, could not think about anything other than his wife and son. His rage cast doubt over everything—even for what he had fought, for what he had given up six years of his life.

Mr. Kaiser's mouth twisted at the memory, his affability disappearing into the scowl. He stared into the space before him. I looked down at my pen, bit my lip.

"The pain never goes away," he continued, returning to the subject of Dachau. He described how he couldn't talk about it right after he saw it, and then once he returned stateside, no one wanted to hear about it. "There was nothing to brag about; we had survivors from the camps here in Winthrop, so I just sort of divorced myself from it, because I figured what had I got to add, they were the ones who went through hell."

The vibrant man I met at the front door faded as Mr. Kaiser's body sank into the chair, his eyes losing focus. *Bring him back*, I told myself, as the silence became intolerable. I asked, "How did your platoon happen to enter Dachau?"

He hadn't been with his regular squad, part of the 20th Armored Division. He had been sent to escort vehicles on a munitions run and was heading back on an unfamiliar road. A sentry stepped out of the woods and told his driver to pull over because of enemy fire ahead. They fell in with a group from the 42nd Infantry Division and came upon a double barbed-wire fence. Some bodies in striped pajamas lay there.

"We had no idea where we were, and then we're coming up to these gates, and I realize: this is one of those camps we had heard a little about—where they were supposedly keeping Jews. I wanted to get out and see if we could help; my driver didn't want to come with me. He said, 'What do I need with some Jews?'"

When Mr. Kaiser got out of the truck and walked into the camp, it was as if he had entered hell. The second barrack he went into had hundreds of prisoners lying on shelves, four or five high, covered with some straw. They were too weak to get up; some could barely turn their heads. Their eyes were the only indication

What liberators at Dachau found

they were alive. Several banged their tin cups on the side of the bunks because they were too weak to get up. The smell was so overpowering, he became sick and ran out.

"Out in the courtyard, I couldn't move," he said. "My mind froze; the shock was complete and total. Especially when we saw the crematorium—with these piles of bodies, stacked five bodies high...."

His voice, which had been getting quieter and quieter, broke off. He put his head down into the cup of his palms, his shoulders shaking. He then excused himself, stood, and left the room. My hands were up around my glasses to hide my tears. His words echoed in my head, overwhelming my thinking.

Seconds later, his wife, Cyma, walked into the room. She was a tall, graceful woman, quite a bit younger than her spouse, her hair just beginning to gray, her step sure and energetic. She asked how her husband was doing.

"I'm afraid I've stirred up a lot of pain."

"Don't worry," she told me. "It was his decision to talk with you. It's as if he needs to talk about it. After never saying a word about it for twenty years, he hasn't stopped talking about it in the

Dachau crematorium

last twenty. But I guess that's what trauma is."

"Has he talked about it with your children?"

She paused. "The children? I don't know; I guess on some level, but not directly. He's never sat down and told them anything. It's all reading between the lines. They learned more from reading an interview a newspaper did with him."

When Mr. Kaiser returned to the room, his wife offered us some kugel and iced tea.

"Wonderful!" I answered, listening enthusiastically as her husband told me what a great kugel his wife made.

Mrs. Kaiser's remarks about her husband not having shared his experiences with their children had magnetized my thoughts, and my mind flipped through questions that might get him to talk about that. I asked him how he thought witnessing Dachau might have affected him emotionally, and how he dealt with it.

"Humor helps," he answered—words I had often heard from my father, especially as I got older. Mr. Kaiser told of how he found humor in things that had absolutely none—like having spent a night sleeping next to what he discovered in the morning to be a dead German. "I lost my faith," he said. "How could God exist if this could happen?"

God took on a whole different meaning for him, he explained, becoming only a personal conscience to do what is morally right, rather than any kind of supreme being.

"I just lost it when I saw bodies stacked up, the killing—it hurts, it hurts, it brings back memories that just don't go away. Every once in a while they just appear...."

He lifted his hands in front of his eyes. The room pressed in against my chest.

"Did you have any idea beforehand what you'd find in the camp?"

"No," he answered, his voice flat, as he continued to look off to a corner of the room. "There was no psychological preparation whatsoever."

This echoed the comments of Johnny Marino and Ed Zebrowski in their interviews with the Holocaust Museum in Houston. I told Mr. Kaiser that I was not sure why, but I thought for my father, seeing Nordhausen was emotionally overwhelming.

"I was sick to my stomach, but I don't think I was traumatized."

When I brought up the influence his experience might have had on his children, Mr. Kaiser acknowledged they had been affected somehow, if only because he was a moralist. "I've always taught them to act like good Jews, to respect their elders." I could not see the connection he was making. He mentioned his son's strong sense of justice, so I asked how old his son had been when he first heard of his father's war experiences.

"I didn't involve him in any of that until he was about thirteen or fourteen," he answered. "I guess I wasn't free to talk to him about it. Some part of me still wants to hold back." He paused. "I just can't.... He asks questions I don't want to answer some-times—like 'Did you ever kill somebody?'" He took out a hand-kerchief and wiped his eyes. "I guess even after all this time I can't open up." He put his hands over his eyes, apologized, and again left the room.

As I looked at the delicious kugel Mrs. Kaiser had brought me, I thought about the intensity of discomfort arising in Mr. Kaiser as he considered talking about his experiences with his son. I wanted to know what feelings he had been having, what thoughts, what regrets. Why it was possible for him to talk with me, but not with his own son about his war experiences?

He reappeared, smiling, re-energized, and told me how after his interview with the project at Hillel, he began speaking to school groups. He presented the students with a "what if" scenario, asking them to imagine that all the people in their town were lined up and killed in one day. Everyone they knew on their street, the street beyond that one, and the one beyond that: This was what went on in Nazi Germany. "You should see some of the letters I got from some of those kids. Would you like to see them?"

I really didn't, because I could almost predict their contents and wanted to stay on track with the interview. But I indulged him. As he disappeared, his wife invited me into the kitchen for some water. Standing there chatting with her and their daughter,

George Kaiser, 2004 *(courtesy Robin J. Coles)*

Rachael, who was visiting for the afternoon, I felt like I was in my own family's kitchen in Metuchen. These people were of my culture. We spoke the same language of the heart, carried the same worries and troubles.

"You promise me the next time you're in Boston that you'll come for dinner," Mrs. Kaiser said.

"Yes, I'd love to," I assured her from the heart.

Mr. Kaiser appeared with his hands full of letters, all bound together with neatly tied string. He presented them to me. They felt like ten pounds.

"I'd actually like you to keep them," he said. "They can help with your research."

"Keep them?" I was stunned. "Oh, no, I can't...."

"Yes, I insist."

I stood awkwardly, uncertain what to do next. I turned to the table where my glass of water stood, to Mrs. Kaiser, who had retrieved my raincoat from the closet.

"Here," she took the letters from me so I could put my coat on. I felt like the dutiful ten-year-old once again.

After I thanked Mrs. Kaiser for her sweet hospitality, her husband walked me down the block to the corner, where Burke and the boys were waiting in the car. We walked in silence, small talk unnecessary. As we shook hands goodbye, his eyes brimmed with sorrow. I felt an urge to take that from him also, but I reminded myself that all that I had carried for my father had not lessened his own melancholy. As I got into the car, I turned and waved. As we turned the corner, Mr. Kaiser was still waving back.

"Well, how did it go, Mom?" David asked. "Did you learn anything new?"

"David, give her a minute," Ray said.

I bowed my head and wiped my eyes.

"No, it's okay," I turned and smiled at them. "He is a wonderful man, and I feel privileged to have talked with him. It was more valuable than I even imagined. Thanks, guys, for doing this for me."

"Sure, honey," Burke said. "We had fun. Right guys? We raced up and down the beach and got a lot of energy out."

We headed out of town, passing neighborhoods of row houses gray with soot, screens torn, windows broken. I thought of how, after the war's end, these all-but-abandoned neighborhoods had been vibrant. Full of promise, embodying the hopes of a generation.

I slipped into a daydream, seeing in my mind another building—a police station. I'm getting out of a black-and-white police car. Walking into a three-story brick building, going up a long wooden staircase that opens up into an enormous room with arched opaque windows, sitting down in a row of attached wooden chairs, the kind where the seat flips up when you stand. My mother sits next to me.

I'm five years old.

My mind froze. The shock was complete and total. There was no psychological preparation whatsoever.

"Don't let them take you," my mother pleads. "If you go, I'll never see you again!"

Her face was white, her eyes wide with the future.

Burke leaned over and said in a soft voice, "You okay?"

I jarred myself back to the present.

"Yeah," I managed to say. Then I shifted my thoughts. "It's all so sad. These men are full of sadness. I feel like I just left my father standing there with Mr. Kaiser."

I tried to shake loose the images in my mind by jotting down the man's phrases: *Even after all this time I still can't open up.*

The memories just don't go away. They just appear....

Some part of me still wants to hold back.

Mrs. Kaiser telling me he never talked to their children about Dachau: *It's all reading in between the lines.* And yet he talked to *me*—to a point. He had talked to classrooms of children, giving them the image of everyone in their town being lined up and

killed. But to his own children he said nothing? Was he protect-
ing them? Why?

For thirty-six years Mr. Kaiser did not tell anyone that he had
been among Dachau's liberators, that he had seen the walking
dead, the crematorium. Thirty-six years of locking up those
images within himself. *You don't talk about it.* His perception that
some levels of suffering become insignificant in comparison to
others: *We had survivors from the camps here in Winthrop, so I just
sort of divorced myself from it, because I figured what had I got to
add, they were the ones who went through hell.*

Like Joseph DeLuca, he tried to divorce himself from his emotions, with an implicit recognition of the impossibility of divorce.
The pain never goes away.

Mr. Kaiser's wife saw he was traumatized, and her forthright-
ness to me indicated her opinion was no secret. Why would he
need to deny it? I had observed him *avoiding* talking about
Dachau. As soon as he got close to the pain, he left the room.

I knew it was the same pain my father had locked away.

While I was in law school, I decided to ask my father about my
mother. On a return visit to New Jersey, I set out one day to have
lunch with him at his office. When I walked into the lobby, he was
standing outside the examination room, his arm around the
shoulder of an elderly man.

"Leila!" he boomed, a smile spreading on his face. "This is my
smart daughter," he said to the patient. "She's in law school,
preparing to be a great constitutional scholar."

A few minutes later it was just the two of us at the small table
in the office kitchen, spreading peanut butter over bread.

"So tell me," he said, "how are you liking the study of law,
which is so suited to your fine intellect?"

I swallowed a bite that felt dry as paper.

"I still have my doubts, Dad. It's not at all what I thought it
would be."

"Give it a chance. You gave up on graduate school too quickly. I don't want you doing that again, as soon as you start feeling unhappy. The great thing about the law is that you can use it in so many ways. A law degree will benefit you no matter what." He pointed at me as if his finger could push the words into my head.

"But I never get to use my writing in a way that feels true to myself. I'm having to change everything about the way I think and write."

"You're a wonderful writer, but writing isn't a vocation, Leila. It will serve you in your work, and work is everything." He looked into my eyes as if his could imprint his point of view on my mind. "Because no matter what else happens in your life, you always have your work." He kept a lock on my eyes until I nodded assent.

When we finished eating and took our dishes to the sink, I took a deep breath. "Dad, I need to tell you something."

"What? Tell me. I'm listening."

"I've been seeing a counselor—at the university. It's free. I had such a hard time this past January, having a lot of nightmares, being depressed. It all seemed to catch up with me."

He didn't reply, so I plunged ahead. "We've acted as if nothing bad happened to us or as if everything that went wrong didn't affect us, but it did, and I'm trying to figure out how it did."

He turned his face away from me, out the window in front of the sink.

"So, Dad, I really need to know what happened to her—to my mother?"

Silence.

"Can you tell me, Dad, please?"

Tears ran down my father's face—tears falling onto his beautifully pressed light blue Brooks Brothers shirt.

"I can't talk about it—not yet," he said in a voice so soft I leaned over to hear him. "Maybe someday...."

I wrapped my arms around him, my own tears spotting his shirt. Within two seconds, he pulled away. "We can't cry. We have to be strong. We can't stop now, after all this time."

I held my breath, pushed ahead.

"Do you have any photographs of her? Any letters that might help me know her?"

He shook his head. No.

The last time I saw my mother was in a police station, days after my fifth birthday. We had been shopping for white sneakers to go with my prized possession, a turquoise poodle-dog skirt she had given me for my birthday. But instead of bringing us sneakers, the sales clerk appeared with a policeman who escorted us into a black-and-white car with a red light rotating on its roof. Over the years, I learned my mother had acquired the habit of shoplifting, and this time was one time too many.

In the backseat of the police car, my mother clutched my arm as if we had been dropped out in the ocean, and I was her life-saver. "Stay with me," she gasped in my ear. At the station, the policeman led us up a long set of dark, wooden stairs into a room full of empty benches.

My mother gripped my arm harder. "Whatever you do, Leila, don't leave me," she commanded, as if I were planning to do something bad like the time I bit the boy next door soon after my father and brothers moved out. "Don't let them take you. If you leave, I'll never see you again!"

Another policeman appeared, his hand separating me from my mother. I did not know how to disobey his calm firmness. His other hand wrapped itself around my shoulder, pulled me up from my seat, guided me towards the stairs.

"Leila, don't leave me, Leila!" My mother's screams followed me down the dark steps.

I did not turn around.

At the bottom of the steps waited my father—a short, trim, dark-haired man in a light-gray suit. I recognized him from his hands, the middle finger of the left one missing its top half. His hands were holding his gray felt hat with its black grosgrain ribbon. I followed him out of the station, through the parking lot, and into his black car, where he announced that we were going back to the apartment my mother and I had been living in so I could pack up my clothes.

At the apartment, I packed my socks, dresses and pajamas. I left the poodle-dog skirt lying across a chair. I somehow knew that the life it had been part of had ended that afternoon.

Twice I asked my father where she was and when she was coming back, but his face turned to stone, his lips pressed into a frown. I stopped asking. It was as though my brothers and I had sprung full-grown from our father's head, because no one in our town, not the teachers, not my rabbi, not the neighbors, ever mentioned her again.

I worked hard at exiling her image from my mind. But my father did not make it easy. Every evening, as we sat down to dinner, he placed two albums—enough to last the course of the meal—on the stereo. One album was the Yale University Whiffenpoofs, which included the song: "A Motherless Child." The refrain "sometimes I feel like a motherless child" repeated like a sewing-machine needle driving into my temple. Yet only I seemed to hear the words.

I adored my father. How could I not? He was the town's beloved doctor who cared for the oil-refinery workers, the storekeepers, the tailors, the ditch diggers—the Slovaks, Puerto Ricans, African Americans, Poles and Litvaks. He not only healed their wounds and reassembled their bodies, he boosted their spirits. On weekends he took me along on his rounds at the hospital where every patient's eyes lit up when he entered their room. "Dr. L.! I knew you'd come by today." They told me how lucky I was, how I had the best man in the world for a father.

Yes, I told myself, I am lucky. And on those many Sunday afternoons when he put Alan and me in the car and drove the fifteen miles from Perth Amboy to Princeton, where we would get out, eat at the Holiday Inn, and then return home, I would lie down on the front seat, snuggle my head up against his thigh, and pray he would stroke my hair. Many times he did, the weight of his hand on my head creating a place in the world for me, giving me the strength to get through another week of our housekeeper's taunts and pinches.

My father did have letters from my mother. Letters that he made sure we would find soon after his death.

After his death, Alan and I drove to the Rahway Savings and Loan to retrieve his will. The bank was eleven miles from his office in Perth Amboy, extra miles he drove once a week because the Rahway Savings and Loan had given his father, Raphael, his first loan, making possible Raphael's transition from itinerant peddler to storekeeper.

After signing our names to the register, Alan and I followed the bank clerk into the steel vault that held the safe-deposit boxes. When we opened the box, rather than vellum certificates or notarized legal-sized white paper greeting us, we saw three yellowed letters bearing the same loopy cursive handwriting. One was addressed to our father at his office; the one to Alan and the one to me had our Water Street address on them, the house we lived in before our mother left our lives.

"They're from our mother," Alan said.

He might as well have said Abe Lincoln had sent them. Our mother never wrote or visited us after she went away. The postmark on mine showed a date of September 8, 1959—six weeks after I last saw her—from Marlboro, New Jersey, a town about twenty miles from our Water Street house.

I turned it over. Written across the back flap was the name "Clara Levinson." My throat clamped shut to keep my heart from jumping out. I put the letter in my purse and only later that day, alone in my teenage bedroom, opened the flap that had been opened years before.

Dearest Leila,

How is my little Princess today? What have you been doing while Mommy has been in the hospital? Mommy is feeling a lot better and hope I will be back home with all of you real soon. Ask Robert to write you a letter so that you can mail it to me. I sure would love to hear from all of you so very much. All my love to you, Princess.
Love and XXXXX,

Mommy

I imagined why my father might not have given this to me when it arrived in 1959. He must have known she wasn't coming back and wanted to protect me from false hope. I could forgive him for that, but what explained his not giving it to me a few years before when I had asked him for letters from her?

Two days after I had gone to his office asking for answers and letters, he had come into my bedroom.

"If you're going to do therapy, you might as well do it right and get the best person you can. The Blue Cross I have will pay for it, understand?"

Over the months of interviewing the veterans, I came to see why that statement had astounded me. My father had been able to recognize and express, not for himself but for me, that I had a wound, and it could be healed. Yes, I quickly told myself, I may have been wounded, but that doesn't mean I was traumatized.

Eli Heimberg:
Repairing the World

The rabbi recited the memorial prayer for the dead, and then I wept without control.

—Eli Heimberg

Eli Heimberg and a child from the Displaced Persons Camp.
(Eli Heimberg collection)

After a torrential thunderstorm the night after we left Mr. Kaiser's, my family and I woke in our motel room to a sparkling morning, crisp sunshine filling a cleansed sky. And I remembered, as the olive-green drapes and polyester floral bedspread in varying shades of mauve came into focus, that I had another interview to do. What would I hear today? The evident pain on Mr. Kaiser's face the day before, the perspective his words had triggered for me, made me want to turn over and go back to sleep. I envied my husband and sons who planned to spend the day at a beach.

The Heimbergs lived in a small community of new condos, the separate airy and light-filled units all oriented to a park-like open area that resembled a village green.

"Come in, come in," said Mr. Heimberg, about the same five-feet-six-inches as my father's height, opening the door before I even reached it. His pale, spotted hand clutched the railing of the steps, which made the strength of his handshake surprising. Inside, his wife's caregiver was situating Mrs. Heimberg in her wheelchair, as they were about to go out for a walk.

"My wife had a stroke a few years ago, just as we were getting ready to begin our long-awaited travels," he told me, the reflexive lifting of his shoulders to his ears and holding out of his up-facing palms expressing acquiescence to life's irony.

Mr. Heimberg led me into his study—a cross between a museum and a World War II library. Over the couch hung a huge map of Europe, "42nd INF. Rainbow DIV" printed in large letters in its upper left-hand corner. Illustrated with small pictures for each of the important places, the map showed the route the 42nd followed through Europe after landing at Marseille in December 1944.

Bookcases lined three walls, the titles all indicating the Holocaust or the war to be their subject matter. Framed photographs of a young, dark-haired Eli Heimberg in his uniform, along with framed insignias and certificates from the U.S. Army, covered the remaining wall and surface space. Our subject surrounded us.

"You need to understand that it wasn't my experience at Dachau that left a deep impression on me," he said as we sat down, "but my time at the Displaced Persons Camp in

Landsberg. To see how quickly people became well again and hungered to fend for themselves was uplifting and inspiring."

I replied that he was lucky to have worked with survivors after the liberation.

He nodded, his eyes a blur behind his deep glasses.

"It must have been a shock when you saw Dachau," I said, trying to nudge the subject forward.

"I was the assistant to Rabbi Bohnen, a wonderful man, who was one of the chaplains for the 42nd Division," Mr. Heimberg recounted. "We knew to expect horrible things when we came upon Dachau, but nothing like what we found. There was no way to prepare ourselves for it. More horrifying than the ovens were the bodies in the boxcars on the track leading into the camp. One man, who must have been trying to extricate himself, was reaching out from among the bodies. He was frozen in death, as if asking, 'Why me?'"

He then began telling me about going into the barracks, where most of the Jewish inmates were, his words almost exactly what he had used to describe the memory for the book *GIs Remember*.

The train of death the GIs found at Dachau

"Most of the prisoners were so weak and close to death that they couldn't stand. They were lying on these wooden shelves, hundreds of them side by side. Rabbi Bohnen told them *Ich bin ein rebe American* (I am an American rabbi), and then there came a wail from the men as though they were letting out all their emotions they had pent up for years."

He broke off and tucked his chin down into his chest, which was visibly rising with a deep breath. "When the rabbi and I could speak, we reassured them help was coming for them," he continued. "The rabbi recited the memorial prayer for the dead, and then I wept without control.

Rabbi Bohnen with children at a Displaced Persons Camp
(Eli Heimberg collection)

"When we left late that afternoon, I felt I was waking from a nightmare; my mind was numb. But I began to think but for the grace of God, if my parents hadn't left Europe in the early 1900s, I would have been among the dead."

He paused, and a surprising smile unfolded on his face. "I adopted a dog during the war, a Chesapeake retriever that went with me everywhere, sat at the back of the jeep. At first the newly freed Jews were terrified by him, because Germans had used dogs to inflict terrible harm on the prisoners, but then the Jews laughed when I told them his name was *Hundt*, German for dog. The prisoners said he was more of a human than any Germans they had known."

I asked if he told his wife about what he saw at Dachau.

"Yes, I wrote her letters." He pointed to his desk as though they were sitting there but I only saw the computer and a pile of books and notebooks. He also sent photographs he had taken at Dachau, but his wife wasn't able to look at them, and once he returned, they didn't talk about it. "There didn't seem any reason to," he said. But then a friend reported that on a business trip to Germany, he met a German who had been a lieutenant during the war and who asserted that the Holocaust was a "Jewish fiction." "At that moment," Mr. Heimberg told me, "I decided there was reason for me to talk about what I had seen. That's why, when I got your letter, I called you so there can be one more book with eyewitness testimony."

When I asked if he and Rabbi Bohnen talked about what they had seen after they left Dachau, he said he asked the rabbi how God could allow such evil and suffering. "His response, which satisfied me at the time, was that we aren't individuals but civilizations in contest for survival. Though the Nazis killed all these people, they still didn't win, and that's what matters. Life must go on." (Why, I kicked myself later, did I not ask if that answer satisfied him now.)

He and the rabbi requested assignment to the Displaced Persons Camp, where they thought they could make a difference for the survivors. They advised the newly designated displaced persons to form a council for self-governance and organize elections, all of which they took to very quickly. Mr. Heimberg became a mediator between the council and the army, negotiating with the army or the local Burgermeister (mayor) to obtain for the religious Jews in the camp such religious necessities as kosher meat. "This raised another controversy," he chuckled, "between the religious Jews and the nonreligious ones. The nonreligious ones thought that the camp getting these two cows would result in less meat for all, and we had to assure them it wouldn't."

The religious Jews began to want *challah* for their Friday night dinner, their normal bread being brown bread. As many soldiers found brown bread preferable to the army's standard white bread, Mr. Heimberg arranged for a mutually pleasing trade. "A lot of my arranging depended on the good graces of the general, an excellent man, who was willing to go out of his way to provide necessities to the people. He ordered a supply officer to get some items that would help the people gain confidence in their appearance again. 'Where am I supposed to get soap and toiletries?' the guy asked in disbelief. 'The whole Austrian economy has collapsed.' 'Just get them!' was the general's answer." Mr. Heimberg smiled.

He suddenly began talking about a five-year-old girl at the Displaced Persons Camp. "Her father had been killed in a concentration camp. I picked her up and asked her mother if I could give her a candy bar. When I gave it to her, she bit into it, wrapper and all. I realized she had never eaten candy before."

His smile evaporated, his thin lips tightly pressed together. We sat in silence as Mr. Heimberg looked down at his hands, cupped together. One circled over the other, palm over back of hand over palm.

I grabbed at a question. "Do you ever dream about the camp?"

"Yes." He looked up, into the air before him. "I have one dream that I've had many times. I'm driving a truck, a big one, up to the gates of the camp, and the entire bed is full of candy bars."

As I was leaving, he gave me a copy of the interview video he had given to Hollywood filmmaker Steven Spielberg's Shoah Foundation, along with a *Haggadah* (the book that contains the readings for a seder) from the Passover seder that the 42nd organized for its Jewish members in April 1945—before they found Dachau. Then Mr. Heimberg followed me outside, where Burke and the boys were waiting, the ocean having proved too cold for even wading. Mr. Heimberg leaned into the car and held out a bag of candy. "Here, boys—here are some chocolate mints and trail mix for the drive. You must be good and hungry by now." He wrapped his arm around my shoulder. "You make sure to have some of those mints. They're delicious."

Burke got out of the car to shake Mr. Heimberg's hand, and they began talking about Burke's work, which led to a fifteen-minute conversation. David was anxious to move on, so I got in the van and resumed my role as mother—distracting him with the prospect of swimming at the motel pool later that day. After I hugged Mr. Heimberg one last time, we set off, passing scrubby fields that salt winds have scoured for centuries, followed by protected meadows and then pine forests as we drove west into Rhode Island before heading south towards New York City.

I had not imagined the possibility of a recurring dream that was not a nightmare, that the psyche could become obsessed with a *good* memory. "Mr. Heimberg is a *mensch*," I told Burke. There is no higher compliment a Jew can give someone than to call him a *mensch*, a good, righteous human being.

Mr. Heimberg's daughters later confirmed my impression, telling me how much their father had valued *tikun olam* or

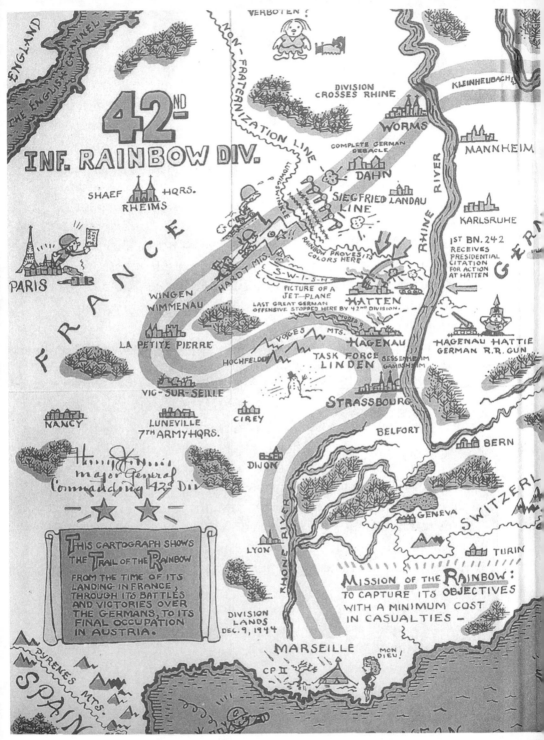

42nd INF. Rainbow Division map

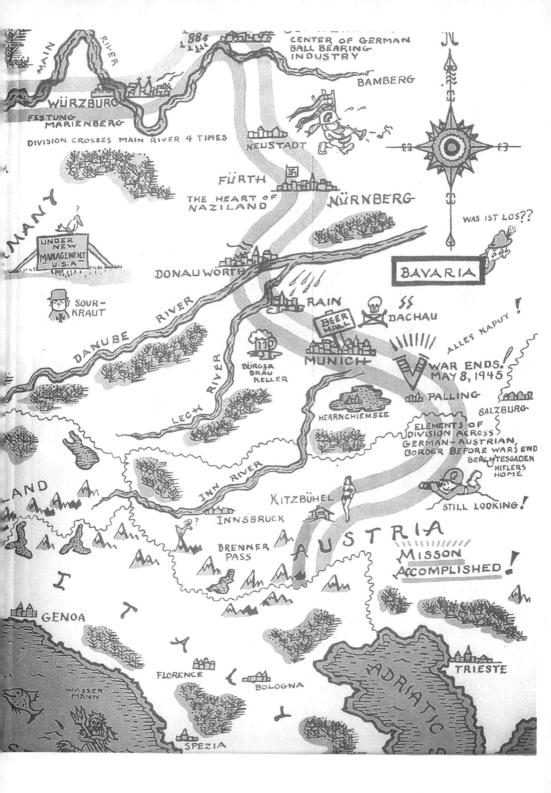

"repairing the world." At his draperies factory, he employed many Portugese immigrants whom he treated with great respect, encouraging them to educate themselves by setting up after-hours English classes. On hot summer days, he gave them breaks in his air-conditioned office. Recently, he has been sponsoring refugees trying to gain U.S. citizenship.

Perhaps positive responses to trauma are possible, I thought. It reminded me of the inscription my stepmother had chosen for my father's headstone: "Knowing the good, he has done it." My father was a *mensch*—tirelessly and unwaveringly treating the workers of Perth Amboy, far removed from affluent communities. Yet, why was it that every semester, when I share with my students the stories of the veterans I interviewed, when I tell them of Mr. Heimberg's dream, I choke back grief? Is it the way the five-year-old lays her thin arm lightly around the young Mr. Heimberg's neck? Or the guardedness in her eyes? Or is it the image of Mr. Heimberg opening his arms, lifting her, handing her a candy bar?

Once I got my driver's license at age seventeen, I often took the fifteen-minute detour to my father's office, the chance for a conversation with him worth the extra time. But that time came with a price: seeing the attention he gave his patients.

Like Tommy Borowski. When the door to the examination room opened, my father emerged with his arm around the stooped shoulders of a weathered man wearing a thin flannel shirt and stained canvas pants. My father's eyes enwrapped the man's leathery face.

"I know, I know, Tommy. It's hard for us little guys to stay afloat, but you've got to keep the flag flying." (At least he used the same cliché with them.)

"What else can I do, Doc? I sure appreciate what you do for me. You're one of the last ones who's not in this for the bucks."

My father chuckled, his hand touching his own temple before

pointing up to the ceiling. "I'm in it for you, Tommy, and that sweet wife of yours." He then gestured toward me. "Tommy, here's my Leila, my smart girl. Leila, Mr. Borowski and I go back, what, Tommy? Thirty years?"

"Thirty-four, Doc." He extended his hand, years of oil darkening the nails. "You're the apple of your father's eye. Every visit he shows me that photo you took of the rainbows."

This information threw me. My father showed off my photography, one of my "avocations?" Was Mr. Borowski talking about the same man who never acknowledged my interests, my grief, or my depression?

One Saturday, about a year after I last saw her at the police station, my mother was supposed to come visit us, and my brothers and I got dressed up and waited in the living room for her. I was almost heaving with nervousness. We waited and waited, the minutes feeling like needles in my brain. I finally ran upstairs and tore off my nice clothes, vowing I would never let her see me again.

I don't know how long it was afterward that she tried to burn down the house on Water Street where we had lived together as a family. One evening, about two years since I had lived in that house, about eighteen months after I had last seen my mother, the phone rang, which it never did while my father was doing his rounds at the hospital. "Oh? No!" I heard our housekeeper say. "Really. My goodness! Yes, of course. Of course, I will. Right away. You can rely on me, doctor." She walked into the living room and snapped shut the Venetian blinds. "Quick! Away from the window. Turn off the light! Robert and Alan!" She yelled up the stairs as she locked the front door. "Turn off all the lights and get down here right away."

Was this the nuclear bomb we had been drilling for all year at school, running down into the basement and crouching with our heads down into our knees?

My brothers appeared from upstairs, wide-eyed with bewilderment. "Your mother's back in town," Doris said. "She's broken into your old house and tried to burn it down, and God knows what she'll try next."

"Burn our house down?" Alan echoed.

We huddled in the dining room at the back of the house in the dark, for which I felt grateful. No one could see my tears. That night I couldn't fall asleep, the roses on the wallpaper leering at me.

At breakfast, questions burst from Robert. "How did she do it, Dad? How did she try to burn down the house?"

My father's voice emerged from behind *The New York Times*. "She turned the thermostat all the way up."

"Huh?" Robert looked at Alan and me, his face scrunched into a question mark. "How would that burn the house down?"

"The furnace exploded."

"Wow!" Robert yelled. "Blowing up the house! She *is* crazy."

"Enough!" my father's voice boomed as he hit the table with his fists, still holding the edges of the newspaper. "You will not say another word! Do you understand me?"

For the next few weeks, Doris showed up at school every afternoon to walk me home, her eyes darting about as we passed the row houses. I realized even she was afraid.

During the years after my mother never came back, my father was hardly ever at home, leaving us in the care of Doris—our very own Wicked Witch of the West. She and the house we moved to on Market Street were a package deal, two parts of a whole, both ugly inside and out. Wedged between a two-storied dentist's office and a vacant lot, the house sat on a major intersection, and all of its windows looked out onto brick walls or the barren backyard that didn't hold even a lonely swing. During the summer, weeds sprouted up, growing as tall as the ones Jack had climbed to find the ogre.

Our ogre was inside the house. I like to think my father didn't

Seven-year-old Leila on Halloween in front of
the house on Market Street, Perth Amboy.

have many people to choose from, or that when he was home,
Doris seemed adequate. Only after he walked out the door did she
turn into a steel-haired succubus, complete with warts and thick
arms, her few pleasures in life smoking cigarettes and making me
miserable.

Doris could see through walls. "Do you and Alan think you're
pulling the wool over my eyes? I saw you out there with that box
of cookies. No dessert for either of you tonight." For dinner, she
served gristly meat, succotash, or bony fish, and we had to sit until
we ate it. She told the mothers of my friends that I was sick and
could not come over to play. She pinched my shoulder blade as I
dried the dishes after dinner, hissing in my ear, "You better hurry
if you're going to see that television program."

After watching a program, I would go upstairs to bathe—on a
good evening being able to do it alone, on a bad night needing
my hair washed. On those nights, Doris followed me and dug her

gnarled fingers into my scalp as I wrapped my arms about my chest. She laughed. "What do you have to hide?"

All I could do was pout, about which she always remarked, "Your face is going to freeze like that some day, and then you'll be sorry." Then she would try the line, "You're so much prettier when you smile," as if prettiness was reason enough.

I learned how to hide, little things at first: toy marbles in cracks behind the bed, candy in my sneakers. I was especially protective of my Kennedy cards, which came four to a pack, each card showing a photograph of the First Family. I imagined President and Mrs. Kennedy to be my parents, a fantasy encouraged by Caroline also having dark blonde hair and dimpled cheeks. My favorite card showed her in a white bathing suit standing next to her father, his eyes full of love and pride, a barrette holding her cropped hair out of her eyes. They shimmered with happiness. That card I kept between the mattress and the box spring so I could look at it when I dared not close my eyes at bedtime.

The Kennedy family

To get my pink ball that I played with at recess to and from school, I resorted to what seemed my only option. Before school ended, I would go into the bathroom and slip it into my underpants so I could get it past Doris once I was home. Before going down to breakfast the next morning I did the same and once at school hid myself in a corner of the playground so I could slip my hand up my dress and into my underpants to retrieve the ball. Each time my face burned.

Then I tried to hide myself. The laundry hamper worked for a while until Doris discovered it, her face twisted in a smirk. "Are you crazy?" she said.

Reading was my salvation: *The Secret Garden* and *The Little Princess* by Frances Hodgson Burnett, books whose characters, so similar to me and Doris, revealed that not only was my abhorrence of Doris justified but that I could prevail. Best of all, reading allowed me to resist her tyranny right under her nose, invisibly transporting me out of the house.

Over dinner once, Ray asked if there were any foods I hated.

"Lima beans," I said. "I will never again eat a lima bean."

"What are they?"

"Big fat mealy beans that get stuck in your throat. I had a housekeeper who loved to serve them, and my brothers and I *had* to eat them."

"What if you didn't?"

"That wasn't an option."

Both Ray and David crinkled their faces.

"Boy, was your housekeeper mean, Mommy!" exclaimed David. "You should have told on her!"

When the boys jumped up to choose their popsicles for dessert, Burke asked if I ever did tell my father how Doris was when he wasn't around.

I bristled. "Once."

"And?"

My husband looked at me, waiting. I resented being asked to tell this story. I suspected Burke already knew what I was going to say. "Well, it was at his office. I guess I was in law school. I think I asked why he let her spend five years taking care of us."

"And then?"

"And he held his hands out to his side, his palms up. He scrunched up his shoulders."

"That was his response? He didn't even say anything?"

I shook my head no.

"How did that make you feel?"

"Feel? I don't know. Frustrated, I guess."

"Frustrated. Just frustrated?"

I squeezed my hands around my cup of tea.

"What do you want me to say? That I was angry? That I hated him?"

"I want you to say what you felt. Don't you think it would be healthy to take him off his pedestal?"

I got up, threw down my napkin and walked away.

The next day as I was driving down the highway, Ray and David singing the song they had made up about a little toadie, Burke's questions rang in my head like a clapper against the sides of a bell. How could my father have handed us over to Doris? He must have seen her cruel spirit, her deception, her sadism. He must have seen my sadness and loneliness, that I never played with friends, that I so hated being sick I hid my coughs in pillows—despairing when he pronounced I had to stay home. He must have noticed that I began trembling when, at the end of a summer in the Adirondacks, we drove back to Perth Amboy, my spirit withering like tomatoes in a frost.

Why did I never tell him? Did I hope he would see through my constant pleading, "Please, Daddy, please, let's leave Perth Amboy." He must have understood my request, because when we finally did move away from Perth Amboy, he left her behind.

Perhaps I got lost in my hatred for Doris and couldn't find the way out to tell him. I never even told him that she talked about my mother, that she told me I couldn't do anything right. That it was no wonder my mother left me.

My foot eased off the gas pedal. I loosened my grip on the steering wheel. Perhaps I did not trust that my father would do anything about her. Maybe continuing under her rule scared me less than finding out he wouldn't do anything, even if I asked. Then it would have become impossible for me to pretend I was safe.

I remembered the paperweight sitting in a box up on the highest shelf of my closet, which I had taken from my father's desk in his office.

During the years with Doris, I stole many things: a friend's tiny doll with moveable arms and legs, a blue and green plastic *dreidle* from my Hebrew School teacher, a rhinestone red barrette from a classmate's desk. Even a gold ring with a green stone from a cousin. And the glass-domed paperweight.

All those things, and the only time anyone noticed was when I stole money from the richest kid in town.

In her pink-and-white frilled bedroom, she dumped the money from a big silver piggy bank onto her bed: half dollars, silver dollars, a long stream from the mother lode. I reached out and clutched as much as I could, scanning my friend's face for a reaction. When I didn't see one, my legs walked me downstairs, where I opened my fist into the pocket of my coat hanging in the hallway.

That evening, as I sat reading on the living room couch, Doris walked over to the coat rack and began putting my coat on a hanger. The coins jingled, causing her face to register surprise. My throat closed up. She thrust her hand into the coat pocket and pulled out the coins, her eyes beaming with delight, as if she had discovered a whole family of mice.

"And how do you explain this, Missy?"

I played dumb, dumber than dumb, and kept it up for a good two or three days. She finally got the truth out of me by telling me, "Your mother was a thief, and look what happened to her. You don't want to end up like that, do you?"

That evening, as I excused myself from the dinner table, my father said, "Go get the money you took and put it into the *tzedakah* box." Other than the absence of pork from our kitchen, this metal blue box, adorned with a map of Israel, was the most tangible evidence of our being Jewish. Into it we put money for charity, performing one of the required *mitzvahs*, daily good deeds God requires of Jews. Every week we dropped one of our coins from our allowances into the metal box for Israel, to help turn the ancient Jewish homeland into a secure Jewish state.

I dropped the stolen coins in, one at a time, focusing on the names on the map: Haifa, Jerusalem, Tel Aviv. Maybe the coins, rattling against the metal, would travel across the ocean and buy trees for the desert.

My stealing stopped until the following summer at camp, soon after my ninth birthday. In the arts-and-crafts bunk, I noticed a beautiful paperweight someone was making—a collage of small pieces of brightly colored glass that would go under a convex piece of clear glass. One day, even though the assembled mosaic pieces remained unattached to the glass top, I took the paper-weight and hid it in my trunk. When I gave it to my father after camp ended, he bound the top and bottom together with surgical tape and kept it on his desk. Whenever I saw it, shame flushed through me.

Perhaps some part of me had hoped he would recognize the improbability of a nine-year-old making something so intricate? Perhaps I did too good a job of pretending I was fine.

Once, when I was in college and tried to tell my father about my depression, he said, "We Russian Jews come by melancholy honestly." Perhaps that inheritance was more a function of history than of genes.

Maurice Paper:
A One-Two Punch

I was never the same. I was never the same.
— Maurice Paper

(Chic Paper collection)

The morning of the third interview, as we woke up in my father-in-law's house in Columbia, Maryland, David began complaining. "*Another* interview?"

"I'll take you into Washington," Burke said. "We'll be good."

"Oh, *that's* not boring," Ray interjected.

"Boring? Washington boring? When did you become a teenager?" I tried to tease him.

But as I drove to the interview and looked out the window at the colonial farmhouses, all well maintained, exuding the impression that happy families lived there, David's words rang true for me also. Another interview. How could I have ever thought I could do eight within ten days? My ability to listen with concern and compassion already felt close to depleted. I wanted to lie on a beach and sleep in the warm sun.

I pulled up to a condominium building surrounded by fields that echoed their former life as a farm. As I walked up to the front door, knowing what I might hear, the walls of my stomach pressed together.

The names of the building's residents, listed in the lobby, jolted me. Each one was Jewish: Abrams, Davidowitz, Davidson, Finkelman, Gershen, Levy, Schwartz.... I rang the button next to the name Paper. As I stood in the hallway a deep voice called out. "Is there a Leila out here? Come down to your left."

The man who appeared looked like my Uncle Max: Tall for a Jewish man of Eastern European parents—about five-feet-ten— with a broad body and more hair than most of his peers. His strong, open and smiling face welcomed me.

"Come, we're down here at the end."

Mrs. Paper, leaning on a cane, stood in the doorway of their apartment. Next to her husband, she appeared birdlike, tiny, but her vivacity filled the room. When I walked in, I saw that these people were kindred spirits. A glass case next to Mrs. Paper brimmed over with china figurines and other *tchotchkes*—small objects with no function. In the living room, the bright yellows, deep reds, and royal blues of antique glass vases and dishes, displayed against a large picture window, drew my attention. Little ceramic elves nestled in a bowl on the dining table. "I've had those since I was a little girl," Mrs. Paper told me. I love to collect china *tchotchkes* also, but they drive my husband crazy. Yet these two people seemed of one mind about the plethora of objects.

"Our passion has been traveling to Europe to find our treasures," Mrs. Paper said. Her hand waved in the air. "Aach! What we didn't buy I could kick myself for. London's flea markets thirty years ago—we didn't know what a steal the china and fabrics

Chic & Cis Paper, 2007 *(Chic Paper collection)*

were. When I think on the bargains we passed up...." Her palm flattened against her chest. "Now there's no such thing as a bargain, especially in flea markets."

As we shared stories of great opportunities lost, Mrs. Paper opened a bedroom door and out bolted a barking dog that immediately placed itself at my feet and yapped away. Mr. Paper—Chic, as he asked me to call him—sat down on the couch next to me and began hushing the dog, to no avail. I pulled out my tape recorder.

"That's just like the one I recorded Matt's *haftorah* on!" Mr. Paper exclaimed. (Haftorah is the portion from the Bible, usually the Prophets, read after the Torah on Saturday mornings.) Wanting to make sure his grandson became *bar mitzvahed*, a desire that puzzled me later when Mr. Paper described his lack of religious sentiments, he recorded the short selection from *Prophets* that the *binai mitzvah* boy or girl sings after the Torah reading. Learning the portion's words and cantillation is the hardest task of becoming a *binai mitzvah*. His round face shining with pride, Mr. Paper *kaveled* not just over Matt's performance on his big day but over his grandson's superb character. (*Kavel* is a Yiddish word with no comparable English corollary: to express tremendous pride or personal satisfaction from another's success as if it were one's own.)

The M. Paper I had first contacted after finding a phone number in the Baltimore white pages turned out to be their grandson, Matt, who when I told him my purpose, enthusiastically gave me his grandfather's number. "He's a great guy with an amazing story," Matt said. I wondered if this liberator had shared his story with his children and grandchildren.

Mrs. Paper answered when I had called the number. Home by herself, once she heard the purpose of my contact, she shared her perspective of how her husband had handled his memories of witnessing Dachau.

"Oh, he buried it all those years," she told me. "Never said a word, not a word, even though I knew from letters he wrote home right afterwards that it had been awful. So he wrote he had seen it, that it was unbelievable, that he couldn't begin to describe it to me, and then I saw a few photos he had taken. But he never said a word once he was home, and I didn't want to cause any more pain by bringing it up. Then the American Jewish War Veterans did that exhibition ("GIs Remember"), and they interviewed him because he had donated his uniform and some other things that were on display. All of a sudden, in the middle of an answer, he just broke down. Just started sobbing like I'd never seen. And since then he's been able to talk about it."

I soon discovered that her husband did not quite agree with this estimation.

Mr. Paper's talent as a storyteller emerged as he began recounting his years in the war. Animated, hands gesticulating, he put his bear-sized body into the telling. Always a quick study of languages, perhaps from having heard at least four in his childhood home—Yiddish, Hebrew, Polish, and English—he became useful to the army as a translator, a job that put him in odd situations.

Somewhere in France, his commanding officer asked Mr. Paper to interrogate a Nazi colonel they were holding prisoner. As was true of many Jewish GIs, knowing Yiddish enabled Mr. Paper to understand German, as the former language is a hybrid of German and Hebrew. The colonel seemed to be cooperative, so Mr. Paper went with him, taking along another GI, "a little German guy," as a back-up interpreter.

They went into a tent and as Mr. Paper pulled out a cigarette, the colonel asked for one. Inhaling, he said, "*Ah, das is gut,*" sat down, and proceeded to answer every question, though the expression on his face became more and more perplexed. At the very end he stood up and said, "I've heard a lot of languages, a lot of accents, but what kind of German are you speaking? I can understand most of it, but some of it's not quite right."

Mr. Paper answered, "*Ish American un Jud*" (I am an American Jew), and the Nazi spit at him. "As I'm wiping my face, and I'm madder than hell, I said to my sergeant, 'Leave him alone, he belongs to me.'" But in the time it took Mr. Paper to wipe his face off, his sergeant plunged a dagger into the Nazi's back. "The guy's eyes were still open, but my sergeant has his arm around him, and I…" Mr. Paper let out a hearty laugh, "…I thought he had his arm up his back but, as I got up, I saw he was dead."

When Mr. Paper reminded the sergeant that that was against the Geneva Conventions, he answered, "Captain, you can court-martial me if you want; we're fighting for two years, and this god-damn jerk is going to spit in your face?"

As they carried the body out under a blanket on a stretcher, the colonel walked over and asked what the hell happened. Mr. Paper explained that after the questioning, the "SOB" had a heart attack.

The colonel responded that Mr. Paper was a lying bastard—and to get rid of the body.

Mr. Paper laughed hard, hitting his knee with his palm.

I asked if he had been ordered to go to Dachau because he spoke Yiddish.

He leaned his chest back against the couch and hushed up the dog, which had started yapping as he laughed. "In Africa, I was on General Eisenhower's staff, and one day he called me in. 'Son—' he called me 'son—' 'On your form it says you can read Hebrew but don't know what you're reading, and you can't speak it at all, but you speak Yiddish, understand it, and can read with some comprehension. What the hell is the difference between Hebrew and Yiddish?'

"'General,' I answered, 'It will take me more than five minutes to explain the difference.' He said, 'I don't care. Sit in my chair. I want to know the difference.'"

Mr. Paper explained that Yiddish was the street language of the Jews while Hebrew was the synagogue language. Even though Yiddish is written with Hebrew letters, it's a different language from Hebrew, because of all the German mixed in.

"He liked my explanation," Mr. Paper said with a smile.

He then skipped two years forward to when he was a captain in Munich and the GIs had discovered Dachau. General Eisenhower, now five stars, remembered Paper and ordered him to Dachau to communicate with the inmates about how the U.S. government would provide for them. All Mr. Paper knew, as he rounded up ten guys to accompany him in a jeep to some place in the woods ten miles outside Munich, was that they would find a prison full of typhus.

"I didn't know what I was going to face. I didn't know where I was going!"

I leaned forward. "They didn't tell you what kind of camp it was?"

"Nothing." Mr. Paper turned his hands palms down as his hands moved away from each other as if he were flattening a sheet.

"Not even the shape people would be in?" I asked.

Prisoners of Dachau upon liberation

He shook his head no.

"Had you heard stories?"

"Sure. What they were doing to the Jews—putting them in concentration camps. But we thought they were like our internment camps. When I saw it, this completely changed my life. I was very affected by it."

Troops had entered the camp some hours prior to when Mr. Paper had arrived. The inmates were desperate for food, desperate to leave the camp, but his orders were to tell them they could not leave. He reassured them that in forty-eight hours they would have doctors and nurses and food and clothing. "We're going to make you people again," he told them. One prisoner asked why they should listen, why they should believe him.

"Because I talk Jewish," Mr. Paper had responded.

The prisoner said, "So did Eichmann."

Paper thought of a solution; he asked the prisoners to test him. After a couple of minutes one of the skeletal men asked, "How are you called up to the Torah in *shul*?" When Mr. Paper answered,

Survivors of Dachau

"Yitzhack ben Zev," the prisoner looked around at the others and said, "Only a Jew would know that."

"A Jew with a uniform? A Jew as an officer? Unheard of!"

"Was it difficult to deal with what you saw?" I asked.

"Oh, sure, very hard." His hands floated out in front of him again, palms down. "You were so affected by this...."

This sudden switch to the second person, as if Mr. Paper was speaking of someone other than himself, struck me. Over the next several interviews, I would notice how other liberators also made this switch at the same moment: when they spoke, or tried to speak, of their reaction to the camps.

Mrs. Paper interjected, "I don't know how they ever got through."

"And I was an officer," her husband continued, as if an officer should be tougher, less affected by witnessing atrocity, as if he had failed somehow.

Again, his wife spoke. "When I looked at the photos he took there, that he sent.... We gave them to the Jewish War Veterans."

I tried to return Mr. Paper to his train of thought, telling him how difficult it seemed to be for liberators to talk about what they witnessed in the camps.

"Yeah, it breaks you up."

"Well, I'll tell you," offered his wife. "He said very little about any of this when he came home. He ducked under beds when an airplane went over. Still doesn't go to fireworks. But we...he...doesn't really talk about war experiences unless I ask specific questions. He was terrific in his letters, all of which we lost in a hurricane's flooding. But then this all started to come out when he was interviewed in Washington for the Jewish War Veterans' exhibition."

Mr. Paper opened a photo album and pointed out a picture of himself as a young man in civilian clothes.

Mrs. Paper continued, explaining that the interview in

Washington had been the first time she had seen her husband break down. "They had to stop the interview, and afterwards he's been talking about it since."

I felt I was trying to grab a trout out of a stream as I asked Mr. Paper if talking about it had helped him. Instead of grabbing the intended tail, my question scooped up the fish by its belly.

"I was never the same. I was never the same," he said, looking at his hands. "I couldn't go back to school. I had every chance in the world to go back to college. I had every intention to go. I couldn't do it."

"He said, 'I just can't,'" his wife added. "He said, 'I cannot sit there; it's so pointless.'" During the war, she had also been through difficult experiences, losing her mother to cancer, and then after the readjustment to one another after Mr. Paper's return, their first child was born with mental retardation so severe his intelligence wasn't even measurable.

"Yeah, that kind of closed in on us, too," Mr. Paper said, his voice barely audible.

"But then we had two normal children who made up for everything," said his wife.

"Yeah, it was worth living this long just to see kids like that," Mr. Paper said, going on to explain that their first child's mental retardation resulted from oxygen deprivation during birth, a consequence that a caesarean section would have prevented. When the son turned nineteen, Mr. Paper removed him from the home because of how much of the family's energy he sapped. "She," he nodded towards his wife, "wouldn't let go."

"He was a beautiful baby," she told me.

"I haven't been to a synagogue, as a member, in years and years, not since our younger was *bar mitzvahed*," Mr. Paper said. Anger punctuated his words, his face closed. "People can talk themselves into explanations. Like her uncle—telling himself kosher meat is healthier. What the hell was he talking about?" His burning eyes met mine.

"Did Dachau undermine your faith?" I asked.

"I went away a twenty-year-old boy and came home four years later a forty-year-old."

"And then to have your first child be so terribly handicapped."

"Yeah," Mr. Paper laughed with bitterness, "that really crimped it all—put a finishing touch on it." His hands jabbed the air, the palms still facing the floor. "How we made it through that, I don't know."

"Humor got us through it," his wife said.

"To come home to this... I was finished. I was finished. Thank God I was self-employed."

When I asked how he felt in anticipation of being interviewed by the Jewish War Veterans, he said he hadn't thought about it beforehand. "They had my raincoat and hat in the glass case, and there was one of those telephones hanging next to it. So I picked it up and heard myself telling a story. Then people around me began asking me questions, and all of a sudden—for some reason, I broke up. I don't know why."

"Well, you know why?" His wife's tone was kind and maternal.

"It just, it got me in the gut. I couldn't talk. It doesn't happen often."

His wife explained that her husband talks a lot but keeps feelings deeply hidden. And when he does talk, very often the feelings come out. "He's very even tempered, doesn't fly off the handle," she added.

"Was it different after that?" I asked. "When you talk about it?"

"I don't talk about it."

"After that interview, he did," Mrs. Paper insisted. "He started to talk; that was the first I heard the details."

"I never told her anything about it," Mr. Paper said.

I was in the middle of something but I didn't know what.

"You did tell me that you went," her voice took on a hard

edge. "I knew that you had been in Dachau. And you did show, well, it was quite a while later that you sent the pictures home, and I thought, *Oh my God, if this is what was there....* His way of coping was to push it down, the way you do with things when you don't want to face, and it became habit. He wouldn't think about it."

"What happened when your sons got to high school and started learning about the Holocaust?" I asked, thinking of my own son's questions.

Their second son, Bucky, was interested somewhat and asked questions, but the younger one asked very few. Matthew, Bucky's son, had asked his grandfather more questions than both sons. Mr. Paper had assembled a complete book of photos and explanations that he planned on bequeathing to Matt. "He's that kind of kid. Nobody has asked me the amount of questions he has."

"Did Bucky or Matthew recognize that seeing Dachau had been traumatic?"

"I don't know of anything that was more traumatic in World War II. Maybe if I had not been Jewish it wouldn't have affected me, but being Jewish, I was terribly affected. My mother's entire family all wiped out. Only a fifth cousin remained."

We sat in silence, Mr. Paper's words filling the room around us.

Walking out the lobby, through the parking lot, the air now hot and damp, I tried to surface from a gyre of emotions by latching onto one thought.

I was never the same.

This was the finishing touch, the one-two punch.

I don't know of anything that was more traumatic in World War II.

The contradictions of the Papers' remarks swirled in my head. Each was able to see some piece of the truth that the other wasn't: that the son was hopelessly retarded, that there was no help, that the other sons were being harmed, that they had to send their challenged child to an institution. In the 1950s and 1960s, the man had to be the strong one, when even a man who had not seen Dachau might not have had the strength to confront the hopelessness of their son's handicap. To see his first-born son impaired by retardation after returning from Europe and witnessing Dachau—how could his faith have withstood the blows?

And yet he taped his grandson's *haftorah* for him.

Humor got us through.

"You need a sense of humor to get through life," my father told me the last time I saw him. "Just be happy. That's all that counts."

This from a man who had always preached career, career, career, do great things, reach for the highest rung. What had shifted in him during those last few months?

I had never seen my father happy for more than an occasional few minutes. From the humor I have observed in my family and among Jewish friends, it seems that it was a defense against admitting misery, rather than a means to happiness. What humor can undo the Holocaust or even the wounds from witnessing just a piece of it? Jagged steel framed Mr. Paper's laughter. His humor seemed to mask his rage, to distract the listener, to disguise the pain.

We must be strong, I heard my father telling me as I sat out on the curb in front of the Papers' building, trying to collect myself before I went back to my father-in-law's house.

My father had had his own one-two punch after the war: His siblings cut all ties with him when he returned from Europe and revealed he had married a *shiksa*. The younger five acted on the directive of the oldest sibling, Jacob, who took on the mantle of family patriarch once their father died in 1938. Because he had helped fund my father's medical school education, Jacob felt entitled to write him, "What is this I hear about you falling for some gal over there? You need to have your head examined. You're coming back here to Perth Amboy to give back what we've sacrificed for you."

Rube, on far right, and his brothers before shipping out to Europe.
From far left: Alfred, Leon, Jacob and Jacob's wife, Malve.
(Reuben Levinson collection)

So my father left his love behind in Edinburgh and five years later began courting a woman in Perth Amboy named Clara. She did not return his interest until the government "convinced" him that he would be better off enlisting in the army as an officer than be drafted. When she got word that his unit was shipping off for Europe, she got on a train in New Jersey going to Forth Worth, and showed up at my father's boot camp, Camp Bowie. All this I learned during a rare solo visit my father made to my home in Austin. At a dinner party in his honor, I overheard him telling one of my friends, "I actually got married in Texas."

"You got married in Texas?" I said, once the guests left.

"Yes, your mother and I eloped."

I didn't know what shocked me more—that he said the words

"your mother" or that he revealed they had eloped. But what he did not reveal, what I only learned from my mother's sister when she contacted me after my father's death ("I didn't feel I could get in touch with you while your father was alive") was that my father placed a condition on their getting married—that Clara not tell anyone until he returned from the war.

As well as being a *shiksa*, Clara was from South Amboy, to boot. For my father's siblings, that defined the wrong side of the tracks.

How could his siblings cutting him off not have felt like the finishing touch for my father? In whom could he confide, find acceptance and understanding? He was alone with the images in his head, images of which he dared not speak even if someone had been willing to listen.

I'm not sure when my father's siblings began talking to him again. Maybe they took pity on him when rumors began spreading about crazy Clara. Maybe one or two of them helped to spread the rumors.

When she started falling apart, he was busy putting himself back together. Busy with his work, his practice. Perhaps by the time he recognized the crisis, it was too late. Or perhaps he saw his wife was unraveling but had no idea what would help. Because what had helped him?

"You always have your work," he told me many, many times. Work provided the only constant, the only relief, the only refuge. It kept his mind from snapping.

The street I was driving down did not look familiar: open fields, a new subdivision under construction. I had been driving several minutes with no awareness of where I was going. Sweat slipped my hands down the steering wheel. I pulled the car over, got out, and sat on a curb, my head in my hands.

...the finishing touch...

I saw myself sitting on the couch in the living room on Market

Street, Doris eighteen feet away in the kitchen. A book was on my lap, but I was not reading. I was imagining my future: I would have an adoring husband named Daniel, a daughter named Claire, a son named David, and we would live in a cozy cottage in the country with a horse in the pasture. I was Cinderella; Doris was my wicked stepmother and stepsisters all rolled into one. My Prince Charming awaited me in my future, the reward for my childhood of misery, the balancing out for all the bad things that had happened to me. I would find him; I would do it right.

Instead, my husband had known his own version of abandonment and my two sons did not fit into society's predetermined niches. Diagnosed with ADD in second grade, Ray struggled with school and became increasingly depressed. In high school, where teacher after teacher told me he was but one of their one hundred and fifty students, he was diagnosed with mild depression. When David was in second grade, he was diagnosed with Pervasive Developmental Disorder with co-morbidities of anxiety, obsessive-compulsive and mood disorders. Triggered by the slightest frustration or disappointment, his rages were always directed at me, the anger like acid pouring over me. Every year the boys' schooling required vigilance and constant involvement that, along with not having the support of an extended family, left me exhausted.

Feelings of hopefulness only led to bitter disappointment. I didn't realize I was training myself to expect setbacks until friends in high school began calling me cynical. After I became a mother, some people began describing me as negative. Just as I had when my father called me smart, I felt dissolved by words.

In 1964 my father finally moved us away from Perth Amboy and Doris. A thick lawn and trees surrounded our new house in Metuchen and our street had no traffic. After returning from summer camp, I walked into my new bedroom to find a white-lace canopied bed, white lace curtains against vivid flowered wallpaper, and a light blue dresser. I had gone from being Cinderella to a princess. I looked for the carriage of dolls that had sat under the basement stairs in Perth Amboy—dolls my mother had bought me but which Doris never let me play with. Now I could.

"Dolls?" my father's face creased, his eyes narrowed. "You're too old to play with dolls. I gave them away."

Alan's Steiff animals and marbles, my Kennedy card collection, and my comic books also did not make it to our new house. But Alan and I hardly had time to take stock of our gains and losses, because within a week, my father announced that Alan was going to a prep school in Connecticut where our older brother Robert had been for the previous three years. Perhaps it was the new house that released me from the unstated rules of our family, because for the first time I protested, wailed, pleaded. "Please, please, let him stay with us!" Alan promised he would do well in public school, that he'd still get into Yale. We reminded our father that he himself had gotten into Yale from a public school, but none of it moved him. "I want to give you the best advantages to succeed," he told Alan. "You'll thank me some day."

Every moment not in school I spent outside. Then one evening, as my father pulled into the driveway, he rolled down his car window, the creases in his forehead and his narrowed eyes signaling trouble. I slid out of the apple tree.

"Have you done your homework?"

"I don't have any."

"Well, get upstairs and open a book. In Perth Amboy, you were always reading. Now you're always outside running around. I've had enough of your tomboy behavior."

My father and I no longer went on Sunday drives or watched *Saturday Night at the Movies* together. We sat at the dinner table in silence.

Then, at the YMHA where my Hebrew School met, we began

running into Mrs. Kelsey, a widow who had been everyone's favorite fourth-grade teacher at my elementary school in Perth Amboy. The first time we met her as she waited for her children, my father's eyes lit up, and from then on, his eyes scanned the lobby as soon as we walked in.

My father suddenly began smiling. He stopped asking me about my homework and what I had read that day. When he took me to the camp bus that June, rather than looking wistful, he exuded ebullience and energy. A week before Parents' Weekend, the news arrived in a letter: "I've been taking Mrs. Kelsey out this summer. She's a very sweet lady. Why don't you write her son Gene and daughter Kathy at their camp? Here are their addresses...." On Parents' Weekend he told me. "Mrs. Kelsey is going to be your new mother."

Sixth grade became the best year of my life. I had a loving mother at home who didn't mind that I climbed trees. My father smiled and talked at the dinner table and often patted me on the back. My spirited and caring teacher challenged me, his eyes sparkling as I caught his enthusiasm. My new sister Kathy encouraged me to speak up for myself, and my new brother Gene was proving to be a great playmate who appreciated my athletic skills. My pretty mother, in her vividly printed and colored Gucci short dress, was always waiting for Kathy and me at three o'clock in front of the school and came along on our class field trips. Golden rays of grace were streaming down on me; at last I knew life's goodness.

But the following autumn, the happiness evaporated, as though the thin membrane containing us had broken open, allowing our old melancholy back in. Its presence was most palpable at the dinner table, where my father's pout enveloped us like a cloak. He kept his eyes on his plate and refused to speak. My stepmother had become skilled at making monologues into conversations. "You know who I ran into today at Metzky's fruit market,

Rube? Martha Schwartz. Remember Mitzie Glover? Martha's her siser. Abe Cohen's girls. She was telling me the city is letting a group tear down that old warehouse on Washington Street—the one that Izzy once leased near the water—to build some condos. Can you imagine condos in Perth Amboy? What next, time shares?"

She laughed, the sharp edge of her "hah" like an arrow speeding down the table. I did not know if I should jump in and agree that condos in Perth Amboy were ridiculous or pretend that she and my father were having a conversation.

This silence differed from what Barbra Streisand or the Yale Whiffenpoofs had filled. That silence had resulted from the exile of all our thoughts. This silence came from a stubborn, angry withholding.

In the spring, I fell out of a tree while trying to retrieve a ball for my brother. Our neighbor, into whose yard I fell, picked me up and drove me to my front door. One leg had a jagged cut, while I could not stand on the other one.

When my father returned from the office, he stood at the end of my bed and pointed at me. "If you weren't a tomboy, this wouldn't have happened."

School became a prison, the math hieroglyphics, French sheer agony, English sheer boredom. I lost my smartness, the answers no longer dropping into my brain like manna on the Israelites in the desert. When my teachers handed me yellow warning notices, I wondered with fear what response my father would have to Ds when he had already expressed "disappointment" over Bs.

When I showed the notices to my stepmother, I wanted her to say something that would cushion my fall, but her mouth tightened. "You're failing? How could you be failing?"

"I don't know. Really, I don't," I said.

"You've got to find a better attitude. You understand?"

I nodded my head. "Would you tell Dad?"

She stood there, not answering, looking at the ceiling, and then she sighed, a long sigh. "All right. But you have got to promise not to let this happen again." I nodded my head, and at that moment she and I entered a dynamic that continued for many years—where she became the intermediary with my father when I feared his response.

A few nights later, the door to my bedroom opened; thank God I was at my desk doing homework. My father stood in the doorway wagging his finger at me. "I expect you to do well in school. You understand?"

"Yes."

"You've a good mind," he said. "Put it to use."

My jaw clenched as I nodded again.

I managed to stop failing but as the silence in my home grew, so did a hole in me that I tried to fill with food, stopping at the Chicken Little store on the way home for French fries or an ice cream cone from Costa's. But neither French fries nor ice cream lessened the headaches that started pounding as I walked home. There seemed no way out of the misery.

One evening I was alone in the den watching the 1960 post-Holocaust drama *Exodus* on television. The garage door went up; my father was home from the hospital. Without taking off his coat, he sat down next to me on the couch and put his hand on top of mine. "How are you doing, Leila?"

I shrugged my shoulders, keeping my eyes on Paul Newman's blue ones as they beamed from his tan face.

"You haven't seemed happy lately. In fact, you haven't seemed happy in some time. Is anything wrong?"

His words surprised me so much that I didn't think before answering, "I don't know. Nothing seems to work out."

"We've been through too much for you to be miserable," he said, his voice holding back anger. "We've had more than our share of heartache. I'm going to do whatever I can to make things better for you." He reached up and took my chin in his hand. "Starting with your acne. We're going to get you a dermatologist. You're too pretty to go around with these cysts marring you." And he stood up, as if that closed the case, and walked away.

Soon afterwards I recognized that I wasn't the only one suffering. Our family occasionally took Sunday drives, and one Sunday afternoon we were driving back from Princeton, on Route One, and passed the Moddess sanitary napkins plant. Huge white letters stood on the lawn, spelling out "Moddess, because...," the "because" in italics. Gene, who was only nine, asked, "Because why?"

No one answered, and he asked again, "Because why?"

My father whipped his head around, his eyes bulging like an overheated horse. "You be quiet, do you hear me?"

Gene flattened against the seat and tucked his chin into his chest, biting his lip, squeezing his hands together in his lap. Air whooshed through a tunnel that had opened up through my head. What was wrong with my father? What was he thinking? The car became a ticking bomb for the rest of the excruciating fifteen minutes to the house, and when we pulled in the driveway, we flung the doors open and rushed to our rooms. Through the wall I heard my father in Gene's room: "What the hell did you think you were doing back there? Trying to embarrass your mother and sisters? Don't you ever let me hear you talk like that again. Do you hear me?"

My stepsister was sitting on her bed; I was standing, frozen, next to my desk. Neither of us looked at the other. My heart shrank.

My father became unapproachable. Immediately after dinner, he retired to the couch in the den to watch Walter Cronkite present that day's number of American troops killed in Vietnam. At breakfast, he spread out the newspaper around his cereal bowl, first reading the stock market report, and then, as he poured his remaining cereal milk into his Lipton tea, turning to the front page, its headlines announcing to me how many American troops had been killed in Vietnam the day before.

When Martin Luther King, Jr. and then Robert Kennedy were killed, no one in my house cried. Alan and I went down to the train tracks and waved as the train carrying Robert Kennedy's body up to Boston passed by. I felt hope leave me as the train slipped behind the trees.

Sitting on the curb a few blocks from the Papers' condo, my body felt like a spent balloon that had been inflated to the breaking point—deflated and re-inflated until there was no elasticity left.

I was not discovering my father through my interviewees. I was discovering myself.

My childhood had trampled my spirit, had frozen and col-lapsed time into that moment in the police station, my mother's voice forever calling me back.

The police station stood as clear in my mind as the gates of Dachau were for Mr. Kaiser, Mr. Paper, and Mr. Heimberg.

What was that image preventing me from seeing? Was I doing a terrible job of parenting and did not even see it—a thought more excruciating than the failure of life to deliver a "happy ever after?" Had my fearfulness, my anxiety, my insecurity affected my mothering? What might I be transmitting to my children? Maybe I was the source of David's anxiety. I knew there had been costs for one child of my trying to meet the needs of the other, but per-haps the costs of real consequence were those from my childhood. Nausea twisted my stomach, and I bent over, trying to throw up. Nothing came out besides tears.

When I walked into my father-in-law's house, he and Burke were watching the Democratic National Convention on television. Theresa Heinz was on the screen speaking about the selflessness of her husband, John Kerry.

"Why should we care what his wife thinks?" Burke's father said.

"Well, Dad," Burke responded, "it really wouldn't matter to you if it was Mother Theresa up there praising Kerry, you still wouldn't vote for him. So you're not the most objective person."

Roger laughed. "You've got a point, Burke."

I walked upstairs to where Ray and David were playing Game Cube on a television Burke had rigged up for them. They both greeted me.

"Was it a good interview?" David asked.

"It was enlightening," I said.

"Enlightening?"

"She means it helped her to understand her dad better," Ray translated.

"And even myself," I added, though when I saw the puzzlement on both their faces, I regretted the words.

The boys turned back to the television screen, the fact that their mother might not understand herself probably more information than they wanted.

That evening, as I lay in bed, an image surfaced of myself as a six-year-old sitting on the elephantine boulder in the parking lot of my summer camp. Parents' Visiting Day. Cars spill out of the lot onto the field around the social hall, down along the tennis courts. Groups of girls and parents are walking down to the lake; the welcoming ceremony is over—next is the day's first activity. I turn back to face the road, where a black car appears. My heart leaps, but the car doesn't turn into the lot. *Maybe he's dead. No, he can't be. Maybe he had an accident. Maybe he was killed. No, no, he must be all right. I can't be an orphan.* My fingers curl around the cracked edge of granite and squeeze.

Four black cars later, one turns into the drive. The rush of joy flips my heart. My balding, dark-haired father emerges and raises his arms to the sky, his eyes beaming.

"Leila!" I rush to his embrace.

The month before I turned six, my father drove me into New York City. We parked the car amidst towering buildings that blocked the sky and walked to a building named Grand Central Station that reminded me of a birthday cake with fancy frosting. Inside was a huge ballroom with people running everywhere, a man's voice booming numbers and town names, a deep blue sky draped over the ceiling. All the stars in the sky connected into shapes I had seen in books: a winged horse, a huge bear, an enormous cup, a blindfolded woman holding plates on strings. I had entered a fairy tale.

My father sat me in what looked and felt like a closet, but he told me there was a camera looking at me. "Smile," he instructed. "It's taking a photo of you so I can see you even when you're off in camp."

The word "camp" puzzled me.

"Ticonderoga Overnight, Track Four" boomed into the air, everyone around us jumping from their seats. The blue of my father's eyes darkened as he pressed a coin into my palm.

"Okay, Leila, here's a quarter for the porter. Make sure you give it to him. Ask any of the other girls if you need help."

A crowd herded us down dark steps into the station's basement, where a train stretched out like a black leopard ready to spring forward.

Taken in Grand Central Station

"I'll be up next month to visit," my father said. "And I'll write. Be good." He patted my back and handed me a small overnight bag, and it was then I realized that whatever camp was, he wasn't coming there with me.

Girls urged me up the steps into the train. Girls of all ages, but every one of them older than I, ran down the aisles singing and shouting, "Hello," "Hi," "You're back!" Someone opened a door and said, "This room is yours. We'll be right next door."

I sat down and held my breath. The train moved into pitch black. I squeezed my eyes shut and my hand tighter around the quarter. When I had to take a breath, I opened my eyes: The darkness had left, taking the city with it. A black man with a big smile and gray hair in a gray uniform and a red hat appeared at the door.

"Well, look at you, all by yourself. They send 'em younger and younger. May I get your bed ready, miss?"

Like a magician pulling a rabbit out of a hat, by lifting the seat and moving a latch, he made a bed appear out of the wall, sheets and blanket already in place.

"Never been on a Pullman before?"

I shook my head no.

"You'll like it, I promise. It rocks you to sleep, just like in your mama's arms. Now if you need anything, you be sure and press this button." He pointed to a black buzzer on the wall. "I'm the porter, and I'll help you."

I wanted to hug him as I handed him the sweaty quarter.

"Why, thank you, miss. Pleasant dreams."

When I woke up the next morning, the train was standing still. I looked out the window and saw tall trees, only trees. Then I remembered: I was going to some place called camp. Was camp a forest?

As a GI, the American poet Anthony Hecht helped to liberate Flossenburg concentration camp. His poem, "The Book of Yolek," begins with descriptions of the glories of camping but then continues:

Whether on a silent, solitary walk
Or among crowds, far off or safe at home,
You will remember, helplessly, that day,
And the smell of smoke, and the loudspeakers of the camp.

Wherever you are, Yolek will be there, too.
His unuttered name will interrupt your meal.

Flossenburg corrupted forever the word "camp" for Hecht, a liberator who expressed how "the suffering, the prisoners' accounts were beyond comprehension. For years after I would wake shrieking." In 1959, he suffered a breakdown and was hospitalized. Perhaps poetry helped to heal him. At the very least, it provided a place in which he could attend to his psyche's wounds, acknowledge what he had lost.

"Love, my love" my father said to my answering machine the day before he died of a massive coronary.

I never heard him say, "I love you."

Yet his eyes sparkled, his arms shot skyward every time I stepped out of the airport gate. The Saturday morning phone calls, the letters tucking away $20 bills, the questions about my diet, my sleep, the composition book listing the stocks—he had shown his love as much as he was able.

He was unable to speak the words or wrap me in his arms and hold me tight.

He returned from Europe a casualty.

Al Hirsch:
Lamination

Yes, it changed me. Times I wondered—did you ever change, did you ever change back?

—Al Hirsch

(Al Hirsch collection)

107

Burke was packing bottles of water and fruit, preparing to take the boys into the District while I went off to my fourth interview.

"Do we have to?" David whined.

"Hey, maybe there'll be some good souvenirs," Ray reminded him.

"Will there be any rock shops?"

"You bet," Burke said, summoning enthusiasm. "At the Smithsonian."

Secretly glad to be missing the sightseeing, I smiled and headed to a neighborhood only ten minutes away that had been built for veterans of World War II. Mr. Hirsch moved his family there in 1969.

He and I had corresponded via emails for over six weeks, his notes revealing a warm and intelligent man with a sardonic wit who had little patience for fools. In his most recent email, he had asked if his daughter, Lisa, might sit in on the interview, and the prospect of sharing another child's response to her father's history intrigued me. Lisa answered the door of the modest, well-kept brick home on a cul-de-sac, perhaps one of the first cul-de-sacs in the country, I thought, as I looked at the nearly identical brick homes. Although geraniums adorned the outside of the house, the closed curtains in the living room, the unmoving air, the blue-and-white plates anchored on shelves told me the woman of the home was no longer alive.

"I love blue-and-white china," I commented to Lisa.

"So did my mother. This was her collection."

Mr. Hirsch did not look anywhere near his eighty-six years. He still had a good deal of dark hair, a strong voice, erect carriage, and a vigorous handshake. Lisa exuded a youthful spirit in a t-shirt and shorts that revealed toned legs. Like myself, she wore no makeup, which along with her open smile put me at ease. A visual artist, she immediately expressed appreciation for my undertaking my project with the GI liberators.

They showed me a shadowbox full of medals that, along with

Bodies GIs found "stored" at Ohrdruf
(*Al Hirsch collection*)

a Bronze Star, contained a photograph of the piles of bodies in a camp. "It was Lisa's idea to frame those," Mr. Hirsch told me. Lisa explained she and her dad wanted to make sure the medals would "be preserved, not ripped apart." As we sat down at a walnut table in the middle of a bright kitchen with crisp, ruffled gingham curtains, Mr. Hirsch expressed that he had always been willing to talk about Ohrdruf, the camp he had helped to liberate as a member of the 89th Infantry.

"Wasn't I?" He looked at Lisa for confirmation.

"I think maybe," she answered, "but there's a point—you're not raising kids, you're retired, you can catch your breath and start reflecting more."

When I asked Lisa at what age she became aware of her father's war experiences, she told me that photographs of Ohrdruf, the very first concentration camp in Germany that the American GIs came upon (the Russians had discovered Auschwitz three months before), had always been a part of her life. In their basement, along with clotheslines for drying their laundry in the winter, a vacuum cleaner, snow boots, and a metal cabinet full of Passover dishes, was a shiny metal Army trunk bursting with fancy dresses, feather and veiled hats, and high heels that once belonged to Lisa's mom and her sisters for them to play dress-up.

"The pictures of Ohrdruf were in there so I saw them," she said. "I grew up seeing them as long ago as I can remember. It wasn't like, 'What are you doing in that trunk?' No, I was always going in there."

Photographs, all but indistinguishable from my father's— images of endless heaps of tortured corpses—had been a part of Lisa's landscape since she could remember. As her father placed on the table several sheets of paper covered with double-spaced

Ohrdruf *(Al Hirsch collection)*

print, I made a note to myself to ask her more about the photographs later. "It's a lot easier to write it than to say it," Mr. Hirsch told me as he picked up the pages to read, his voice occasionally wavering.

After viewing the concentration camps, we returned to where our 50 mm antitank gun was parked and I started to wonder where hatred like this is born. Where and why does the intense passion to hate drive one to mass murder? My thoughts were interrupted when I was told to get going because our squad was pulling out. I was more than ready to leave this gruesome place. We loaded up and got in the truck once again. We drove along with no one speaking; there was no need to. Each of us was lost in our own thoughts, and each remembered what we had witnessed. The experience and recollection was etched in each face. Over and over again the same cruel brutal memory of carnage, torture, and disregard for life flashed through my brain. As we rode further from that place of torment and deeper into Germany, the words of the poet Edward Markham echoed through my head:
"O masters, lords and rulers in all lands
Is this the handiwork you give to God?"

This punctured the air with ferocity, even as his eyes remained on the paper.

After a few seconds of silence, I turned to Lisa.

"Do you feel that your father's having been a witness to Ohrdruf influenced you?"

"How can it help but influence you—knowing your place in the world...." (This answer and others that would follow as I had noted in previous interviews used the second person.) "That's why we're here in this little *shtetl* [of Pikesville] to isolate ourselves, but I think it was one more way to say 'watch out for the world.' It was never said that way, but we knew."

Knew what?

It wasn't until I got home and transcribed my tape that I saw her answer. Lisa's father had communicated to her indirectly what mine had spelled out: *Don't think it can't happen here.* We lived with no guarantee of security, even if everything around us seemed to indicate otherwise. (Of course, that is why my father so wanted me to become a Constitutional lawyer: I would help to

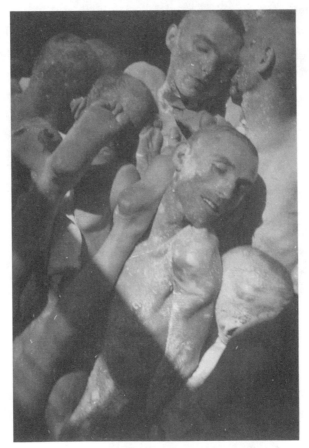

(Al Hirsch collection)

preserve liberty within our country and would become an instrument of our people's security.)

Rather than following up on his daughter's comment, Mr. Hirsch revealed his focus. "I was very bitter when I came back. People seemed so oblivious, unconcerned. 'Oh, aren't those concentration camps terrible.' I heard them say more about going to a bad movie: 'Wasn't that picture terrible!' I just couldn't understand that they couldn't understand how terrible it was. The intense hatred that I witnessed there…. How can people hate so much? Like in 9/11."

Ohrdruf had left Mr. Hirsch with an unrelenting need to comprehend the heart of darkness. I wondered if he had always had a philosophical mind.

"Did seeing Ohrdruf change you?" I asked.

"Oh, yes, sure. It had, when, like I say, when I came back it had. To see what men—my fellow man—was capable of. To see how really unconcerned a good portion of the population was; it was just something they had read about. Well, of course, they couldn't feel it like I did. Yes, it changed me. Times I wondered—did you ever change, did you ever change back?" (There was the second person again.)

"I lost my faith," Mr. Hirsch said. "Though I tried to find it again."

Lisa suggested that perhaps his loss of faith resulted from the horrible ordeal they had gone through of Alzheimer's killing her mother slowly over seven years.

"No," he spoke in clear calm words, "it wasn't because of Mommy, no. When I came back, I tried going to synagogue. I just couldn't."

It seemed the loss of faith, at least among the Jewish GIs, had been universal. My father never showed a modicum of faith, never said a blessing, never looked at the mezuzah at our front door, never even mentioned God, only going to services for the High

The ashes of Ohrdruf's victims *(Al Hirsch collection)*

Holy Days and his parents' *yartzheits*. Yet, he vehemently insisted my brothers and I become *bar mitzvahed*, or confirmed.

Mr. Hirsch's words then took a mysterious turn. "Some people get more, some less. It's something that just evolves. I'm eighty-six. It just laminates; you know. It's one thing that happens on top of another, then all the memories are glued together. And one day you wake up and say to yourself, *You know what—it's a sham.*"

I wondered to what "it" referred.

"I have Dante's *Inferno*," he added. "I'm reading it, and it's a wonderful book. It hasn't scared me one bit."

How could it, I thought, after seeing Ohrdruf? Many of the GIs quoted in the book *In Evidence* likened the gates of the camps to the entrances and exits to hell, but Dante believed in moral reciprocity and balance, while I sensed that Mr. Hirsch doubted such a moral order existed.

Like Chic Paper, Herman Zeitchik, and George Kaiser, Mr. Hirsch had not felt able to take advantage of the GI Bill, though he did not see his decision the consequence of his war experience. "Security was always the goal," he said. Mr. Hirsch also worked to make his family safe in this "*shtetl,*" as Lisa called it. He made security his priority, denying himself the education for which he must have thirsted. Lisa later told me that he had been taking college courses ever since his retirement.

When Mr. Hirsch mentioned he had married before shipping overseas in 1944, I asked if he had shared with his wife what he saw at Ohrdruf.

"No. She knew I had been through it." (He had sent her the photographs of Ohrdruf.) "She never asked me too much about it, and I never told her too much."

He turned to his daughter. "Did I tell you anything? I told you some things when it would come up—like the smell of lime out on a field. I'd say, 'Hey, that reminds me....' Did I go into detail with you?"

"Um, I don't think great detail," Lisa said, shifting in her seat and looking down at the paper clip she was bending. "I don't think I got huge, in-depth explanations. It was mostly those photos. They're pretty vivid, big time—those faces, those people. You knew."

As if giving me a chance to talk with Lisa alone for a moment, Mr. Hirsch excused himself and left the room. Here was my

A courtyard in Ohrdruf *(Al Hirsch collection)*

chance to see how someone else in my situation had reacted to seeing the photos. I asked Lisa if the photos had scared her when she first saw them.

She kept her eyes on her hands. "I was so young when you first look at it, you don't, you just don't get it. You know, and then it just becomes a part of you. I just looked, it was…horrible when you asked, but this is so young when you're first seeing it, so you're not really getting it."

I commented how unusual it was to have become aware of the Holocaust at such a young age.

"Umm, well…." (Was this hesitation or prevarication, I wondered.) "Maybe it matters in my art to get a bigger picture of man and humanity, the fragile existence of life."

She later sent me a note with additional thoughts about the impact of the photographs.

I found the photos in my father's trunk at a very early age. They were very tiny black and white images of a horrific event to which at my young age of limited life experiences, I had no yardstick of comparison.   They were not life size, had no smells, no names, and no comparisons to the self-absorbed limited world of a five-year-old. I carried those images in my head and as the world presented itself, I became better acquainted with the seriousness of the images.   They were not my only examples in my young life of the history of my people.   My Bubby lived with us and spoke to me of shtetl *life on her family's farm in Pumpian Lithuania, where they raised cows and traded horses.   Being born in 1880, she told me of the Pogroms that swept through Lithuania and the false accusations against Jews. This was my Bubby's history and her words became my history, layering with the photos in my Father's army trunk.   Through the years, more*

Burned victims, Ohrdruf (*Al Hirsch collection*)

personal experiences laminate to ingrain themselves as my history. Those whispered lessons of Jewish events laid dormant in my uncon- scious mind, until I was old enough to comprehend their meanings.

During my visit to her home, I asked her if she was able to talk to her father about Ohrdruf.

"As I was growing up, my father would always stop and take his time to answer my questions about the war. I could tell that his words were carefully chosen and guarded. I learned I was treading on hallowed ground by the inflections of his tone, the look in his eyes, and his body language. But I never felt I couldn't ask. As he talked, I could see it was really horrible; I mean, I got the idea."

Pressing for clarity, I asked if she had a sense of how seeing Ohrdruf had affected her father. Lisa said that he had lost his mother when he was three and his stepmother was killed by a car when he was seventeen. "So he's just had this role, and so this is life, and this is just one other thing—one terrible event out of many he's had."

I repeated for her the earlier words of her father that he came home a different person than when he left.

"I don't know," she said. "You know that age of twenty—you can be somebody one year, giggly and a teenager—and then, boom, you're an adult. So I don't know, though there are certain aspects that he won't talk about if I ask. He'll shut down." She had thought his writing about it would enable her to understand the full picture.

Though her answers sometimes frustrated me, when I later grappled with a surprising range of trauma among the GI libera- tors, I came to appreciate the information about her father's early traumas. But sitting in their kitchen, I felt as if I was butting my head against a clear partition.

Mr. Hirsch walked back in, and somehow we began talking

about the forthcoming presidential election. His political views caught me by surprise. I had not imagined someone with similar history to my father's could have such a different political orientation, and my surprise slipped from my mouth, breaking the rapport. I left their home with the sense that I had screwed up.

"Just listen and be open," a friend had counseled me about doing the interviews before I left Austin. "Just let them talk."

I envied Lisa for her father still being alive, for her palpable closeness with him, for having access to his past. Here was a father who communicated with his daughter, who shared himself, who had allowed a close bond to form. But I wondered if that bond had heightened Lisa's sense of life's precariousness.

Many of the liberators stated that their desire to protect their children kept them silent. I understood this motivation. I have not shared with my children stories of my own painful childhood out of a fear that introducing too soon the world's potential for loss and cruelty would warp their spirit. And though my sons are now young men, I have yet to share specifics.

Hadn't my father's photographs taught me that silence does not shelter a child?

As I drove away, I wondered about the nature of the liberators' trauma. All the men I had spoken with were soft-spoken, stable, hardworking husbands and fathers, while people with post-traumatic stress disorder (PTSD) are unable to function because of violent anger or extreme depression. People with PTSD are addicted to drugs and/or alcohol, are volatile and unpredictable. Maybe the veterans were no more traumatized than I had been by strangers separating me from my mother suddenly and permanently.

Yes, they all showed signs of depression, of melancholy, but did that constitute PTSD? What did it mean to "never be the same?" To have come home a different person than the one who left. Did they mean that literally?

Seeing a bookstore in a strip mall, I pulled into the parking lot and bought two books on trauma. Then I went to a coffee shop and spent the rest of the day reading.

I bought two books on PTSD—*Trauma and Recovery* by Judith Herman and *Waking the Tiger* by Peter Levine, both considered seminal on the subject. Levine and Herman take a broad view that trauma pervades modern life. As long as an event instills feelings of terror and helplessness and seems to threaten annihilation, it traumatizes a person. Traumatic events are extraordinary, not because they are rare, but because they overwhelm someone's ability to function. (This differs from The American Psychiatric Association's definition of trauma stated in *The Diagnostic and Statistical Manual of Mental Disorder* or *DSM IV*—standard classification of mental disorders used by mental-health professionals. It defines trauma as the consequence of events outside the range of usual human experience that involve "actual or threatened death or serious injury or a threat to the physical integrity of the self or others." As well as military combat, the DSM cites violent personal attacks such as rape, natural or man-made disasters, and torture as trauma-inducing experiences.) Herman and Levine believe that common situations such as emergency-room visits, routine surgery, falls, and car accidents can be traumatic if they are horrible and scary enough to be, or even appear to be, life-threatening.

According to Herman, victims unconsciously blame themselves for having been attacked as they want to believe they had some control, some ability to have prevented what happened from having happened, that they had overlooked taking some precaution, been too flirtatious, or taken too much risk. Believing one's self to be at fault is more tolerable than acknowledging our fundamental vulnerability to life's random violence, because then we would always be vulnerable to more destruction. Nothing we could do would make us safer, a reality capable of inducing madness if fully acknowledged.

Herman breaks traumatic experiences into three components: 1) being taken by surprise, 2) feeling trapped, 3) and the experience results in utter physical and mental exhaustion.

Herman explains that human beings, like all animals, are biologically wired to experience fear when danger looms, but with trauma, a feeling of terror continues even after the danger is gone, as though the terrifying event is still occurring.

I envisioned my father again, wagging his finger. "Don't think it can't happen here," his words echoed. "Always have your passport up to date." He never felt safe.

There are three categories of symptoms of PTSD, consequences of being traumatized that may not manifest themselves for months or years after the event and may come and go over years. The first such category is "intrusion" where the victim relives the event, the memory returning in minute detail, so detailed that the person feels as if they have time-traveled. (My memory of the day in the police station was extremely detailed, but, I assured myself, never did I think it was still happening.) Often sensory cues—sounds, smells, or images—trigger the memory. Recurrent nightmares are common. (But I hadn't heard any veteran liberator talking about nightmares. Mr. Heimberg had a recurring dream, but it wasn't a nightmare.)

Avoidance or "constriction" is the second category of symptoms. The person avoids anything related to or capable of reminding them of the traumatic event. These symptoms often involve victims numbing themselves emotionally. (My father never showed any emotion other than occasional outbursts of anger. But that's true of many people, I thought.)

The third category is "hyper-arousal," where the person is constantly irritable, on edge, jumpy, prone to panic attacks and insomnia, always expecting danger. (I tried to remember if my father had been constantly irritable. Why had I avoided bringing up subjects like the Vietnam War, race relations, Nixon, and my birth mother that were likely to displease him? Why did I use my stepmother as a go-between?)

The ultimate consequence of trauma, Herman claims, is that it shatters one's connection to others. The trauma profoundly and irreparably violates core beliefs, values, and self-image, which had bridged that individual to community, family, and friends. So not only does the victim's sense of self become damaged, but they are left feeling utterly abandoned and unloved. (My father had kept our family together. Yet how loved did he feel?)

While in high school, I spent a Saturday in New York City and brought back a necklace, a piece of costume jewelry, for my stepmother. I gave it to her as she and my father sat watching the news.

"Isn't it lovely!" she said. "Don't you like it, Rube?'

My father gathered up his newspapers and stood up in one swift motion, wordlessly leaving the room, the flopping of his slippers on the stairs signaling my parents' bedroom as his destination.

My stepmother and I looked at one another, her compressed forehead and lips mirroring my own discomfort.

As I lay reading on my bed that evening, the door to my room burst open, my father standing in the doorway, pointing at me. "You could have gotten me something also. All I do for you. I don't think that's too much to ask."

As the title of her book indicates, Herman lays out a path for recovery. Survivors must receive attention and assurance. Re-integration back into their community.

Back at my father-in-law's house, after everyone else went to bed, I stayed up, doing more research on the computer. One website discussed how trauma often results in disassociation, a change in the victim's consciousness. The site quotes the Yale psychiatrist, Dr. Dennis Charney: "It does not matter if it was terror of combat, a hurricane, or auto accident. All uncontrollable stress can have the same biological impact: victims of devastating trauma may never be the same biologically."

I clicked the red X on the Internet window, turned off the computer, and sat in front of some television sitcom until I could not keep my eyes open.

I did not want to admit that my father had been traumatized. Because I did not want to admit that I had been.

Witnessing the Holocaust changed the liberators—forever. Nordhausen irreparably changed my father. The man I knew (or what I knew of him) was not the Rube Levinson who his mother Lena had raised, who had courted Clara; not the Rube who had gone off to Europe. Perhaps that man would have been a loving father, seen my need to grieve, and noticed my depression.

Perhaps his good aspects, the soft, warm man whose eyes could laugh, were what I had known of my father's pure soul, his *neshamah t'hora*. I knew, when I first saw my father's photograph, my body knew, that what the photos recorded had defaced his pure soul long before I ever had a chance to be held and loved within it.

While this possibility disturbed me, it was not really all that new. I had begun to suspect that the man I knew was more a product of witnessing Nordhausen than he was the man who had gone off to Yale, a poor son of poor immigrants but on his way to realizing the American dream.

No, this disturbance went deeper than that.

This was about me as much as about my father. This was why I had not been able to take in Dr. Charney's words: "All uncontrollable stress can have the same biological impact: victims of devastating trauma may never be the same biologically." Who can tolerate knowing we have been altered forever, damaged forever, deformed? That we have lost that pure soul God granted us at birth?

I thought of a dream I had had during my years in law school of a child, in a house, alone after first her mother, then her father, leave. In the dream, I see her through the window. She is deformed, her face contorted, her body twisted, and I cannot bring myself to go help her.

This was why Lisa stirred me up. Her not recognizing or acknowledging (which was it?) that finding those photographs when she was a little girl had shaped her world view, struck a nerve. The glass partition against which I had been hitting my head was my own refusal to see myself clearly, honestly. To see that a direct link existed between my trauma and my father's. At the heart of all the murkiness was an unwillingness—or was it an inability?—to see clearly.

The next day, I took my sons to a neighborhood pool, and as I watched their torsos, one long and lean, the other short and square, spring up and over into the water like seals, Mr. Hirsch's choice of the word "laminate" echoed inside of me. *Some people get more, some less. It just laminates. All the memories are glued together.*

I had the feeling that follows watching the first installment of a PBS murder mystery: the facts are laid out, and just as the primary suspects emerge, the segment ends, leaving only frustration and churning suspense. Who is the murderer?

Or, in this case, what has been murdered?

It just laminates.

What laminates? Mr. Hirsch had used the word to express the idea that one's experiences layer on top of one another, and it becomes impossible to say how one specific experience influences us. But the word had a profound resonance within me, as it seemed to capture an essential aspect of trauma. Trauma laminates. It laminates the moment of trauma. Every sight, smell, and sound of it. It laminates the part of ourselves that cannot separate from that moment, that comes into being as a result of that moment. Encased, shielded, coated, unfading, cutting off access to the heart underneath, the flowing blood.

We laminate photographs and documents to preserve them, making them unalterable. Lamination is a potent preservative. The word reminded me of how psychologists describe the experience of a traumatic moment, calling it "flashbulb" memory that records indelibly every sensory aspect of that moment. The stored photographs were the external representation of the internal images that sixty years had not diminished one iota.

For the liberators, time compressed and collapsed every smell and sight of entering the camp into a deathless alternate reality that has co-existed alongside their post-war lives. The lamination of traumatic memories encases them, seals them away, taking away all emotions but melancholy.

And, I realized, that is what explains the inability to see clearly. The lamination from trauma obscures the ability to see: to see the need for stories. The veterans could not see that the sadness seeped through the plastic coating of silence, that sadness without story brings unpredictable consequences. They could not see they were cultivating amorphous grief, grief that has no beginning or end. They could not see they were placing the photographs where their children could not help but find them, and in finding them but having no story to connect with them, they would create their own. And to create a story is to become a part of it.

Leila Levinson

George Tievsky:
No Words Can Convey

I didn't talk about it for forty years. I could not talk about it because words could not convey the horror....

—George Tievsky

Two days later, I awoke to a feeling of dread. The excitement I had felt when I had first set up the interviews with liberators had vanished. And now I had to prepare myself for doing another in a few hours.

"Maybe I'll call him and tell him I'm sick," I told Burke as I hunched over my cup of tea.

He gave me a look that confirmed how out of the question that possibility was.

I tried to inspire myself by thinking that my next interviewee, Dr. George Tievksy, might be able to reveal some specifics of my father's experience at Nordhausen.

127

Scene of field medical station in France, sometime after D-Day,
during a lull between battles

While most of the veterans were, like my father, sons of Yiddish-
speaking immigrants from Eastern Europe, Dr. Tievsky had also
become a doctor.

Tievsky's father, like my grandfather, had emigrated from what
was then Russia and is now Lithuania to become a shopkeeper.
Like my father, Dr. Tievsky excelled in public school, which
opened doors of opportunity, only to find himself up against the
barrier of anti-Semitism that almost kept him from going to medical school. It is easy to overlook, when studying the Holocaust,
that in the decades leading up to World War II, Jews in America
suffered intense discrimination. A wealthy Jewish benefactor created a space for Dr. Tievsky at an American medical school while
my father crossed the ocean to go to the University of Edinburgh
Medical School.

The war interrupted the beginning of both men's medical practices. Under the threat of being drafted into the infantry, both volunteered and became officers. ("Much better to be an officer than an enlisted man," Dr. Tievsky would tell me.) Both men left behind new brides when they shipped out. But unlike my mother, who was an unknown quantity to my father, Dr. Tievsky's bride, Priscilla, had been his best friend and proved an invaluable confidant when his war experiences threatened to overwhelm his mind. Like my father, Dr. Tievsky treated survivors of a concentration camp as he was a physician with the 66th Field Hospital, which was attached to the 42nd Division, one of the two divisions that liberated Dachau.

He met me in the lobby of his condominium in Chevy Chase. Even his stature brought my father to mind: short but consequential, carrying an air of confidence and gentility, even elegance. Though his white hair and wrinkles bespoke his eighty-seven years, his quick step and strong handshake did not. "Please," he extended his hand before him to the elevator as if he were rolling out a red carpet. The apartment echoed his elegance: hand-blown glass vases full of flowers, silk drapes, enameled Arts and Crafts-style copper lamps, and embroidered fabrics from the Far East.

On a dark wooden coffee table in front of two Queen Anne chairs lay a banker's box full of what looked like sets of cards, each stack sandwiched between pieces of archival paper. Dr. Tievsky removed the rubber band holding one set together and spread photographs out on the table, the black-and-white faces of camp inmates in narrow beds floating up from the gray tones. To explain the photographs, Dr. Tievsky referred to yellowed letters, tied with ribbons, that he had written his wife from Dachau. I pulled my chair up close so I could see what he was looking at. Like Al Hirsch, Dr. Tievsky began reading to me, choosing one of the letters he wrote his wife from Allach, a subcamp of Dachau:

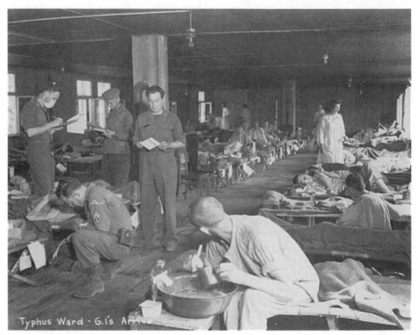

Typhus ward at Dachau

A number of my patients stopped to shake my hand and express their appreciation. They wished me a speedy return home. "Time will pass and it will all be over soon," one said. "Yes," said her friend, "that is what she told me when we rode the freight cars for days and that is what she said all the months in the concentration camp. Jews will always live."

He told me that, though he arrived at Dachau a week after its liberation, the smell of death still permeated the camp and the survivors seeming all but dead. "Some years after the war, when I was in practice and would see a patient with a tattoo, I would ask 'What camp?' One day a patient said I wouldn't know it—a camp named Allach. When I said I was there, he got pale, and I could feel blood drain from my face. He had us over for Shabbat dinner and told us that when GI gunfire got near, the guards left, so he and some other prisoners walked out, got themselves a car, and drove around. They saw one of the camp guards, pulled him into the car, and they drove through the night, trying to decide what way to kill him to prolong his agony. Talked about it all night, by the time...."

Dr. Tievsky's wife entered the room with a tray of iced tea. I commented that she had played an important role in her husband's processing of his experience.

"I didn't talk about it for forty years," Dr. Tievsky interjected. "Nobody knew it. Nobody—just Priscilla. I couldn't talk about it—because words could not convey the horror, and words would almost be sacrilegious—that to try to describe it to anybody was just a disservice to those who survived. I didn't talk about it until the Liberators' Conference of 1981."

"But you showed the photographs to the children," his wife reminded.

"That was later, when they were old enough. I cannot recall ever speaking about it until I heard Elie Weisel say at the conference, 'You must bear witness.' Before then I *could* not speak about it, *could* not talk about it. Only with Priscilla could I, and that was such a relief, not to be alone with those images."

He looked down at the photographs of stick-thin people with closely shaved hair lying on cots, Army blankets tucked up to their waists. When I asked what age his children were when he first showed them the photographs, he looked up as if he had forgotten my presence.

"I guess they were in their teens."

"How did they respond?"

"Well, they didn't verbalize much. They internalized it, I guess."

Dr. Tievsky added that they do not bring the subject up now, nor do his grandchildren. He hadn't talked about it at all with the youngest two, seventeen and sixteen years old. "Their father was

Medics at Dachau

the one who asked me; I haven't pushed it myself. I knew that if I had to speak, I wouldn't sleep well the night after. Just remembering all this...brings bad dreams. I won't sleep well tonight."

Guilt cut through me. It was bad enough stirring my own bad dreams.

I wanted to understand the relationship between talking and dreaming, as it seemed to run counter to my hypothesis that silencing bad memories results in bad dreams, the psyche's release. But how much was he really telling me? He opened the door a crack, showing me photographs, reading the letters. Words still eluded him.

Dr. Tievsky had used his intellect to fence in the demons. He had spent a great deal of energy and time the previous years trying to understand the hatred that gave birth to the Holocaust. While anger about American indifference to the genocide of the Jews fueled Al Hirsch's need to understand, for George Tievsky, it was witnessing, just days after Dachau's liberation, anti-Semitism within his own division.

He took out several sheets of paper and began reading:

Answering a knock on my door, at the newly liberated Dachau concentration camp, I saw the face of my Jewish medical corpsman silhouetted against the blackness of the night. He was crying bitterly, and through his sobs I heard the unbelievable: "Captain, the men in my squad tent are Jew-baiting me." It was the figurative ninety-ninth blow in those weeks of horror.

"I had to resolve this." He looked up at me. "How could such Jew-baiting go on in the face of the ovens? How? Why the Holocaust? You ask me what would have helped when I came back. First problem I had was I couldn't talk about it. A second problem was reading prayers in the *siddur,* reading the *Chumash* [the bound version of the Torah] where God tells Abraham and Moses, 'You shall be a great nation, you shall be as the stars in the sky, the sands in the ocean.' How could I say those words now? And third, how could I resolve these Christian Americans Jew-baiting this fellow in their own tent?"

Resolution came from reading *Constantine's Sword,* which led him to conclude that Christians resent Jesus for what he asked of them: to live in righteousness for the betterment of their fellow human beings. It was the same answer Andre Schwarz-Bart presents in *The Last of the Just.*

From that point Dr. Tievsky went on in a stream of consciousness about meeting Jan Karski, the courier from the Polish Underground who carried first to London, and then to FDR, photographs—the first incontrovertible evidence of the Nazis' genocide of Europe's Jews.

"Karski told me how in his meeting with FDR in July, 1943, FDR said to him, 'You Jewish people....'" George's voice broke here, and for a few seconds he could not speak. Then he went on to relate how Karski informed Anthony Eden about the extermination plan. "Karski said Eden got up, went over to the window, lifted the curtain slightly—there was a black-out—turned around and said, 'Mr. Karski, has it ever occurred to you that when Jews come, they bring their anti-Semitism with them?'

"When Karski came to America to tell Felix Frankfurter and Brandeis about the camps, they first told him he was lying, then apologized and said they couldn't believe what he was saying. FDR told him the U.S. would win the war and reconstitute Europe and help rebuild Poland, but his final words to Karski were, 'I'm not going to worry about the Jews; this can't be a war for the Jews.'"

I thought of the absence of reference to the Holocaust during the WWII Memorial dedication. The public representation of the war still precluded the fate of the Jews.

Dr. Tievsky then changed the subject completely, though what he said provided insight into my father's experience. As a general medical officer, Dr. Tievsky was the first one to see patients after they were taken off the field, blood pouring from all extremities. Once, a medic handed him a wounded soldier's wallet that flipped open to show a photograph of a pretty young woman holding a baby. Tievsky knew that the soldier, in deep shock, had only a few hours to live, that the pretty woman was already a widow, the infant fatherless.

When I asked him how he kept his emotions intact, he responded by talking about where his division went after the four weeks of treating survivors at Dachau.

"There was a big war still going on, and we were supposed to go to the Pacific." He looked at a letter. "June 1st…we were on a train for days to southern France. A man I valued told me he was thinking of turning himself in as a psychotic. We were being shipped towards the Pacific, where they expected huge casualties. But then the bomb was dropped, changing the world forever. In war things happen. Some men get it easy; others get the worst."

These words echoed Mr. Hirsch's. *It gets laminated, some more, some less.*

I left Dr. Tievsky and his wife in the kitchen preparing the Shabbat meal. Exhaustion saturated me. Despite all the similarities between this man and my father, I did not feel any more able to imagine what my father had gone through in Nordhausen. I found myself with pieces that inched me closer to understanding but could not get me past a firewall of incomprehension. The pieces demanded decoding before I could begin to interlock them and see why these veterans still could not talk about what they witnessed.

The photographs substituted for telling. *It was such a relief not to be alone with those images.*

The Holocaust came into the homes of thousands of GIs. It came through photographs, two-by-three-inch black-and-white snapshots taken with Kodak Brownies or stolen Leicas, *Because no one will believe this.* These GIs were the first soldiers to have cameras, which they used to record where they had fought, what they had seen. In immutable detail.

Some GIs sent the snapshots home in lieu of words so their families might at least know what their sons, husbands, and brothers had witnessed. But the wives and mothers often threw those snapshots away, because how could they let such images reside in their homes? Perhaps such a response was wiser than one might at first think.

Because, in the homes of the liberators who held onto their photographs, the snapshots took up a large space, whether on the coffee table in an album or a trunk used as a coffee table. From the beginning, Al Hirsch's photographs made their way into his household. Eli Heimberg kept his in an album on a high shelf, not accessible to a young child but perhaps to an older one who, if determined and curious enough, might ask questions.

The meticulous organization of George Tievsky's photographs reminded me of my father—how he kept his office immaculate, his shirts pressed and starched, and his attire formal, even on weekends. He arranged photographs of my summers at camp in an attractive blue leather album that he kept on a shelf in the den. Yet the war photos remained crammed into a shoebox stored inside a trunk.

Just as reading from his letters about his time in Dachau was easier for Dr. Tievsky than recounting the experience, showing photographs was easier than telling. All he had to do was untie the ribbons. Even though Dr. Tievsky never talked to his children about the photographs, his meticulous care showed his family the space Dachau occupied in his heart.

My father's storing his photographs in a trunk in his office basement seemed a compromise between discarding them—as had Chic Paper—and hanging onto them. Placing them in the trunk seemed to express a wish that one day my brothers and I would discover them and understand. Their presence revealed his desire, at least subconsciously, to reveal himself and to share—finally—the images that haunted him.

Mr. Hirsch's word "laminate" expressed a contradiction, a paradox. The lamination occurs both involuntarily and by choice. Lisa had used the word "protect" to describe her father's intention; he was compelled to protect his children. But the unconscious, particularly when intense emotions are locked away, manages to express its conflicts in ways all but impossible for the traumatized person to recognize or control.

The lamination that followed the witnessing of Ohrdruf—and Nordhausen and Dachau and every other camp—obscured the liberators' vision, preventing them from seeing the possible consequences of their choices. Especially the ones they made about how they stored their photographs— both physically and mentally.

Like crumbs leading us into the wilderness, the photographs showed us where our fathers were during the war and what they saw there. Nicholas Nash, the son of a GI who was among the liberators of Mauthausen, remembers his sensitive and cultured father often screaming during the night. When Nicholas was fourteen, he began to get an idea what might explain his father's nightmares when found a packet of photographs in his father's library—gruesome images his father recorded upon entering Mauthausen. Sensing that questions might trigger his father's volcanic temper, Nicholas avoided the subject. (His mother spent much energy shielding her children from her husband's anger, sending them off to neighbors on days when he was especially distraught.)

After the acclaimed television miniseries *Holocaust* was broadcast in 1978, Nicholas's father set off to Mauthausen, insisting that he go alone. When he returned, he contacted other veterans from his unit, but to his family he offered no information. "We [Nicholas and his two sisters] were well trained not to ask, as asking might reawaken things. There was always something that lay behind the eyes that you knew you'd never get to."

As well as leading the children of liberators to the awful knowledge, such photographs led many grandchildren to it as well. One young man told me that after he came upon his beloved grandfather's images, "I felt horribly alone with them. I tried to talk to other kids at Hebrew School, but they didn't want to hear about the photographs, and I didn't feel like I could talk to my grandfather, as he never brought up the subject himself. So I was stuck, alone, with images I couldn't get out of my head."

Steven Lenger, the son of Paul Lenger, a GI liberator with the 89th Infantry Division, described deep affection for his father, who had enlisted in the U.S. Army after fleeing his native Germany in 1938. "Yet, even with our closeness, there was a part of him that was like a dark closet he could not open up. And that came from seeing Ohrdruf, not from what he knew in Germany before he left."

A current of recognition ran down my spine. I knew that closet door like the back of my hand. And then I understood. My father's photographs were my true inheritance.

Edgar Edelsack:
Disturbing the Seabed

Here I was, twenty-one, having seen colleagues blown up as they tried to de-arm German mines, being put on a detail to load bodies of frozen GIs onto trucks, so I was a very hardened soldier. But to see Mauthausen was something very, very emotionally...something that to this day I haven't made peace with.

—Edgar Edelsack

Edgar Edelsack collection

"It was very difficult. I was not prepared for Mauthausen." The quiet voice of eighty-one-year-old Edgar Edelsack broke,

139

tears cresting his eyelids and flowing down his cheeks. "To this day, I'm not prepared for it."

We sat with his wife, Charlotte, on the back deck of their Washington, D.C., home that overlooks their garden—the focus of Edgar's time since his retirement from his career as a physicist. I had heard Mr. Edelsack in an interview on National Public Radio, and the sadness in his voice, the humility about his role, moved me to call and ask him if I could come talk with him.

On his deck, drinking iced tea, he first talked about going to work for the government after the war—after Hiroshima and Nagasaki—because he wanted to do what he could to prevent another war. His face creasing with the weight of purpose, he said, "You have to join the enemy if you're going to try to change the enemy." After V-J Day, happy to return to graduate school and move on with his life, he boxed away all his memories. "But I never really made peace with Mauthausen, as is evident today, so those memories you carry on for the rest of your life."

Mauthausen was a large camp in a network of work camps that produced stone for an envisioned model Aryan city. The starving prisoners quarried granite that they then carried on their shoulders up a steep embankment known as the "Stairway of Death," their inevitable deaths as much the Nazis' purpose as the quarrying of the rock. Intelligentsia and political prisoners, which included many homosexuals, comprised the prison population until 1944, when the compressed deportation and genocide of Hungarian Jews swelled the camp's population, many of whom were subjected to medical experimentation. Death came by injection rather than the gas chamber.

The 11th Armored Division found thousands of walking dead when they liberated Mauthausen on May 5, 1945. Over the prior six months, the Nazis had forced prisoners from camps in the east on death marches to Mauthausen, Buchenwald, and Dachau to prevent their liberation from camps on the Eastern Front.

Epidemics of typhus and starvation had decimated the inmates.

"Here I was, twenty-one," Mr. Edelsack said, "having seen colleagues blown up as they tried to de-arm German mines, being put on a detail to load bodies of frozen GIs onto trucks, so I was a very hardened soldier. But to see Mauthausen was something very, very emotionally...something that to this day I haven't made peace with."

His voice broke. He looked down at his hands, pressed together on the table. I wanted to reach out, take one of them, and whisper reassurance that he was not alone. War presumes the possibility of defense, an even-handed combat; but in the camps even children were brutalized. Every moral code proved meaningless, the dignity of the human spirit a joke.

"What I saw there mirrors what we see in pictures of it: emaciated people of just bone and skin." Mr. Edelsack's voice broke again. "I provided food, K-rations, cigarettes...and took many photographs over the two days I spent there." He stopped, looked down again at his hands, fingers interlaced. "Very difficult. The pictures I took were so emotionally disturbing that after many years I gave them away. I couldn't face looking at them. The whole subject is one that I have subjugated, that I haven't talked

Mauthausen, May 1945

about to Charlotte very much or my family because it's one that always brings tears up."

Again, my questions were causing a good man to cry. After decades of avoiding any painful subject with my father, here I was asking Mr. Edelsack to face what was in the photographs, the ones he had given away because he could not face them.

A few minutes later in our conversation he contradicted himself.

"The Mauthausen experience—I somehow haven't chosen to relate to it. Until this [interview] came up, I hadn't thought about Mauthausen. I thought so adversely about it that I got rid of the pictures. Every individual faces trauma differently. I've tried to make peace with it and move on."

Like Mr. Kaiser and Mr. Paper, he could not see that his effort, almost palpable, to find peace had failed, that giving away the photographs had not erased the images from his mind. Perhaps his not speaking to his wife, his son, or his grandchildren—"My

Edgar Edelsack before the section of the World War II
Memorial honoring the Battle of the Bulge
(Edgar Edelsack collection)

grandchildren have asked about the Depression, FDR, and so forth, but they haven't asked about the war"—was a strategy, conscious or not, to keep the images from rising in the mind, a process he at one point likened to disturbing a sea bed. "It's like sand that settles, and if you go [to reunions], it stirs up the sand. But if I thought there was something useful, as there is in your case, I'm delighted to have it stirred up."

Well, maybe not delighted. His politeness and sense of duty were second nature.

Like George Kaiser, Eli Heimberg, Chic Paper, and George Tievsky, Edgar Edelsack was willing to talk with me to help to keep the Holocaust in the public's memory. He risked stirring bad memories to help prevent another genocide. But as soon as all these men began describing the bodies or the emaciated survivors, they broke off, the images too overwhelming to face.

Maybe some day, I heard my father say.

I asked Mr. Edelsack if he thought not speaking about Mauthausen affected his coming to peace with it. Only months later, after many re-readings of the interview's transcript, did I see his answer: "My field is nuclear physics. I worked with [Edward] Teller—he's been here at the house. One of the emotional experiences I had was going to the museum at Hiroshima and seeing what transpired in a few moments: 80,000 people were killed. I will never forget the wall that had imprinted on it the silhouette of someone vaporized by the bomb. I was reduced to tears like I was just now talking to you."

The answer was indirect, just as my husband described many of my own to be. But when I connected this answer to what he had said about wanting to do what he could to end all wars, I saw his life's work had been, at least in part, his response to Mauthausen and the wall in Hiroshima. Trauma pushed him to do what he could to prevent more atrocity. I thought of Mrs. Paper's comment about her husband as I was leaving their home: "He's the kindest person I ever met, and I think the war has a lot to do with it. After the war, if he were driving along and saw a car broken down, he'd immediately stop. He puts himself out for anyone, which, I think, is a result of what he went through and what he saw." Eli Heimberg demonstrated the same *menschlekeit*, being the best employer anyone could imagine. My father was known to the Perth Amboy community as their Marcus Welby, the doctor who cared about them as well as for them.

Trauma underpinned their kindness and commitment as well as their silence. Their work was what they could do to help mend the world. Perhaps this explained the difference between the public man and the private.

"You're different with your friends," my son David told me one evening after I got off the telephone. "You laugh with them. You never laugh with us."

His words punched my stomach.

"Of course I laugh with you. What are you talking about?"

"No, you don't. You're always serious, like we depress you or something."

I wanted to swipe away his words, press the delete button. But, as I walked upstairs, I wondered if he was right. Was I one person with my family, and another with my friends—just as my father's patients had known an entirely different man from the one I knew?

With the people I loved and trusted the most, I allowed my demons to emerge. It was a natural function of family trust and intimacy. Perhaps the veterans considered such intimacy dangerous, capable of allowing the demons to emerge, and so resorted to silence as the best means to keep them locked away.

That, in combination with another force operating on them in the 1950s: the John Wayne ethos of being strong. Strong men don't cry. Strong people don't give in to pain, don't fold under the pressure of sadness, grief, loss, anguish. They pony up.

During the winter vacation of my sophomore year in college, Robert asked me to come into Alan's room for a minute because he needed to tell us something. Alan and I sat down on his bed while Robert stood before us, the late December sky gray and flat through the window behind him. "Our mother died in October," he said. I began crying, the first time I had ever cried in front of my brothers. I was still crying when our father joined us.

"You have to be strong, Leila," he said. "These things had to happen. There was no other way. She just couldn't face what she had to. She was weak. We did what had to be done." The tears kept coming; I couldn't look at him. "She loved you. She showed that by letting you live your own life. Do her honor by fulfilling yourself. Do her name good."

I wanted to stop crying but couldn't. Robert and my father left the room. Alan sat next to me until the crying stopped.

My father had three phrases that he repeated so often they were a family mantra:

Keep the flag flying.

Reach for the highest rung.

In this family, we pick ourselves up by our bootstraps.

During my teenage years, Dad had made fun of our next-door neighbor "shrink" who practiced out of his home. Sometimes he peeked out the front window as the man's patients arrived or left. "That poor soul would be better off spending his money on a new car than on telling Gerald Mayer his problems," he'd say, shaking his head. "At least then he'd have something to show for it."

Though he never said it, I knew he thought that going to therapists showed weakness, and if our family was nothing else, we were strong. Being strong was what made my father, my brothers, and myself different from my mother.

But things changed in my second semester of law school. I

became unable to get out of bed and attend classes. A nightmare began to recur, robbing me of the refuge of sleep. I walked endlessly about my eight-hundred-square-foot house, dropping glasses and plates as if my hands had no muscles. My lifelong terror of going crazy like my mother seemed to be coming true.

Sometime in the second week, knowing I could not keep my father out forever, I answered the phone.

"What the hell is going on? Why haven't you been answering the phone?" he demanded.

"I've been miserable with school," I said, squeezing the phone cord. "I'm thinking of not going back."

"You're what? You're thinking of quitting? The world is not your oyster, Leila. You need self-discipline. You need to make your way in the world on your own two feet. I did not raise you to be a princess." His began yelling, his agitation increasing with each word. "So pull yourself together and get back in there."

I agreed.

Five years later and after my father's death, when I found the letter from my mother, I learned why he had used the word "princess." I had been her princess. He was afraid I was proving to be like her and that I was losing it like she had. Like he refused to remember *he* had. Like I had always been terrified I would.

Nat Futterman:
The Terror of Looking

The thing that got me was when I looked at the leaves on the tree. I said what the hell is the matter with them? The leaves were gray. I rubbed one, and it was covered with ash. And, you know, wha, wha, what is this? And then when we walked through the gates....

—Nat Futterman

Nat Futterman and his wife, Harriet, after the war
(Nat Futterman collection)

In her book *On Photography*, Susan Sontag claims that when we take photographs, especially in a foreign land, we rely on the camera to see for us. We place the instrument between the land-scape and ourselves, so rather than our mind receiving the deep direct imprint of what lies before us, the film records the image.

Unlike the other veterans with whom I had spoken, Nat Futterman did not take photographs of what he saw when he walked through the gates of Buchenwald. His only photograph is of the gate itself, because the American officers of the divisions that liberated Buchenwald prohibited the GIs from taking photographs. And though none of the veterans had been able to say more than a few words about what they witnessed, Nat Futterman said even less, freezing at the moment when he stepped through the gate. Without a camera to mediate the scenes before him, they imprinted themselves deeply upon his mind and soul, intertwining with even his conscious thought.

Buchenwald lay atop a wooded hill within a forest outside of Weimar, once the epicenter of Germany's rich culture. Goethe, Bach, Schiller, Klee, Kandinsky, Liszt, Moholy-Nagy, Nietzsche, Strauss, and Schopenhauer—even Rudolf Steiner, the creator of the Waldorf School philosophy—all lived there. In Goethe's beloved woods, a mere eight kilometers from Weimar's center, the Nazis built a concentration camp, complete with a crematorium.

Mr. Futterman met me at the New Rochelle, New York, train station, wanting to save me a taxi ride to his house. Over the phone he had told me to look for a five-foot-ten-inch balding man with wire-framed glasses. As I got off the train, I saw him leaning against a low stone wall, his hands clasped together and resting atop of it.

As we pulled out of the parking lot he said, "I'm not sure how much I'm going to be able to say about Buchenwald." I looked over and saw tears running down his face. But before I could think of an answer, he began explaining how he had once met the other Nat Futterman, the one whose name I found at the back of *In Evidence* and who I thought I was calling when I reached the man next to me instead. We knew I had reached a man other than the one listed in the book, because that one had served with the 32nd Armored Regiment, 3rd Armored Division, while the one next to me had served with the 10th Infantry Regiment, 5th Infantry Division. Of all strange coincidences, two Nat Futtermans had liberated Buchenwald, and they both now lived in Westchester County. "So it was fate," Mr. Futterman frequently repeated, "that I was the one you contacted."

His wife, Harriet, greeted us at the door and joined us in the study, which brimmed over with Mr. Futterman's collection of

Mr. Futterman (upper right) with his fellow soldiers
(Nat Futterman collection)

war memorabilia: Napoleonic helmets and swords, ribbons and medals, World War I helmets, pistols. Mr. Futterman began telling me about how he enlisted at age seventeen because on his first date with his wife, an enlisted man shamed him by calling him an "F-1"—someone whose physical limitations prevented him from qualifying to enlist. Mr. Futterman spoke of how his business took him back to Germany in the 1970s, where he observed that the country had barely begun to face its past.

His intellect and skilled narratives swept me into his stories, and I all but forgot my purpose. But when he recounted overhearing a German colleague making anti-Semitic remarks, I asked how he thought witnessing Buchenwald shaped his values and priorities since the war.

"It's, it's very difficult to put...to put into words."

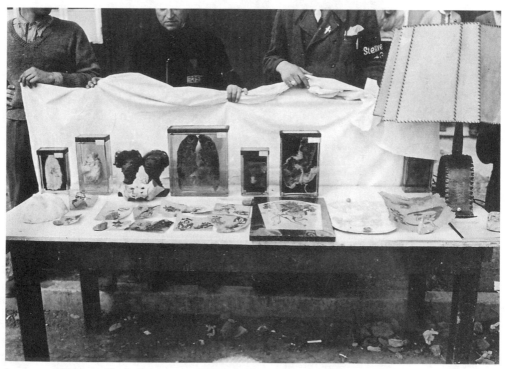

Mummified and tatooed human parts GIs found at Buchenwald.

Mrs. Futterman, who until that moment had not said anything, began a verbal duet with her husband. "They did not speak
of it because they were supposed to be men who were matured
from this; they were all young."

"I was a kid."

"He was a kid. He spent his nineteenth birthday in a hospital,
wounded."

"Let me tell you something about the average GI, the grunt
soldier. We didn't know where the hell we were, what we were
doing, where we were going. It was a day-by-day thing. Certainly
the officers didn't explain anything, just: 'Do your job, carry the
radio, come to me when I ask you to.' Do this, do that. One day
this officer shows up and asks who can operate a radio. So stupid-
ly, I raise my hand and he tells me to come with him in his jeep.
And we drive and drive. I don't know where the hell we are. Then
all of a sudden, you could smell that something was wrong. Smell
it. The thing that got me was when I looked at the leaves on the
tree. I said what the hell is the matter with them? The leaves were
gray. I rubbed one, and it was covered with ash. And, you know,
wha, wha, what is this? And then when we walked through the
gates...." He stopped talking and spread his hands out before

Buchenwald gate *(Nat Futterman collection)*

him, as if they could block the image.

"I have a picture of the gate at Buchenwald, but nothing more. It was so...."

His wife asked if he wanted her to retrieve the photograph album.

"Sure, aah...." He squeezed the inside corners of his eyes with his thumb and index finger.

"That's why he doesn't talk about it," Mrs. Futterman said. "Doesn't talk about it."

"It's very hard to even think about it because it was so overwhelming just when you walked through those gates...."

"He was eighteen years old," his wife reminded me.

"...and saw what was going on...."

"I mean, how old are your children? You know...."

"It was so overpowering," Mr. Futterman continued, "that we didn't know what to do. Nobody knew what to do. How can you help these people? Soldiers started to feed them rations, and I said, 'That's the wrong thing to do. You'll kill them; don't do that.' And, and they were...they came over and kissed our feet. It was incredible."

Tears ran down his cheeks; his voice cracked. "And, and the sights—this has to be hell, this cannot be this world. Can't be...." His hand pushed at the air as if he might exile the memories, the images.

I asked if he talked about it after leaving the camp.

"Aach. Everybody was just stunned. Nobody could talk. We couldn't even talk to each other. It was so...so horrible. But then you get angry, you know—the anger was so intense. They brought the Germans from the nearby town—to go in there and clean up, move the bodies, these—I don't know what to call them—these *finks* who lived next to the camps and claimed they had no idea what was going on when the smell was unbelievable for miles around. We made them dig the grave and carry the bodies

Mr. Futterman, far left at end of war
(Nat Futterman collection)

into them. Their looks of discomfort...they all knew. They just preferred to pretend they didn't know. Then you get angry...."

He shifted into the second person at the same point the other veterans had—when describing his emotional reaction to the camps.

After the war, Mr. Futterman went to Cornell where he roomed with another veteran who had been a refugee from Germany just before that country's invasion of Poland. But they never said a word about their experiences. While the silence continues to the present day within his family, he sees this as the consequence of his children not being interested. *They never ask questions; only my grandsons do, occasionally.*

Several months later, I spoke over the telephone with the Futtermans' daughter, Joan. She expressed that although the

Holocaust was part of her family's history—most of her mother's Hungarian relatives were murdered, and the numbers on the arms of those who survived were etched on Joan's memory—what she knew about her father's role she learned from her mother. "'That's why daddy went to war,' my mom would tell me, 'to free people in the concentration camp. Someday he'll sit down and tell you himself.'

"But when?" Joan asked in deep frustration. "He's eighty."

Her tone quickly changed as she described how her father wanted to nurture a joyful, optimistic atmosphere in their home and avoided sad or morbid topics. "My father is very soft, mushy. His joy came with tears. When I came down the steps in my prom dress, he cried. Joy came very easily."

The description brought to mind my father's observation that

Sign at Buchenwald

melancholy ran in *our Russian blood* whenever we teared up at happy occasions.

A few moments after Joan said her father never spoke of Buchenwald, she indicted our generation for not caring more about what our fathers did. "My brothers listened to anything about the war with half an ear. This says more about our generation. If it's not about us, we're not interested. Our generation has this sense of entitlement." She connected this attitude to what she saw in the enclave of Jews she lives among in Westchester County. "They have no personal relationship with the Holocaust; it's generic. There's no intimate understanding." Two sentences later, she said, "Knowing where my dad has been is disturbing."

I wondered if our generation has always sensed, but feared, what our fathers held within their silence about the war. Joan mentioned that her father was a fitful sleeper, and Mr. Futterman, himself, told me he often dreamed of Buchenwald's horrors. Perhaps it was not only our parents' silence about the camps that kept us from asking questions; perhaps we also sensed we would hear more than we wanted to know. Perhaps we were, to some degree, culpable in our parents' isolation. Because once these veterans began talking, the memories poured out, each recounting eliciting another.

"I can't believe this, I'm remembering something else...."

Mrs. Futterman assured him, "It's okay. Tonight you'll put it away, but now it's good to remember."

"Ghosts, there are ghosts in the room," David said to me one morning years before as I went to take him out of his crib, a morning after I had had my nightmare.

Perhaps I had sensed the ghosts hovering around my father the morning after he dreamed of Nordhausen. I was beginning to think that he and I mutually benefited from his locking away his memories of Nordhausen.

The following spring I organized a commemoration of the camps' liberation at the university where I taught. Four of the six veterans were from Dallas and Houston; I only had funds enough to invite one of the men I had interviewed in the northeast, and I invited Mr. Futterman. He surprised me by readily agreeing.

At dinner the evening he and his wife arrived in Austin, they told my husband and me about their recent trip to Belgium in honor of the sixtieth anniversary of the Battle of the Bulge. The Belgian and Luxembourg governments and people treated the veterans and their families like royalty, showering them with feasts and gratitude. During a visit to a cemetery of American soldiers, Mr. Futterman wanted to locate the marker of Lennie Miller, a fellow member of the 10th Regiment.

"He was an only child. And his mother never was able to find out how he died." Mr. Futterman pulled from his pocket a photograph of a grave marker on which a Star of David was chiseled. "The cemetery was vast. I would never have found his marker, but of all crazy coincidences, we met a fellow at a reception who turned out to be the director of the cemetery, and I mentioned my interest in finding Lennie's marker. The next day he called with its location. But I don't have anyone to tell, as he was his widowed mother's only child."

He took out of his pocket two more photographs of men in World War II uniforms. The three of them had been buddies since childhood, and they went off to war together. Though one of them became a POW, he never talked about his war experience, Mr. Futterman having discovered only recently through reading an article in the Sunday *New York Times Magazine* the details of his friend's imprisonment. As his friend was Jewish, the Nazis sent him to a slave-labor camp where in nine months, 290 of the original 349 Jewish POWS died of starvation and overwork.

"I had no idea," Mr. Futterman said.

Along with the photographs, he showed me thirty-one pages

he had printed from a website of a fellow liberator's account of liberating Buchenwald.

"Can you imagine?" Mrs. Futterman exclaimed. "Thirty-one pages of memories of that place? Maybe he made it all up."

A few minutes later, after we all commented on the restaurant's great mango margaritas, she turned to me. "Leila, you're an intelligent, knowledgeable person. Why do you think these men never talked about the camps?"

"That's what I'm trying to understand," I said.

GIs inspecting gold items, including teeth, taken from Buchenwald victims

The next day I got the chance to ask what she thought the answer might be.

As the other veterans were not arriving until that evening, I drove the Futtermans to the small town of Fredricksburg in the Hill Country, which retains the period flavor of its mid-1800s German settlers. Their opposition to slavery resulted in the community's isolation after Texas seceded along with the South. Now the town capitalizes on its history, its main economic base being tourism and antiques. When we entered one store, I winced; everything was from Germany. While there was nothing from World War II, many books and uniforms were from World War I.

"See this guy," Mr. Futterman said, pointing to a photograph in a book. "He was a hero from the first war, and it was his support of Hitler that endowed the Nazis with much of their initial legitimacy. Son of a bitch. Let's get out of here." He slammed the book shut and walked out of the store.

As we waited for sandwiches in a delicatessen, I took a deep breath and asked Mr. Futterman if he thought he'd be able to talk about Buchenwald at the commemoration the next day.

"Yeah, yeah, I will." He looked down at his hands, palms flat on the table, thumbs wiping the surface. "I'll tell the students to beware of some government telling them about glory, about signing up for war."

A few minutes later, I took another deep breath and asked Mrs. Futterman if she had ever asked her husband what she asked me the night before: "Why don't the liberators talk about the camps?"

"He says because the kids don't ask. But right after Joanie talked to you, she said to him, 'Tell me about it, Dad,' and he answered, 'You don't want to know.'"

"They haven't asked me," Mr. Futterman insisted. "When we got back from Belgium, they didn't ask. All those years they saw the medals and never asked."

Nat and Harriet Futterman, 2008 *(Nat Futterman collection)*

"But perhaps you gave a nonverbal message over the years not to ask," I suggested, working hard to keep my voice quiet and kind, "and so now there's a dynamic of you thinking they aren't interested and they think you don't want to tell." I told them about remarks I had heard Elie Weisel give the week before, where he described how, during the 1960s, many of his students at City University of New York were children of survivors. He found himself bridging the "chasm of silence" between these students and their parents. "The students thought their parents did not want to talk; the parents thought the children did not want to hear."

Mr. Futterman looked off into the space before him, his hand squeezing his temples.

"No, no." He shook his head slowly. "They don't want to hear about it."

What, I wondered all the rest of the day, was that insistence about?

When I returned home that evening, Burke asked if Mr. Futterman had taken me through Buchenwald's gates.

"No," I answered. "I think he wants to more than anything. I think he knows that would free him, finally, but he can't seem to let himself see what he found behind those gates. It's as though he's imprisoned by having been a liberator."

The next day I saw why Mr. Futterman wanted to avoid going through the gates, and in that moment I realized why he so reminded me of my father. The morning of the commemoration, he and three other veterans generously agreed to speak with my

GI stands before truck loaded with corpses of victims of Buchenwald, April 1945 *(Center for Holocaust and Genocide Studies, University of Minnesota collection)*

Holocaust Literature students. I had asked the students to prepare gentle questions for the veterans, but as the four men sat
before them, no one raised their hand. Mr. Futterman broke the
ice: "Come on, we can take it."

A student stood up. "So what did y'all see when you got inside
the camps?"

The room went silent. I imagined myself strangling the student.

Gordon Rowe, a retired state judge, came to the rescue. As was
true of many of the veterans I interviewed, the circumstances of
Judge Rowe's war experience involved a weird twist of fate. He
had come upon Dachau, not as a part of a liberating force, but as
a result of doing some "collateral sightseeing," an activity he used
to stave off boredom. When he came upon barbed wire and saw
on the other side barracks and piles of bodies and walking skeletons with green lips (from eating grass), he turned and ran, certain he was hallucinating. (Later, he told me he had never told any
of his fellow soldiers what he had seen: "I just couldn't be sure it
was real." It stunned me to consider what he had held within himself all these years.)

Johnny Marino spoke next, his eighty-two-year-old voice
strong and clear. Months before, his and Calvin Massey's oral histories on videotape at the Holocaust Museum Houston had
served as my introduction to the liberators' pain. Now, Mr.
Marino plunged into a description of the death factory his unit
discovered outside of Landsberg.

"No prisoner came out of that building alive; everyone in there
was dead, and the smell, it was terrible. Terrible. Then we started
coming upon camps everywhere. One had a ravine longer than
this room, full of bodies. The smells were so bad, your stomach
seized up, and this gray dust was falling on us, sticking to our skin.
We had to tie kerchiefs around our faces not to breathe it in. I saw
things…piles of bodies, boxcars full of bodies, people so thin it
looked like skin was pulled over bones, eyes sunken. It filled me

with such hate. I held that hate for years until one day I realized hate is a four-letter word that will eat you up. It makes you just like the people you're hating. I had to replace hate with love. That's the only way to change the world."

This echoed the theme of the last book we had read, *Secondhand Smoke* by Thane Rosenbaum. Its main character, the child of two Holocaust survivors, becomes the prisoner of his parents' as well as his own rage and desire for revenge. Duncan only finds relief from meeting his long-lost brother, who carries no hate in his heart and teaches that the victim can only become truly liberated when they forgive the perpetrator. Forgiveness does not

A victim of Kaufering IV who was burned alive when
Nazi guards locked prisoners in barn and set it on fire to
prevent their being liberated

exonerate the perpetrator; rather it releases the victim from hate.

Then it was Mr. Futterman's turn to speak. Just as he had done when I had first met him at the train station, he clutched his hands together, his body bent forward.

"What I saw... God...." His chest began heaving; he covered his eyes with his hands.

Calvin Massey came to the rescue by telling his story. "At Landsberg, I shook like a leaf. I couldn't stand seeing these walking dead, these zombies. I was in agony because I wanted to help them, but I knew my K-rations would kill them. I wanted to run away, but then a voice came to me: 'What are you afraid of?' 'I don't know what to do,' I told it. 'I can't talk with them.' 'Find one who seems receptive, and go to him and hug him.'" Tears streamed down his cheeks, dripped off the bridge of his nose.

"I went over to one of the people," he continued, "and he fell in my arms, and I hugged him. I never hugged like that before. I hugged and hugged. And then they all came over to be hugged. I'm only sorry I didn't get to hug all of them."

He described other camps he saw, where the Nazis had burned people rather than let them be liberated, where bodies of people lay dead, shot for trying to lick dew off of barbed wire. His tears never stopped flowing.

When he finished, Mr. Futterman said, "Now that we took an hour to answer that, any other questions?"

The class jumped to their feet, applauding. They rushed up to the men, shaking hands, hugging Mr. Massey. "He's a chick magnet," I heard one male student say.

That night, over four hundred people wedged into seats and stood in the aisles, eager and anxious to hear the veterans share their stories. Some, like Mr. Marino and Mr. Massey, bared their souls. Another said more about the Battle of the Bulge than about Dachau. "The others have already told you about that place, so I won't repeat it."

GIs at Kaufering, one of the camps outside of Landsberg

And then Mr. Futterman opened the gate of his memory—a crack.

"I walked in and piles everywhere—of bodies, the legs and arms like sticks. And skeletons, walking skeletons, and one came over to me and kissed my feet. I dare any of you to be able to see such things and not lose it. What I've told you is more than what I have ever told my wife, sitting there, in the front row, and my children, whom I love very much...."

Terror. As alive today as it was in April 1945. Edgar Edelsack had told me as much: *I'm still not prepared for it.* It explained why veterans turned down my request to speak with them. *I just can't....* It destroyed any possibility of God for Al Hirsch, Chic Paper, George Kaiser, and my father. It demanded that Eli Heimberg focus on the Displaced Persons' Camp. My father tried to lock it away in the trunk in the basement.

How did I not recognize that these men were still terrified? That the camps' power had not diminished after sixty years? Images so threatening that even a word might summon their hellish reality.

The Trauma of the GI Liberators

*No photo has ever shown what the soldiers encountered when
they walked through the gates.*

—Carold Bland

Service held for Buchenwald Jewish survivors

Over the next few months, I tried to make sense of the words,
the images, the emotions, the differences between Calvin
Massey's tears of grief and George Kaiser's and Nat Futterman's
tears of anguish, tears that flow when grief cannot. It seemed that
Mr. Massey was an exception, that the liberators, still caught in
their trauma, had never grieved, and denial kept the terror of their
memories intact. Terror seems to exile grief, locking the witness
in an eternal moment of horror.

When the responses began rolling in from the veterans I had

contacted, I had noticed that many of the men who answered were Jewish, even though the majority of my letters went to veterans whose names, at least, seemed to indicate they were not Jewish. The fifty-one interviews I did with liberators had no scientific method. Whenever I came across the name of a liberator, I wrote that person. I identified divisions that had liberated camps, attended their reunions and spoke to whomever was willing to speak with me.

The net result of this approach was that of the fifty-one veterans, twenty-nine were Jewish. Perhaps, I thought, Jewish veterans had more reason to provide testimony to counter Holocaust deniers. But what explained that the two veterans who most openly showed grief—Calvin Massey and Johnny Marino—were not Jewish? Jewish veterans still seemed most captive to the terror of what they saw in the camps. Did being Jewish somehow make a GI more vulnerable to PTSD than their non-Jewish comrades? Was that due to their identification with the victims?

It quickly became apparent to the GI liberators that a preponderance of the victims and survivors were Jewish and had been killed or imprisoned because they were Jewish. (Ascertaining the number of people killed in the camps has not been possible, but historians generally put the number between 3.5 and 4 million. *An estimated 80-90% of these were Jewish.*)

Mr. Heimberg told me, "…but for the grace of God, if my parents hadn't left Europe in the early 1900s, I would be have been among the dead." It was not a huge leap of the imagination for the Jewish GIs to picture themselves lying among the camp victims stacked in piles *like cordwood*, falling out of boxcars, twisted and burned in ravines, or falling down to kiss the GIs' feet. The victims were the Jewish GIs' cousins, their second cousins, their parents' former neighbors, their fellow Jews. "It was only sheer luck that I wasn't among them," a Jewish veteran told me. "That's why I felt empathy." Each of the Jewish veterans I spoke with had much in common with one another, my father included. Children of Jewish immigrants from Eastern Europe, they grew up in Yiddish-speaking, observant homes. They all experienced anti-Semitism from their fellow Americans before and even during the war. Being Jewish underpinned their response to discovering the true meaning of "concentration camp."

But sharing the faith did not necessarily lead to empathy, just as not sharing it did not preclude empathy. And a liberator's emotional reaction had no rhyme or reason: some GIs became enraged and others went into shock, while compassion moved others.

One veteran I spoke with has never been able to forgive himself for the disassociation he experienced from the victims, his fellow Jews, after he witnessed Nordhausen. (He was part of a military intelligence team gathering information about the Nazi weapons research.)

"I was there for a couple of days, two weeks after its liberation. I had a personal, intimate tour of the ovens, and I remember this part in particular: My guide climbs up on a hill and says, 'I'm standing on 6,000 Jews.' I got furious and yelled, 'Get off.' 'What's your problem?' he answered. I pulled him down. I had gotten rid of my Yiddish accent, after having been teased that I couldn't speak German with it. But this was a group that I wanted to speak Yiddish to, but I couldn't find the words, and I was alien and embarrassed. It was a terrible thing that I couldn't speak to them. These were my people—Litvaks—but I couldn't talk to them. My Yiddish never came back.

"When I think of Nordhausen now, I think of this shock and the alienation that I could never forgive myself for. These survivors... I didn't want to be one of those. It was a devastating blow. The 'Yach—don't get that on me' was shattering. Here I was, a social worker who should understand, and *this* was *my* response?"

He talked about other aspects of his war experience, how he came to believe during the war that he and his men were invincible, that it became a comic strip where nothing could hurt them. Then, when he was back stateside, he became devastated that he needed anesthesia for a tooth extraction. "It hit me that I was mortal. Going home, as I walked to the bus, a car backfired, and I fell to one knee, reaching for my pistol that wasn't there anymore. I was surprised to see everyone else around me acting normally. Once I got home, the door slammed—and I did a sitting high jump. That startle reflex lasted for a while...and it has returned. I'll be on the computer, and my wife will come in to tell me lunch is ready, and I'll jump, upset the desk. Things like that. It's been hard for her; I haven't been a very nice person to be around."

Even though this man became a psychotherapist after the war, well-read in research on trauma, he could not extend his learning to himself. Most of what he said belied his claim of having "learned compassion" for himself. As I walked out of his front door, he asked, "Have any other men you've talked with expressed having had similar reactions to survivors?" Apprehension of my answer twisted his mouth, compressed his forehead. I did not feel I could answer with anything but yes.

He had not spoken of the war with his two adult sons. "They'll have the movie (made about his intelligence unit) and the four hours of tapes to see if they want to. One son I would tell, but the other one is too fragile. Sensitive. So much awful things in the world as it is. Why pile more on them?" (Words my own father might well have said of me.)

Was it significant that in the eleven years after the then-five-year-old's father died, the family moved sixteen times, that his older brother, a gifted musician, died at age sixteen, that his mother had witnessed pogroms—state-sponsored terrorism directed at Jewish communities?

Perhaps this man's childhood robbed him of resiliency, ensuring that witnessing atrocity would sentence him to a lifetime of self-recrimination and depression that his instinctual disassociation from the horrors reinforced. But I also thought of an essay I had read by Robert Jay Lifton, a psychiatrist who has written books about the survivors and perpetrators of atrocities. The essay, which appears in *Human Adaptation to Extreme Stress: From the Holocaust to Vietnam*, edited by John P. Wilson, Zev Harel and Boaz Kahana, is called "Understanding the Traumatized Self: Imagery, Symbolization, and Transformation." Lifton sees the issue of death as central to understanding trauma. If we are to understand trauma, we must confront death "personally and conceptually." When someone comes upon a situation that overwhelms them with horror, where the death surrounding them is utterly beyond comprehension, feelings of helplessness flood in, and this leads to self-condemnation.

"Grief and loss tend to be too overwhelming in their suddenness...for them to be resolved." One of the many symptoms is an inability to mourn and an inability to reconstruct shattered personal forms with vitality and integrity. This witness of Nordhausen was the living manifestation of these words.

I was beginning to understand the utter absence of grief in my childhood home.

The tapes from Hillel at Boston University's oral history project revealed that non-Jewish GIs who entered the camps were just as likely as Jewish ones to feel empathy for the victims or shock. John Connors of Arlington, Massachusetts, said of Mauthausen, "The smell...you can block out sights, but not smells. Any GI who smelled something like that got the worst. And the ovens... when we saw them, we were silent, not a word, not 'Oh Jesus,' not 'What is this?' Not 'What have we done?' The ovens imprinted themselves. They stuck with me and are still with me."

Edward Fitzgerald with the 45th Infantry Division said of Dachau, "If we had known anything like this was going on, the war would have ended six months earlier. Our men cried. We were a combat unit. We'd been to Anzio, southern France, Sicily, Salerno, the Battle of the Bulge, and we'd never, ever seen anything like this."

John O'Malley, Jr., with the 84th Infantry Division, said of Ahlem, "Having gone through the war, my emotions were numbed, but I couldn't believe what I saw. The shock was great. You didn't think much about it at first, but after a few years the melancholy felt overwhelming. It doesn't fade, doesn't go away. It's good to keep your mind away from it, to look ahead. If you dwell on it too much, you get in a difficult spot. Even when I look at a photograph I can smell it. The medics went crazy."

Some said they had not gone into shock. "It was so horrible, my mind rejected it. I had no emotional scars because I didn't believe it." That veteran mentioned that he often spoke about his experience to his children. So how was Calvin Massey able to take in what he saw and feel the staggering grief? Might his embracing prisoners have been the key?

I remembered the stories Mr. Massey told me of his childhood in rural Alabama, his tight-knit family, his close relationship with his brother, the quintessential idyllic American childhood that not even the Depression darkened. "We always had 'possum and rabbits and deer to eat," he had said.

Then it hit me. The parents of the Jewish veterans not only came from Eastern Europe, they emigrated to escape pogroms. They witnessed the devastation of their Russian and Polish *shtetls*—the slaughter of neighbors, cousins, siblings, and parents; the rape of their mothers and sisters; and the burning of homes—the massacre of Jews only differing in degree from the more systematic genocide of the Final Solution.

The pogroms resulted from the intense discrimination that

Locations of pogroms of early 1900s

followed Tsar Nicholas I's creation of the Pale of Jewish Settlement in 1835 out of Poland, Lithuania, and the southwestern provinces of Russia and White Russia. Within the Pale, Jews could not live in rural areas or some cities, nor could they be farmers, only petty traders, shopkeepers, peddlers, and artisans. Poverty became endemic, reinforcing the common perception of Jews as parasites. Once the press spouted militant anti-Semitism, the pogroms of 1881 soon followed. After Tsar Alexander I's assassination, rumors quickly pinned the blame on the Jews. In 1881, over two hundred pogroms ravaged Jewish settlements, the authorities condoning the attacks or looking the other way. Over the next three years, the years during which my own grandparents were born within the Pale, pogroms occurred every few months.

A nineteen-year lull followed, during which time my grandparents, Raphael and Lena, grew up in a community that fear and grief ran through like a stream, keeping anxiety constant. In

Aftermath of pogrom in Chisinau, 1903

1903, the year my grandfather left his wife and infant son for America to avoid conscription into the Tsar's army and create a brighter future, the pogroms began again.

The new wave began in Kishniev, some fifty miles from my grandparents' *shtetl*, but the violence quickly spread to the rural areas. During 1903 and 1904, forty-five pogroms killed ninety-five Jews and severely injured 4,500. Property damage was catastrophic. In 1905, the level of violence increased when the Tsar signed the October Manifesto, which promised the establishment of democratic institutions. Six hundred and ninety pogroms occurred, killing 3,000 Jews. One pogrom in Odessa killed 800 Jews and left another 100,000 homeless.

I do not know if my grandmother's *shtetl* was attacked during the two years after her husband left for America. I cannot say if trauma or the loneliness and unhappiness of Lena's life in Perth Amboy caused the dullness of her eyes and the limpness of her mouth in the family portrait taken in 1916, nine years after her immigration. Even without trauma, the elements of her life were unhappy. She did not want to leave her home in Russia and her mother with whom she had lived for the previous three years, and she did not like the cramped quarters and soot and congestion of Perth Amboy.

Her marriage most likely had been arranged, as my grandfather was from another *shtetl* not within walking distance. And according to all his children, he had a fierce temper. In the nine years after my grandmother joined him, she bore seven children. Jews believe sex is a *mitzvah*, an obligation, and the Orthodox proscriptions against sex during the ten days that encompass a woman's menstrual period ensure conception. One of my aunts remembers her mother as always having been tired. In a photograph taken when she was fifty-one, Lena looks close to seventy. Four years later, she died of cancer.

The few times my father spoke of his mother, his adoration was evident in his sad, shining eyes. I saw her melancholy reflected in his, the melancholy he dismissed as Russian.

Although my father never mentioned a pogrom, his emotional history points to such violence having shaped the family's consciousness. If Lena witnessed the violence—or even if she lived in fear of it—security would have become fragile for her. Intensified by her unhappiness in Perth Amboy, her melancholy would have permeated her household, overpowering any sense of optimism, making my father less resilient and more vulnerable to the shock of Nordhausen, as he had no reference for how to overcome such pain. As his trauma set up the circumstances that led to mine, so

Victims, all children of pogrom in Ekaterinoslav, south of Kiev, 1905

had hers set a chain of cause and effect into motion. Trauma leads to trauma. *L'dor va dor.*

But I still was not clear about what made remembering trauma so terrifying that it could create stasis, a "lamination," capable of lasting a lifetime…and beyond.

The following September, I headed off to two division reunions where I met a broad range of World War II veterans, one of whom provided an essential clue. The first reunion was of the 11th Armored Division, of which Edgar Edelsack had been a part. Posted on their website is an account of its sojourns in Europe that includes the following:

> *Oh, yes, thousands, millions of words have been written about Dachau, Nordhausen, Buchenwald, Mauthausen, and the other monuments to the Third Reich. But if the genius of the world, the great word artists of all time were to concentrate and labor for eternity to convey the horror of these places, their impact on the human spirit, they could not succeed. But to see—that would be enough….*

The 11th Armored gathered at a large hotel in Arlington, Virginia, the chrome-and-marble lobby filled with people when I walked in: wedding parties, tourists, and several small groups of elderly men sporting the tell-tale cloth soldier's hat and division badges. I walked upstairs to the hallway outside the grand ballroom, introduced myself to men standing around, and explained I was writing a book about my father's experience as a camp liberator. Would they be willing to help me understand what he went through by sharing their perspectives on having witnessed Mauthausen? Their responses were various forms of no.

Terrible, can't begin to tell you how terrible it was.
Wish I could. Still can't talk about it.

My grandmother and her first child, Jacob, in Russia, 1905

I'd love to be able to help you. Maybe later.
I put that behind me. The only way....
Wiped that from my mind. You get on with your life. That's what
you have to do, just move forward.

"I'd give anything for my husband to get that off his chest," one woman said as she stepped forward from a group. "Maybe if you came to our home in Philly...." She slipped me a piece of paper with her name and phone number.

A young man approached me after hearing my conversation. "Come to my dad's room. I think he'll talk to you." His father, John Rastelli, had just stepped down from being president of the veterans' group. He held out a hand to welcome me as I explained my purpose. Another veteran, Tarmo Holma, walked into the room.

"This young lady wants to know about our coming upon Mauthausen," Mr. Rastelli explained. The two of them began a waltz of one man's memory sparking memories in the other.

"Was it after we went through that town where not a soul came out of their homes?" Mr. Holma asked.

"No, remember," Mr. Rastelli said, "Sal was joking about his plans to find some girl who would be so desperate for a man she wouldn't even care about how bad he smelled?"

"Yeah, we were walking through those woods. Creepy, how there hadn't been a sign of a Kraut for days; but those woods reminded us all of Bastogne."

"Yeah! How could you forget that?"

"And I was up in front and saw those holes. Thought they were just ditches. But got up close and they were huge, twenty by twenty, at least. And I looked down, and the bodies...they were full of bodies...emaciated bodies, skin on bone...."

Tears fell down Mr. Rastelli's cheeks. He placed his face in the cup of his palms over the table and wept. His wife pushed her chair away from the table, and retrieved tissues, which she placed in her husband's hand. The small gesture seemed fluid and natural, as if she had done this very thing many times before.

"And that was even before we got to Mauthausen," said Mr. Holma. "Mauthausen made that pit seem like a picnic."

These two men could talk about their memories and show deep pain, no terror. Mr. Rastelli evidenced that he had grieved often, that his tears were not a rare event.

At the reunion of the 12th Armored Division in Abilene, Texas, I met Carold Bland, a liberator who "pushed" his way out of his terror. One of the most soft-spoken, modest veterans I spoke with—which says a lot, considering all were humble—he still lived where he had grown up in rural Missouri. Before the war he had never traveled more than fifteen miles from his home. Prior to the war, he had never known a Jew. He demonstrated that a veteran did not have to be Jewish to experience lasting trauma from witnessing the death camps. He echoed George Kaiser's remarks that all the death he had seen during the war had made him a tough combat veteran by April 1945. "But [Landsberg] we could not handle. There's no way on earth you could exaggerate what happened there."

Like the other veterans, Mr. Bland broke down as he tried to talk about Landsberg. He changed the subject to his return to civilian life after the war: "That they didn't train us for." Like Mr. Hirsch and Mr. Kaiser, he felt alone back in the States, unable to talk about having seen a concentration camp because people didn't want to hear about it. "They didn't understand, and when I did try to talk about it, people responded as if I thought I had won the war on my own." He had nightmares, depression, and anxiety, which he believes caused his marriage to dissolve. His second wife, whom he married in the late 1960s, would wake him from the nightmares and comfort him. A decade later, the nightmares finally went away.

"I had to push my way through it," Mr. Bland said.

In the middle of our conversation, another veteran, Sidney Brickell, joined us. Though he had fought alongside Mr. Bland during the war, unlike Mr. Bland, Mr. Brickell, who is Jewish, had not suffered over what he saw at Landsberg. "I just went on with my life," he said. "I think about it from time to time, but that's about it." When I asked what might explain the difference between their reactions, Mr. Brickell answered that his friend was more sensitive. But I saw another factor at work, revealed in Mr. Bland's words toward the end of our conversation. "I learned from the war that we're all people. We are all the same. There's no difference between us except the ones we pretend exist for some political purpose."

When Carold Bland saw the dead and walking dead at Landsberg, he was not able to see the victims as "other." It was that sense of common humanity that led to his nightmares, his depression, and his loneliness back in the States. No one else understood—except Sidney, whom he regarded as a brother. "He understands me better than my brother does. Coming here every fall keeps me from being alone with my memories."

There, again, was that sense of being alone with the images.

Mr. Bland told me he believed that talking about his experiences to college and high school students helped to heal him. What he said next arrested my attention. "But if I try to get too graphic, it's pretty hard to keep talking. No photograph can represent my memories, because a photo only reveals so much. It can't enable you to smell, to hear. No photo has ever shown what the soldiers encountered when they walked through the camp gates."

Although his concluding words gave me the final pieces of my puzzle, I did not see it at the time. I was too busy wondering what made the memories terrifying long after the threat they posed had disappeared.

Kay Bonner Nee:
Monstrous Memory

I went into complete shock. God, I remember those ovens with
burned bodies still in them. It was at that point that I sort of
went into shock....

—Kay Bonner Nee

(Kay Bonner Nee collection)

Throughout my project, I wanted to find a woman who had
been among the camps' liberators. I wondered if a woman might
have responded differently to the trauma of witnessing one of the
concentration camps. Though coming of age in the 1960s inculcated

179

in me the values of egalitarianism and feminism, parenthood altered many of my ideas about gender differences. I could not get either of my boys to let a doll remain in the crib for more than two seconds or prevent them, at eighteen months, from turning a stick into a gun as they sat in a sandbox. And I observed women, on the whole, to demonstrate more comfort with emotions and more readily enter therapy.

My father's photographs included pictures of women nurses, but I had no luck locating any of them or the ones listed in *GIs Remember*. Then I came upon an Emory University doctoral dissertation that referenced the oral histories of GI liberators assembled by Fred Crawford and other groups around the country. The dissertation included a reference to Kay Bonner Nee, described as an entertainer for the troops. She had somehow witnessed the liberation of Buchenwald.

I found an address for Ms. Nee in Minneapolis, and ten days after I mailed her a letter, her daughter emailed me that her mother would be more than glad to talk with me. I called Ms. Nee, and though at first she sounded a little puzzled, when she connected my name to the letter, enthusiasm enlivened her voice. We agreed to meet a month later.

A tiny woman whose slight body curved forward from osteoarthritis, Ms. Nee opened the door of her apartment in assisted-living with a smile. "Come in, this is such a delight," she said, shaking my hand vigorously though she did not meet my eyes. As we walked into her living room, she ran her fingers along the wall upon which there were photographs of people my age, either formally posed or playing with their children. As we sat down on a couch, I noticed how dark she kept her apartment, the living room curtains still drawn.

Ms. Nee began telling me about her childhood, how she grew up on a farm in a small Minnesota town that had eight bars but no grocery. Her parents' loss of a son before her birth burdened their already difficult life, and on a doctor's advice, they moved to another small town. After her father failed at farming, they moved to Minneapolis, the eight family members living in one room. Another child died, and two sisters went into a convent, leaving Kay and a brother at home. "All of this was passed down to me," she said in a dispassionate tone of voice.

After attending college on a scholarship, Ms. Nee got a job as a radio director and on-air personality. She greatly enjoyed the work, but then the war began, and eager to go overseas, she began writing to the Red Cross.

Here she stood up, saying we needed more light. She turned and walked over to the wall that separated the living room from the kitchenette, but rather than flipping the switch, she ran her hand up and down the wall, as if wiping it clean with her palm. After three passes, her palm landed on the switch. "Ah, here we go." The overhead light turned on.

I realized she could barely see. She sat back down on the couch.

"Where was I?"

My voice guided her face toward me, and she went on to tell me how she managed, despite being too young, to get accepted by the Red Cross for an overseas assignment. She was not one to let bureaucratic details get in her way.

I asked her why she had wanted to go overseas.

"That's where all the action was."

Her stories of her experiences in the European theater amazed me. Her decent singing voice and stage presence convinced the Red Cross staff in London to get her assigned to the USO as an entertainer, teaming her up with another woman, assigning them a two-ton truck out of which they would work. A piano was rigged to roll out from one side and lowered down with a pulley, so that she and her partner could do a show no matter where they found themselves. The hitch was that Ms. Nee had never driven.

"It didn't occur to the Brits that an American girl wouldn't know how to drive," she said. A "Cockney fellow" taught her how to drive, taking her to a road just before the Waterloo Bridge.

She put on a cockney accent. "He said, 'All right, lady, now you take it.' I got behind the wheel, and I thought, *Oh, dear God, I have got to really do this.* Well, I almost ran us off the Waterloo Bridge. He reached over and pulled the brake, wiped his forehead, and said, 'I say, lady, you ain't never driven before, 'ave you?' And I said, 'No, I haven't but you're going to teach me. This is very important.'"

On D-Day +14 (June 20, 1944), she crossed the English Channel, landing at Utah Beach, then traveled through more small towns than she could remember.

I asked if she ever felt in danger.

"Well, you know, the strange part was—and I suppose because I was young—I had many close escapes but I don't know that I was afraid. I always felt sure, somehow or other, that I would come out of this. If I had been afraid, I probably would have just collapsed, because there was nothing around to give me any comfort."

She was in Paris during its liberation, saw the Allied troops march through the Arc de Triomphe, then got back in her truck to drive to the front lines and entertain troops. That she and her partner were unescorted women, free to travel wherever they chose, amazed me. Even newswomen did not have that kind of access to the battlefront. She did not realize at the time how extraordinary it was that she had the blessing of V Corps (the army corps to which she was officially attached) to travel with few restrictions.

After the liberation of Paris, she and her partner came to Eupen, Belgium, which was eighteen miles from Aachen, Germany, and which, as of October 21, 1944, the Americans controlled. Christmas of that year—one that she would "always remember"—they couldn't set up a show because of the battles.

Kay Bonner, standing in the middle, during the war
(Kay Bonner Nee collection)

But a theater in Eupen wasn't being used, so they called in soldiers who had acting or singing experience. "A great many boys
came in, and we put together a show for troops from all over. But
on December 19, someone ran in the theatre yelling, 'Get back to
your trucks! Don't stop, whatever you do. We are under attack!'"
The Germans had broken through at Moncheaux, only about five
miles from Eupen.

   "We were in danger, especially those of us who weren't soldiers. So we got into our truck and took along another girl. We
drove without our lights, using the tracer bullets of the Germans

that would light up the road enough so we could tell where it was. At one point, we heard German voices, and a shot killed Katie, the girl with us."

"Were you terrified?" I asked.

"Well, no, I guess because it seemed so unreal, as if you were having a strange dream or something rather than the real thing." She and her partner came in contact with others from V Corps, and they stayed at a temporary evacuation center through Christmas.

"What a desolate Christmas it was," she recalled. "New Year's Day, our ack-ack gun shot down a German plane, and the pilot parachuted out. As he was hanging in the air, our boys took a machine gun and shot him down. And I remember thinking: This is what war does, it turns decent people into murderers. These boys can't be blamed because that's what they've been taught. But I'll never forget that miserable New Year's."

About two weeks later, they started again, following V Corps as it moved into Germany. They were the first women across the Remagen bridgehead and continued to do shows in Germany.

Then she saw Buchenwald.

"One morning, I went with the troops. They said they were going to a concentration camp; did I want to come along? It was Buchenwald, full of the most horrible sights I've ever seen."

Unlike most of the other veterans, Ms. Nee kept talking at this point of her story.

"There were remains of bodies in the ovens. A big truck, slat-sided—a big wagon—was loaded full of bodies, waiting to be burned. It was a horrible sight, and the smell of the place was enough to do you in. The fellow who was showing me through took me into this cement, round room with big thick walls, and he said the walls were so thick to muffle the screams. It was a torture chamber. There were big hooks that he said were used to hang prisoners before they were tortured."

Buchenwald, April 1945

She went from this building into one of the rooms where people supposedly slept. The bunks there were four high and close
together, making it impossible to sit up. "There were...,"she held
her pointer finger out before her as if actually counting the bunks,
seeing it all in her mind "...four of these bunks along each side,
with ten people in each one."

On the other side was what she described as the "room of the
living dead," because the people in there were barely alive. Ms.
Nee recalled thinking, *Oh, good Lord, so they've been liberated, so
what? They're all going to die.* "But then I thought, *Yes, but they'll
die knowing they're free, and this is very important.*" An elderly
gentleman reached out and grabbed her coat, saying "American,
American, *gut,*" before he fell back and died.

Afterwards, the GIs brought people from Weimar to see the
camp. When told, "Look, look what you did," the townspeople

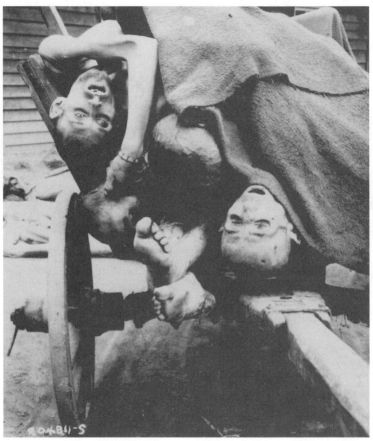

Buchenwald, April 1945

said, "Not us, not us. We didn't even know the camp was here."
The inmates told the Americans the townspeople were lying.
Whenever the inmates had been taken into town to work on the
roads, the townspeople had hissed and thrown stones at them.

I asked Ms. Nee how she responded emotionally to
Buchenwald.

"I went into complete shock. God, I remember those ovens
with burned bodies still in them. It was at that point that I sort of
went into shock, a protective shock, so that as I went through the

rest of the camp, while I was horrified, I somehow…the reality of it was kept from me, so that I could go on."

She recognized what had happened to her psyche.

She only talked about what she had seen for several days afterwards. "Then, when I talked about it, I'd bring the whole thing back and I wasn't ready to do that." When I asked with whom she talked about it when she did talk, she went off on a tangent about how, after V-E Day, she and her partner began coordinating shows. I persisted.

"Well, I didn't talk about it much. I don't think anybody wanted to hear about it. Even my own mother would say, 'Now, Kay, that's all behind you. Forget about it, don't even talk about it.' And, uh, so I sort of shut up. And didn't talk about it for years, actually, until some people started doing research on the camps and got my name somehow, and came to talk to me."

I was surprised she did not talk about it with her husband who was a GI also stationed in the European Theater.

"I told him some, but I didn't dwell on it. It was more or less

Ovens at Buchenwald, April 1945

an area of my life I knew I would have to forget, because I couldn't go on thinking about it. So it was part of my life I had to put behind me. Be careful that it didn't come to the front."

The postwar life Ms. Nee went on to describe was an extremely busy one. She had four children in the five years right after the war while also pursuing her career with public television, where she developed new programming. So, as well as having traveled unescorted through war-ravaged Europe, she helped pioneer the possibilities for women wanting to juggle career and motherhood. I could not comprehend how she had done it all. Perhaps the daily demands helped to suppress unwanted memories.

What she did remain conscious of were the values she wanted to instill into her children. When they were teenagers, she took them to Belgium and Germany so they would realize the terrible reality of war and do what they could to help prevent such a thing from happening again. "I wanted them to be aware that unless they were good and influenced other people to be good, they were in danger," Ms. Nee said. "I think they learned that lesson very well."

But rather than taking them to Buchenwald, she showed them Dachau—and did not mention that she had been among the liberators of Buchenwald. "It was as if the person who saw Buchenwald was somebody other than myself, as if I were looking at it from the outside."

I couldn't censor my surprise at her avoidance of discussing Buchenwald with her children while showing them Dachau.

"There was something that I didn't want to accept, I guess. Even though I had seen it with my own eyes, it was difficult to believe that human beings could be that terrible to other human beings. It just seemed an impossibility."

The room became silent.

Looking at the photographs of her grandchildren, I asked if she had spoken with them about the war.

German civilians ordered by U.S. Army to witness Buchenwald,
April 1945

"I plan to, but they're still too young."

After we concluded the interview and I was packing up my tape recorder, Ms. Nee said, "I stay away from my memories. I don't like to go there, I don't know why. Maybe it's a fear."

My body froze. I tried to sound calm as I asked, "A fear of what?"

"Of the memories destroying me."

I stood, unable to find words. Then I thanked her, shook her hand and walked down to my rental car. After driving around and around a block of large Victorian houses, I parked at a small lake and began walking, following the crushed granite that curved and meandered, taking me farther than my sandaled feet appreciated, but still I kept walking.

Then I drove around other blocks and found a street of restaurants, parked the car, and ate dinner at a Korean one. Afterwards, I went into a bookstore and spent over an hour wandering the aisles. At ten o'clock, with no other option, I went to the hotel and hoped I would open the door to find my sons and husband on the other side. The stale motel odor pushed emptiness into my lungs. I called home. Ray was out with friends; David wanted to know when I would be back. "Tomorrow, honey," I assured him.

Burke asked how the interview went.

"Good."

"Was her response different from the men's?"

"Sort of. I'll tell you tomorrow."

I turned on the television and flipped through the channels. Images of murder and violence kept appearing until I found an old movie starring a gaunt Judy Garland. I turned the light off but couldn't close my eyes.

Maybe it's a fear. Of the memories destroying me.

Was it the thought of my father's endlessly slow death that terrified me as Ms. Nee's words echoed in my mind? Or the memory of my own trauma? But hadn't I always been able to recall that day in the police station to my mind—to see the rows of benches, the windows on the wall, the police car—clearly, vividly?

I thought of Audrey Hepburn in *Wait Until Dark*—the blind woman knowing, though she could not see him, that the murderer sat waiting within her own house. Ms. Nee had a murderer in her home. Did I also? Waiting for me, created out of memory, given substance from the silence of my childhood home.

Lying on the motel room bed, I could not close my eyes, because when I did I saw the two children at the bottom of the ditch at Nordhausen.

I can't get too graphic... Mr. Kaiser had said. Nat Futterman could not go through the gate. Carold Bland: *But if I try to get too graphic, it's pretty hard to keep talking.* Edgar Edelsack: *The pictures I took were so emotionally disturbing that I gave them away. I couldn't face looking at them.*

Lot's wife turned into salt because she looked into the heart of horror. And felt it killing her.

Back in Austin, I shared Kay Nee's parting words with a friend. A scholar of late twentieth-century American Jewish literature, she said, "Just like children of survivors, you and the other children of liberators saw your parents refuse to let their memories destroy them. That takes a lot of energy."

Even if the veterans succeeded in locking away the memories, they could not lock away the fear that the memories might slip through, whether in a dream or awake, maybe triggered by the smell of lime on a newly lined baseball field. Now I knew what about the veterans most reminded me of my father—a palpable fear, signaled by the sudden speaking of themselves in the second person. A metallic coldness, or absence, I mistook in my father for indifference.

How do we live if we fully allow ourselves to see the truth that image reveals?

And if we do not look, how can we free ourselves from a terror that only grows with not looking? Terror seems to demand full exposure, thorough exploration.

The liberators became prisoners of the camps they liberated.

My father, the man who heard my mother screaming at the police station, "Don't leave me. I'll never see you again!" had in spirit never left Nordhausen. His terror had encircled my childhood home with barbed wire.

As we got ready for bed the next evening, I shared my insight with Burke. When I said that Nordhausen had imprisoned my father, Burke sat up on the bed, as if stung by a bee, his mouth open. "You're Hitler's victim, too. Our family is."

His words caught me midstride between the closet and bed.

Emaciated. Skeletal. Lice-ridden. That wasn't *us*. I put my hands out before me, palms facing Burke, trying to push away his words. European Jews—on the other side of the ocean—were the victims. Not we Americans. I was no different from the veteran who forgot his Yiddish when he saw Nordhausen.

A liberator raised me, shaped my world view, my spirit. I absorbed my father's terror and carried it with me into adulthood, into the home I created with my husband and children. Many liberators could not see where their severed spirit resided, just as I had not seen that part of me had never left the police station. *Don't let them take you.* There were parallels between my early years and experiences of the Holocaust as a result of my father's paralysis. I had been separated from my mother at a police station. I had been put on a train to an unknown destination called "camp," and I awoke in the morning in the middle of a forest. My mother had been erased, no sign of her detectable, as if she had never existed.

I began to look for images of Lot's wife. And found a painting done by a German painter, Anselm Kieffer, who was born in 1945. There is no human form in the painting, only train tracks endlessly continuing into the horizon cloaked with an empty sky. Research about Kieffer revealed that a major influence on his work was Albrecht Durer's engraving, *Melancholia.*

When terror makes grief impossible, melancholy finds opportunity. Melancholy is not an emotion. It is a parasite that sucks us dry.

Two months after my visit with Kay Bonner Nee, I came across the title of a book that grabbed my attention: *War and the Soul* by Dr. Ed Tick. After working for over thirty years, first with

Vietnam veterans then with veterans from all the wars of the last seventy years, Dr. Tick does not see PTSD as a mental illness with symptoms of stress/anxiety. Rather, he sees it as a disorder of the soul that results from witnessing or partaking in violence that has no transcendent meaning and that violates the soldier's moral code. As the terror makes safety impossible, the soul flees the body.

Rather than assigning the words "post traumatic stress disorder" to the acronym PTSD, Dr. Tick assigns the words "post terror soul disorder." The soldier has become a "psycho-spiritual" casualty, violence and terror having shattered his or her identity.

Post terror soul disorder made complete sense to me, because in all my therapy, I ultimately remained unable to find the way to forgive my father. I had begun to wonder if forgiveness might be a spiritual act, rather than an intellectual one.

Dr. Tick uses mythology and ancient European and Native American wisdom to explore what the soul is—the source of our will, our aesthetic and ethical sensibilities, our consciousness and identity, as well as of our shadow desires. To try to heal PTSD through traditional psychotherapy and medication alone ignores and denies what happens spiritually to a soldier.

"Society disowns the suffering war creates for its soldiers," writes Dr. Tick, and this "abandonment of veterans is as much a cause of PTSD as the war itself."

I thought of how no one in my family acknowledged what had happened to me in the police station, let alone how it might have affected me, and I knew the truth of Dr. Tick's words.

Veterans suffer, according to Dr. Tick, in large part, because of the huge chasm between how our culture continues to regard war, seeing it as a legitimate answer to conflict and denying how it changes soldiers forever. I thought of Mr. Hirsch's words: "Have I ever changed back?" and Mr. DeLuca's remembering how his mother told him she hadn't gotten the same boy back.

To heal PTSD, Dr. Tick says we must "surround the trauma

with soul." He suggests how that might happen: public story-telling, witnessing of the veterans' pain, holding retreats for veterans after they return but before they re-enter their families and society. At these retreats, elders would create a container for the veterans' traumas and sanctify and purify their consciences, enabling a new identity to emerge.

Was I helping to surround the trauma of Mr. Heimberg, Mr. Kaiser, Mr. Paper with soul by asking for their stories? I prayed I was.

Were they helping me to retrieve my own?

I prayed they were.

Could men who no longer believed in God know the grace of their souls?

Yes, something in me insisted. Yes.

I needed to grieve for my soul. For mine and for my family's, for our losing the possibility of happiness even before our family began. To grieve having lost my father even before I knew him. I had known only half of him, his outline visible; but while he looked present, his wounded soul was not. That part of himself he lost. Nordhausen had severed his soul from him, the part of his being that creates intimacy and feels and expresses grief and love.

I lost a piece of my soul in the police station. Where could I begin finding it again? I had no community of veterans, no group of elders to turn to. Nordhausen. I could begin at Nordhausen. Perhaps, I thought, part of my father's soul still lingered there, unclaimed, unmourned. Perhaps I could put it to rest. Maybe grieving at the grave of my father's vitality and my family's happiness would release me from my terror.

Part Two

Scenes of the Crimes

This shaking keeps me steady. I should know.
What falls away is always. And is near.
I wake to sleep, and take my waking slow.
I learn by going where I have to go.

—Theodore Roethke, "The Waking"

Leila Levinson

Nordhausen

The skin of memory gives way at times, revealing all it contains.

—Charlotte Delbo, *Days and Memory*

View from Nordhausen

As the plane landed in Berlin, I took deep breaths, pushing my palms flat against my thighs. "Relax," I repeated to myself, "you'll do fine." I was only a little less nervous than the last time I had traveled to Germany, back in 1971, as a seventeen-year-old on a bicycling trip. It seemed incomprehensible that a mere twenty-five years after the war, my father had agreed to my traveling to Germany.

That time I entered on a train from Belgium, my anxiety soaring within minutes of crossing the border into Germany. A young man sat down in my train compartment: blond, defined cheekbones, sapphire eyes—the Aryan Adonis. I buried my face in my book, *The Greening of America*, its title providing my neighbor his opening line: "Are you American?" Blood rushed to my cheeks as I realized the book advertised my nationality. Adonis then proceeded to tell me about himself. His East German father had married his Cuban mother while on a Communist-sponsored trip to help Cuba create an irrigation system. After having spent most of his childhood in Cuba, the young man was happy to be living in his beloved Germany. My lack of enthusiasm for his country must have become apparent, because his next question was: "Are you Jewish?"

My stomach lurched. We had only just crossed into Germany, and already my blonde hair and emerald eyes had failed me.

"Why do you ask?"

"Because you're so nervous about being in Germany. Let me assure you, we're very good to Jews now."

I didn't know which was worse: his thinking this would put me at ease or that he might be baiting me with sarcasm.

The next day didn't go any better. The youth hostel, located in a castle, started the day with military marching music, and out in the courtyard soldiers were goose-stepping in formation. I left Germany after three days, a week earlier than planned.

This trip, thirty-five years later, would last only a week, I kept telling myself during the seven-hour trans-Atlantic flight. The seven days loomed larger with every passing hour, the confidence I had felt in Burke's presence fading; my resentment at his work for preventing him from being with me surged.

As I walked off the plane, my heart sped up. That moment after arriving at another country's airport I was in limbo, crossing the line from my familiar world to a foreign one, as I waited for officials to check my passport. I looked outside through the airport's huge windows, a world where people bicycled amidst small cars and buses, and billboards bore German words. I looked up at the monitor hanging between the door to the outside and me. The words ARRIVALS and DEPARTURES brought to mind the opening words of *Auschwitz and After*, the memoir of Auschwitz survivor Charlotte Delbo.

People arrive. They look through the crowd of those who are wait-
ing, those who await them. They kiss them and say the trip exhaust-
ed them...
But there is a station where those who arrive are those who are
leaving...
A station where those who arrive have never arrived, where those
who have left never came back.

"Fine," the German official said after looking at my passport, my last name, Levinson, as good as if "Jewish" were stamped next to it. His one word of English settled down my heart rate.

Standing on the bus outside the terminal, I began to doubt it would take me to Friedrichstrasse or Frederich's Street, where I could catch a subway to my hotel.

"Do you speak English?" I asked a woman with a soft face standing next to me. Her gray hair underscored the vigor of her blue eyes.

"Yes, gladly." She smiled and assured me I was on the right bus, and that she would let me know when to get off. "Are you on holiday?"

"No," I said. I wondered how she would receive the information that I had intended to research my father's experience as a liberator of a death camp. But she didn't. I eased my shoulder blades against the window of the bus as it pulled away from the curb.

The chic clothing of people getting on and off the bus, the swirl of vehicles and bicyclists, the billboards with bold graphics— all of it melted my anxiety. The bus stopped in front of a building of glass and light and air, a humongous terrarium encasing a whole other world of escalators and colored banners, people and stores.

"Nice, *ja?*" the woman caught my eye. "It is our new train station. Just opened."

Before I could agree, another building appeared: monumental columns of old, austere granite, the echo of a dome on its roof, as if the structure had been bombed. The sky was visible between the curved steel beams. The Reichstag.

Again, the woman noticed my reaction. "This is how we remember war. So we never forget."

I hid my satisfaction. Yes, they should see a vestige of devastation, an open ugly wound every day atop the nexus of their power, a physical reminder of the devastation they brought upon themselves. Yet, as I looked at the gaping space between the beams that crowned the pristine Roman columns and immense stairs, familiar melancholy began to fill my chest.

From the outside, my hotel exuded history. Ceramic tiles covered the roof; Dutch-looking arches adorned the windows and door and middle of the roof line; wings arched from the top corners. But inside, the lobby exuded the blandness of a Holiday Inn. As my room wouldn't be available for another eight hours, the receptionist stowed my suitcase in the office, and I headed off to the Jewish Museum, three blocks away. The buildings around me spoke the history of this part of Berlin, just east of where the Berlin Wall once stood. Box-like concrete apartments lined the streets, their only interesting feature the display of occupants' possessions on the balconies: plants, hammocks, bicycles, baby swings, paper garlands, small tables for dining al fresco. Graffiti splashed color onto the walls.

A small street sign emerged from the fringes of one such signature: *Judisches Museum.* As I followed its direction down a

The Berlin Jewish Museum

cobblestone alley, a large mansion appeared, its whimsical yellow façade and curved lines a welcome relief from the gray. But once the building, an eighteenth century former courthouse, fully came into view, its right section jarred me. It looked as if someone had jammed a metal airplane hangar with jagged edges into it. I paid admission and received a brochure that informed me the architect, Daniel Libeskind, the child of Holocaust survivors who raised their son in Poland, named this project "Between Two Lines." Two linear shapes formed the building. One, "The Line of Connectedness," represented the history of cultural interaction and mutual influence between Europe's Jews and non-Jews. A sequence of empty rooms running in a disjointed line made up the second portion, "The Line of the Voids." Their windowless space embodied the absence of Jews in present Germany.

The front door to the museum opened into the old building where high walls and large windows fill the rooms with light. Then arrows leading to the exhibitions took me down a long, enclosed hallway into the new building at the end of which hangs a sign: "European Jews Murdered by the Nazis. Austria—50,000. Belgium—65,700. Bulgaria—50,000."

Oh, I thought, the numbers of people from each country. My knees bent.

"France—77,320. Germany—210,000. Greece—60,000. Netherlands—110,000." My breath left me.

"Hungary—550,000. Lithuania—140,000. Poland—2,900,000.

Two million, nine hundred thousand Jews from Poland.

"Romania—271,000. USSR—1,145,000."

One million, one hundred and forty-five thousand Russian Jews.

Standing there, on German soil, reading these numbers with all the zeros as if some machine could count no higher, I felt dizzy. People stood next to me, reading the sign. They read and moved on. My feet became lead. People pushed past me. Tears flowed down my face. Some people did not even stop to read. I could not move but neither could I stand there. I uprooted each foot and forced my body forward.

The next room displayed a copy of a decree Emperor Constantine issued in 321 that Jews could serve as traders in Germany. Even before the Jewish-Roman wars in 75 AD and 135 AD devastated Judea, Jews established settlements all over the Roman Empire, from Cadiz in Spain to Lyons in France to Worms in Germany. In many ways, Paul Johnson says in *The History of the Jews*, Jewish traders linked the developing town communes of the Middle Ages to the older cities that dated from Roman antiquity. They did this through the very fact of the Diaspora, which created networks between Jews spread over a huge geographical area. This, in combination with their essential skills and work ethic, allowed the Jews to gain important roles in Europe's economy and culture. The display at the Berlin Jewish Museum highlights that Jews played key roles in establishing trade routes in the German cities of Worms and Mainz, harmonious relations between Jews and Christians prevailing until the first Crusade.

The museum does not mention that anti-Jewish sentiments had accumulated over centuries as a consequence of two factors: Christians hearing rampant stories of the Holy Land's reigning Muslims slaughtering Christians, and that Jews allied themselves with the Muslims. The second factor was that as Christianity forbade Christians from charging interest, Jews were medieval Europe's moneylenders.

As Johnson describes, the first massacres began in Rouen, France, and spread in the spring of 1096 to the Rhineland. The bishop of Speyer stopped violence by hanging ringleaders; so did the archbishop of Cologne, but the bishop at Mainz barely escaped the city alive. The Christians of Mainz slaughtered or converted Jewish men. They killed Jewish children so they couldn't be brought up Jews, the same reasoning Nazis used to target children. One thousand women, who had taken refuge in the archbishop's castle, all committed suicide.

So began the first pogroms, the crusaders terrorizing entire settlements of Jews en route to the Holy Land. In the twelfth century, the Jews of England and western Europe who survived such attacks fled for countries in the eastern half of Europe in a desperate exodus, which resulted in eastern Europe becoming the center of Europe's Jewish population. Germany's location on the boundary between western and eastern Europe made it a desirable home for Jews who, over the next eight centuries, played a dynamic role in the region's commercial and cultural history.

An entire room of the Berlin Jewish Museum is dedicated to one extraordinary Jewish entrepreneur named Glikl bas Juda Leib, who managed to sell cloth and jewels all around northern Germany even after her husband died, leaving her with eleven children. Displays explain the banning of Jews from large cities like Hamburg in the 1500s and 1600s, the role Jews played in financing the German court, and the contributions of intellectuals like Moses Mendelssohn, the famous philosopher, and his grandson, Felix Mendelssohn, the composer (who converted to Christianity). The message the museum imparts is that to an extraordinary degree a small minority of Jews shaped Germany economically and culturally. But Christian Germans always regarded this minority with ambivalence, at best, vacillating over the centuries between granting Jews autonomy and rights and stripping them not only of those civil rights but of the very right to live at large within German society.

The end of the nineteenth century brought unprecedented freedom and economic prosperity to German Jews. Toward the end of the museum's exhibition, photographs from the 1920s and early 1930s fill a room. Middle class, assimilated Jews sled, swim, and dance before us, even exchanging presents around a "Hannukah bush." Round-cheeked children with glowing eyes sit in the laps of plump mothers in dark dresses with white collars; mustachioed men in top hats recline with ease on lounge chairs. These people glow with success, satisfaction, and security.

A final room presents the words of ten of the 105,000 Jews living in Germany today. All state how rich, satisfying, and rewarding their lives are, as if this room argues for Jews moving to Germany. In the hall stands a computer on which to answer a survey.

"Do you know any Jews personally?" Yes 29%

"Do you know anyone who is anti-Semitic?" Yes 49%

I walked out into a courtyard Libeskind named "The Garden of Exile and Emigration." Forty-nine pillars of white granite stand in seven rows of seven pillars. Seven is an auspicious number in Judaism. The seventh and last day of the week is the holy day of *Shabbat*. *Shavuoth*, the holiday commemorating receiving the Ten Commandments, means weeks, coming seven weeks after Passover. There are seven major Jewish holidays. Every seventh year the land must lay fallow. Seven by seven is forty-nine, the year Jewish law demands to be a "jubilee year" when creditors are to forgive all debts so people have the chance to start anew. When we lose a loved one, we sit *shiva* for seven days. We say seven blessings at a Jewish wedding. The list goes on. Seven, according to Jewish scholars, means completeness, a subtle irony in this Garden of Exile.

Walking through the pillars, I felt off-kilter and reached out to a pillar to get my balance. It wasn't just the fat cobblestones underfoot that threw me off. As I looked down and then up a row, I noticed the ground was pitched at an almost imperceptible angle, just uneven enough to create a slight imbalance, undetectable until dizziness shut my eyes. I had the sensation of being out on a rolling sea, the horizon allowing no fixed point. I sat down on a bench.

A sign in the courtyard states that Libeskind sought to create in the garden a physical experience of exile and emigration, the disequilibrium of being without a home. But in me it stirred physical memories of waking from nightmares and wanting to get out of bed and away from sleep but unable to, the fear too strong that my legs would not hold me, that the world wobbled beneath me. And if I fell, I would find no bottom.

Back in Austin, a month later, I would read on his website that Libeskind intended the Berlin Jewish Museum's new wing to embody the consequences of the Holocaust. "Only through acknowledgement and incorporation of this erasure and void of Jewish life in Berlin can the history of Berlin and Europe have a human future." "Erasure and void" were more than ideas for me. I had spent a lifetime denying their presence at the heart of my life. Libeskind's physical expression of absence wrenched my gut, spoke to me... *Leila, the individual; Leila, the Jew; Leila, a human being.*

There, in the museum, my body was not yet ready to feel this. I stood up and left the Garden. But the hallway or "road" did not lead me to the exit. Instead it took me to the Holocaust Tower, placing me before a leaden door suitable for a torture room of a medieval castle. *I don't have to go in there*, I told myself. *No, you're here to see this*, another voice insisted. I followed two young women into the concrete room. Dark, narrow, and high, the walls squeezed the space, squeezed out the air, cut off all sound. The only light fell from a tiny window about twenty feet up.

This isn't so bad, I thought as I looked at the walls, the floor, the ceiling. The women and I did not look at each other. Within a minute, a feeling of invisibility pushed against my lungs and they felt as if I had been holding my breath too long underwater. I extended my arms and pushed open the door.

Outside, on the street, the sun cut into my scalp and neck. I sat down on the curb, crossed my arms on top of my bent knees and placed my face in my lap. I wanted Burke. I wanted to feel his arms, his chest. I was not sure I could see what Nordhausen had to show me.

The next day, I left early for the train station. To reach Nordhausen, I got off the sleek bullet train at Magdeburg and waited an hour for another train as the day quickly heated up, the temperature reaching into the nineties, the air thick and stagnant. The old train I stepped into did not have air conditioning. The cars flooded over with friendly Czechoslovakian high school students, who, I soon learned from those who spoke English, were going to a small town close to Nordhausen to spend a month working in an orphanage. Czechoslovakians volunteering their services at a German orphanage inverted my American expectations.

The students stretched their legs on top of their backpacks, spreading their lean bodies over the seats, in the aisles, in between seats; their heads bobbed as the heat thickened into a narcotic. I could not sleep. I tried looking at the scenery.

The train lumbered through monotonous fields, tidy even in their brownness, and small towns. Wind turbines popped up everywhere as part of Germany's commitment to reducing carbon dioxide emissions. After some three hours, "Nordhausen" appeared on a platform sign, and I waved goodbye to my young friends. I deposited my suitcase in a locker in the station, grateful that the post-9/11 mentality that removed all lockers in the States had not taken over Germany. I stowed the locker's fat key in the change section of my wallet and walked into the station's tourism office, where friends back home had told me I could easily obtain a hotel room. "There's always someone in those offices who speaks English," they assured me. They were wrong. No one in the Nordhausen train station spoke English. I was now in the eastern half of Germany, where, under Soviet control, school children learned Russian, not English. The only people I met who spoke English were younger than twenty-five.

With sign language that made me feel and, no doubt, look ridiculous, I communicated my need for a hotel room. I put my palms together as if in prayer under the side of my head while bending my neck. The woman's eyes opened wide, then she laughed, nodding her head in comprehension. Her second phone call succeeded, and she indicated on a map a hotel four blocks away. I tried to ask about transportation to the site of the concentration camp. Remembering Germans had used the words "*konzentration lager*" for the camps, I said "*Konzentration lager Nordhausen?*" Her eyes scrunched up like Roman shades closing as she shook her head back and forth. Perhaps I imagined the aura of friendliness evaporating. My gaze fell to the floor; what now? Mittelbau-Dora. The name the United States Holocaust Memorial Museum uses for Nordhausen popped into my head. "Mittelbau-Dora?"

"*Ah, ja,*" she seemed to exhale, the lines around her mouth and eyes dissolving. I felt ridiculous again, as she pulled out a brochure from a display at the end of her desk, a foot from my face, and handed it to me. It was even in English. "Mittelbau-Dora Concentration Camp Memorial."

So it was Mittelbau-Dora? Not Nordhausen? A woman at the United States Holocaust Museum had told me that the real name of the camp was Mittelbau-Dora, and that the GIs called it Nordhausen because of the camp's proximity to the town, but most books as well as liberators refer to the camp as Nordhausen. The information in the brochure only added to my confusion. "An external camp of the concentration camp Buchenwald, referred to as 'Dora,' was established at the end of August 1943 in the Kohnstein near Nordhausen." Dora, not Mittelbau-Dora? And wasn't the camp in the Harz Mountains, not the "Kohnstein?" The brochure continued: "In October 1944, 'Dora,' under the name 'Mittelbau Concentration Camp,' became an independent camp. It developed into the center of a complex of over forty external camps nearly everywhere in the region."

How did the Nazis keep all these camps straight? What did they call those thirty-nine other satellite camps? Perhaps the GIs made it simple by calling all of the munitions plant's various satellite camps "Nordhausen." It reminded me of Herman Zeitchik's story about stumbling upon a small compound, considered part of the Dachau system, in the middle of the woods that held "only" a couple hundred prisoners.

As the hotel lay in the opposite direction from Mittelbau-Dora, I decided to go directly to the camp memorial. The driver took the scenic route, driving through neighborhoods where stucco row houses abutted the cobblestone streets. Unlike eastern Berlin, Nordhausen seemed to have been spared massive destruction in the war, as most of the buildings clearly predated the era of Communist control.

Some ten minutes later, we emerged from the narrow maze of streets, a bank of hills rising before us. Their puny size made it difficult to believe these were the Harz Mountains, in which the Nazis built their new factory for secret weapons after the Allied Forces discovered the rocketry plant at Peenemunde. Photographs from the 1940s show a long rise with a huge cliff of white rock exposed, but only a mere knob of a hill lay ahead of me.

As if a string pulled my head towards the driver's side of the taxi, I turned. Eight feet ahead stood a boxcar—decaying wood, a large metal bar hanging loose, blackness spilling out of the open door. The car sat on tracks extending into my destination. We passed through two crumbling brick columns.

The driver held up twelve fingers. I counted out the Euros. "*Danke.*" I got out of the taxi, placing one foot, then the other on the ground of the Mittelbau-Dora Memorial—the place World War II GIs refer to as Nordhausen—and lost my bearings.

Before me stretched broken concrete of a vast plaza. A memorial wall with a bronze relief bordered its south side. When I shaded my eyes with my hand, I could see the ruins of buildings in the distance. I opened my backpack to pull out my father's photographs in which bodies fill the same plaza as the one before me. But while buildings abut the courtyard in the photos, not even the outline of those buildings' foundations remained here.

On a rise, a barracks-like structure loomed over the grounds. In the opposite direction I saw a modern silver building that had to be the memorial's reception center. A dozen teenagers, their faces blank with boredom, lounged around the entrance. More teenagers draped themselves along the walls inside the still-crisp hall where a tall thin man peered at me from behind the desk, his thick eyeglasses magnifying his blue eyes into a smear of watercolor. I hoped he spoke English.

"Is a tour available?"

"Only in German," he answered, looking past me as he held out a self-guided tour map. "American?" I nodded. "We have books," he said, sweeping his hand out towards the shelves, "but no tour."

I thanked him and began selecting a handful of books in

English when I overheard him saying, in English, "Would you be interested in seeing a film about the camp?" His arm was directing a man and woman towards an open door. He then turned in my direction and met my eyes. "Would you care to see a movie?" he asked.

Inside the theatre room, in stark, white block letters "The Liberation of Nordhausen" appeared against a black background. I had seen this footage a year before while doing research at the National Archives in Maryland. Shot by the U.S. Signal Corps, it recorded in sharp detail the blurred chaos of bodies I had found among my father's photographs. Yet, even in focus, the hollow faces looked identical, as if they had never been persons with names, genders, families, homes, memories. GIs with blank faces carried the bodies on gurneys, arms dangling over the sides.

The face of a German official, speaking long after the war, filled the screen. "You have to remember the context. It was war; anything was possible." I stood up, leaned on a chair to catch my balance, and walked outside.

Facing the courtyard again, I turned the map around and around. No direction made sense. When thunder rumbled on the far side of the mountains, I looked up: thick dark clouds. I knew I had to get going.

A crumbling foundation to the south of the courtyard reminded me of the Anasazi ruins in southern Colorado and Utah—tiny spaces created by a series of brick walls. A small sign said "Prisoners' cells." Ten feet away another sign said: "Former execution site. Death was by hanging." I pulled a sweater out from my bag and hugged it around my shoulders. A cold breeze cut through the air as I looked at the map again, but it still made no sense. My head felt light, as if suspended over my body; the map's lettering began to blur. I sat down and rested my forehead against my palms.

Occasional thunder underscored the silence of the surrounding forest against which three notes of a bird echoed. I smelled pine. Deep forest. With my eyes closed, I could almost pretend I was in New York State's Adirondack Mountains, where I went to summer camp throughout my childhood. My father and I had both loved those mountains; I still thought of them as home even after thirty years and a house and family in Texas. But here, in Nordhausen, the pine smell and bird's song stiffened my body. How had my father not thought of this place when he sat in his chair, newspaper in hand, surrounded by the balsam woods of the Adirondacks?

The faint outline of a path took me past half-submerged ruins covered with moss, signs sticking up from years of leaves: "Bath house. Here inmates washed officers' clothes." "Depot. Here inmates deposited their belongings." *What belongings?* The path curved; more lumps protruded from the leaves. "Theatre. Inmates could attend movies for a small fee." *With what money?*

GREETINGS FROM ADIRONDACK MTS.   S-525

A man-made road and a little brook
Travel together down the hill,

But the man-made road will somewhere end
While the little brook goes onward still.

© C. T. & CO.

The Adirondacks

Ruins of Mittelbau-Dora's "bath house," July 13, 2006

The path widened enough for a truck to travel. When it looped around trees, I cut a diagonal through the woods, my feet sinking into years' worth of rotting leaves. Again the bird's notes pulled my eyes up to the treetops. A tower of bricks rose from them, a chimney, the number 1944 carved into its base. The brick building emerged complete, intact, compact, the size of a hamlet's schoolhouse. I held my breath, walked up to the front door, lifted my foot, pushed my body forward, placed my foot down inside the doorjamb.

The room was small. As my eyes adjusted to the darkness, faint lines on the wall became visible: a mural with flowers, a sun with childish rays. Flowers and birds with smiley faces. A sign said "Guards' room." My eyes darted over to, then through, the mural-framed doorway.

Ovens.

Black steel doors, brick, steel tracks running down the length

Mural on wall of guards' room in the crematorium

of their bellies. The room swirled. I crouched, my animal-self forcing my sight away, onto a plaque hanging on the wall. Its words, in French, memorialized a prisoner of the camp whose grave resided in the air. A ribbon—red, white, and blue, the French tricolors—lay in one oven's mouth.

The sound that came out of my throat bounced back from the concrete walls. I tucked my face into my skirt. When I looked up, the room still held no one but me. Thank God.

I stood and walked into the next room. Its emptiness poured into a drain in the floor's middle: the dissection room, its clamminess impervious to the cold breeze sweeping in with the approaching storm. Two metal and wood gurneys lay off to the side.

My father stood in this room, in this building, in mid-April 1945. Remembering him, I remembered my purpose and walked out of the crematorium.

Nowhere did I see any sign of the graves that stretched into the horizon of two of his photographs. I returned to the receptionist, who looked up, his face nodding with confirmation of an expectation, even while his mouth remained an unbroken line.

"I was wondering," I said slowly, "where are the graves?"

"Graves?" His eyes opened wider. "I do not understand." The question seemed nonsensical, as we stood eighty yards from the crematorium behind a screen of trees.

"The graves the American soldiers had the town's citizens dig—for the bodies...." My discomfort with the history my words carried (why was I the one feeling discomfort?) broke off my sentence. I showed my father's photographs of the endlessly long, canal-shaped graves, bodies visible within them, GIs standing guard.

"Oh." He took out of his desk a map of the town, and his finger descended to a small square. I bent over to read the tiny words. *Hauptfriedhof.* "Town cemetery," he translated. "Next to our cemetery you will find theirs." But even as the impassive man showed me the location of the victims' graves, I still could not see where my father's photographs were taking me.

In 1943, after the Allies bombed Peenemunde, the Nazis decided to excavate tunnels out of the Harz Mountains' gypsum and granite. For labor they used 170 inmates from Buchenwald Concentration Camp outside of Weimar, some forty-five miles away. With no more than picks, dynamite, and shovels, the prisoners

V-1 rocket

struggled, their lives becoming more wretched than they had been even at Buchenwald. Confined to the tunnels for weeks on end, they existed on scraps of bread, a few sips of coffee, and air filled with particulates. If the prisoners talked to one another, if they picked up a scrap of rubber, they were hanged and displayed, up to twenty bodies at a time, over the paths the prisoners walked. At first, the Nazis transported the dead to Buchenwald for cremation, but the death toll from the tunnels' deadly conditions increased so quickly that Mittelbau-Dora imported more prisoners to build a crematorium. The prisoners also constructed multi-storied wooden bunks inside the tunnels, around 6,000 inmates living in this dark, damp coldness where they had only buckets in which to relieve themselves. Dysentery and tuberculosis became rampant, death omnipresent.

The movie available for viewing at the camp memorial quotes a prisoner, Jean Michel: "The water that oozed from the rock caused a disgusting, permanent clamminess. Some prisoners went mad, others had their nerves shattered from the constant din, the noise of machines, of pick-axes, the bell of the locomotive, continual explosions, and all of it echoing mercilessly in the closed world of the tunnel. No heat, no ventilation, not the smallest pail to wash in: Death touched us with the sensation of choking, the filth that impregnated us." All to build V-1 buzz bombs that hurled balls of fire onto the citizens of London in the middle of the night.

The camp's population rose rapidly from 3,000 in September 1943 to 10,000 by December of that year. Almost half of that number still lived in the tunnels. They included Russian and Polish prisoners of war, French and Belgian resistance fighters, and, of course, Jews, for whom the worst work was saved. In the last several months, the Nazis even sent children to the camp, into the tunnels. "I saw them with my own eyes," says one woman in the film, a secretary for IG Farben, the company in charge of the weapons' production.

I thought of the photograph I had come upon in a book that had pierced my denial about the significance of my father's photographs—the one of the young boy and toddler girl, arms spread-eagled, stars on their coats, lying at the bottom of a ditch in Nordhausen.

IG Farben paid the Nazis for the never-ending supply of labor for the weapons plant inside the mountain. Outside, other prisoners built barracks so even more prisoners could support the plant. By the spring of 1944, a full-blown camp existed: fifty-nine prisoner and administrative barracks, twelve offices, two bathhouses, a hospital area, a prison, a bordello, a theater, and the crematorium. By April of that year, some 17,500 inmates had arrived in Mittelbau-Dora. Within the next nine months, another 17,000 inmates arrived from other camps, surpassing the camp's capacity.

My father's photograph of Nordhausen citizens burying the victims,
April 15, 1945

As the number of dead overwhelmed the crematorium's ability to keep up, prisoners had to burn corpses in pyres. By the time the Nazis closed the plant in late March 1945, some 20,000 people had died there, giving the V-1 rocket the distinction of taking more lives in production than it did as a weapon.

Between that March and the day a month later when the GIs liberated the camp, some 4,000 more died.

And their graves were next to the town's cemetery? Had the GIs transported thousands of bodies five miles to bury them next to the town's own dead? His soldiers respected, even loved General Terry Allen, the *mensch* of the 104th "Timberwolves" Division that had liberated Nordhausen. Allen must have found it unacceptable to make the final resting place of Nordhausen's victims the same place where they had known utter misery and horror.

The receptionist suggested I catch a bus back into town down on the main road. I decided first to take a detour to the tunnel's entrance. The German tour would have allowed me to see inside, but I did not think I could manage being inside the mountain surrounded by people speaking German. I stood before the tunnel's entrance and held up the photograph of my father standing a mere twenty feet from where I stood. The photographer had stood far enough back to include the tunnel's massive entrance in the frame, its size dwarfing my father. I could not make out the shape of his mouth or the look in his eyes.

Sixty-one years separated us, years that had all but erased the signs of what he witnessed here. On the ground, visible in the grass, lay pieces of white rock. I picked one up. It looked like white sparkly granite, grooves running down its side—traces, perhaps, of having been scraped off the rock wall by a pick. A piece of this place, something that witnessed what he witnessed—I put in my pocket. As I looked at the rock-covered slope and felt the rough edges of the white rock in my pocket, an unfamiliar uncertainty surfaced inside me. How much did I want to know?

My father at the entrance to Mittelbau tunnel

I walked out the entrance, past the cattle car, past the intersection with the main road. I walked along the tram tracks where the museum receptionist had told me I could catch a bus. No bus appeared. For an hour-and-a-half I walked, forcing my mind to focus on what was before me. I passed a teenage boy on a bicycle, a bulky bag over his shoulder that weighed the bike to that side. I passed an animal refuge, where creatures resembling miniature elk grazed, their huge antlers covered with a moss-like substance. An older couple, both thick-waisted, walked by, hand-in-hand with a little boy who jumped up and down as he pointed at the deer. Two men and a woman in a *biergarten* drank dark amber beer out of large, thin glasses. A restaurant next door served Chinese food. Noodles, not rice.

By the time I got to my hotel, where no one spoke English, I collapsed on the small bed, craving a warm bath and regretting I had left my suitcase at the train station. I soaked my feet in the tub until hunger urged me towards the station to retrieve my bag and then eat dinner at a café. Inside the empty station, I opened my wallet to take out the locker key, but the coin purse held only three coins, no key. Kneeling down on the floor, I emptied my purse. No key. I thought of every step I had taken since putting

Medics entering the Mittelbau tunnel

the suitcase in the locker: I had taken out my wallet only in the cab and at the camp memorial bookstore. The key must have fallen out in one of those places, but how did I not notice?

With no way to get my bag, I walked to the café and ordered a small pizza, anxiety overwhelming my ability to appreciate its flavor. Large groups of people, enjoying the now pleasant summer evening and each other's company, surrounded me. The sun no longer in the sky, I looked at my watch. Nine-thirty. Only an hour, at the most, of light was left. I paid my tab and walked towards the cemetery, my feet sore, my thighs aching as I passed my hotel and then some Soviet-style apartment buildings. This part of town had been bombed. Ahead lay the neon and fluorescent lights of car dealerships, glowing like UFOs amidst hundreds of new cars, all small. Beyond those islands of light, the road disappeared into darkness. No cemetery.

Again, as it had that afternoon as I passed the cattle car, my head turned on its own accord. A narrow road passed between

The cemetery for Nordhausen's victims

the dealerships. A mere five yards farther, a low stone wall emerged from the shadows, a small hill rising on its other side. The road continued up the hill, becoming a dividing line between the empty hillside where I stood and a hill covered with rows of white stone crosses, reflecting the fading light. If that was the town cemetery, then where I was standing—this hillside—had to be the victims' cemetery. But only tall trees covered the slope. Could trees grow this tall in sixty years?

I walked up the hill. At its crest stood three white walls at right angles to one another, forming a triangle, with an inscription carved into the granite: "May this be a worthy resting place for the victims of Boelcke Barracks and Mittelbau Concentration Camp." German and Hebrew versions appeared over the English along with a quote from Prophets: "May the earth not cover their blood."

Boelcke Barracks? Another name, this one not at all familiar. The list of names for Nordhausen got longer.

As the dim light evaporated, I walked back down the hill, where ten feet from the memorial walls an eighteen-square-inch white stone protruded from the ground. Its words were in French:

Salon sa volonte
ici ont ete deposes
les cendres du derorte resistant francais
Ernest Gaillard
Commander de la legion d'honneur
Officier des arts et letters
Detener dans les camps
Nazis de 1942 a 1945
Decede en france
Le 11 Aout 1976

"Here lay, according to his wishes, the ashes of Ernest Gaillard, Commander of the Legion of Honor, Officer of Arts and Letters, detained in the Nazi camps from 1942 to 1945, who died in France on the 11th of August, 1976."

A survivor, a prisoner of war, had his ashes brought back here for burial.

Standing too quickly, I became dizzy but felt compelled to hurry before the light completely vanished. My eyes scanned in both directions like a metal detector, but I only saw grass and trees. My head throbbed from looking intently into the darkening atmosphere. The familiar ache of hopelessness filled my chest.

Then my sandaled foot discovered it: a white stone, four inches wide and six inches long, sunk into the ground, its surface flush with that of the soil. Four feet over I found another one; four feet over, another. An entire line emerged as I walked across the hillside, identical stones appearing every four feet. At the edge of the field, just before a line of trees, two stones forming a ninety-degree angle capped the row. Seven feet downhill, two more stones lay similarly angled to face the ones uphill. These marked the end of a row of graves! As I now anticipated, as I turned and walked back east, I found another line of stones, each four feet apart, running parallel to the line seven feet north. Rows of seven stones lying seven feet apart. Seven by seven. My body vibrated. These were the graves in my father's photograph. Just below was the second one, echoing the photograph: the two canals of bodies.

I stood at the upper northeast corner, the spot where my father stood when he took the photograph, the town's distant rooftops barely visible over the tall trees. I knelt down and touched the earth, my mind reaching for the words of the *Kaddish* that might speak to this field of dead. In the middle of a word, I looked up—the darkness was parting around something white farther down

Nordhausen citizens digging graves for victims of the
concentration camp, April 15, 1945

Funeral for victims of Mittelbau-Dora, April 18, 1945

the hill—another stone, another line of stones, another two parallel lines of stones. Another row of graves. Before I heard my thought, another line appeared, another row. Four rows of graves covered this hillside, the entire hillside, the reality of 4,000 bodies swallowing my breath and mind.

After forty-eight years, grief pitched me off my feet. The difference between my father's trauma and my own dissolved with the remaining light.

It took passing the rotting boxcar in front of Nordhausen, walking through the brick columns, becoming disoriented, and stumbling upon the crematorium for me to begin to gain a sense of the onslaught of incomprehensible sights the GIs experienced. I thought of the odors no one but the survivors and the GIs will

Nordhausen citizens digging graves for concentration camp
victims, April 15, 1945 *(Getty Images)*

ever know. Any one of those moments would overwhelm most of
us; the barrage was more than any mind could take in.

Words of survivors came to mind. How upon first entering
Auschwitz, Mauthausen, Buchenwald, they could not take in the
meaning of the thick black smoke or the prisoners' shaved heads
and tattooed arms. If they did fully take it in, they would have
snapped. To survive, the mind shielded itself.

The cemetery reinforced my sense that the liberators' experiences parallels that of the survivors'. As I walked to my hotel room, Ernest Gaillard's wish echoed in my mind the words of Charlotte Delbo: *None of us should have returned.* Also a French resistance fighter, she spent thirty-five years after her liberation from Auschwitz finding words to describe the imprisonment and its consequences. The Nazi death machine had wrecked the survivors' souls, and though they did all they could to encapsulate and lock up their memories of the horror, Delbo described how the memories had a life of their own, spontaneously surfacing, disfiguring the survivors and those they loved.

Forty years before the academics even knew to want the words, Delbo created them. She saw that membrane around traumatic memories permeable beyond control.

I live next to Auschwitz. It is there, unalterable, precise, but enveloped in the skin of memory, a permeable skin that isolates it from my present self. Unlike the snake's skin, the skin of memory does not renew itself.... Alas, I often fear lest it grow thin, crack, and the camp get hold of me again.... The skin gives way at times, revealing all it contains.

I wondered what broke through Ernest Gaillard's skin of memory during the thirty-one years after his liberation from Nordhausen. That he chose to rest alongside those who died in the camp spoke to the effect of his three years of imprisonment. It was evident that he believed a part of him had never left the factory of death, that his physical survival belied his loss. Yet, I believe that by acknowledging that loss, he opened new possibilities for his children's future. In asking that his ashes be brought back here, Gaillard acknowledged what Nordhausen had taken from him, the burial bringing together the splintered halves of his being. Even if he had never mentioned Nordhausen, his request alone communicated his loss to his children and all who come to this place, freeing them from the vise of silence.

Gaillard's children and I might recognize one another, like long-lost cousins. This place claimed a piece of my father as well. For him, it was the part that could have recognized his wife was becoming an alcoholic. The part that could have consoled his children and cried with them. The part that felt compassion, grief, affection, tenderness, and playfulness. The physician could not heal himself.

I do not mean to equate my father's trauma of witnessing Nordhausen to that of Gaillard, who lived through three years of its torments. But neither do I share the opinion of many of the camp liberators I met that their pain is not significant relative to the suffering of Holocaust survivors. Rather I believe there is no value in comparing one person's pain with another, as suffering has no hierarchy. The usual response I heard as a child when I dared voice my unhappiness was: "Look at the crippled person hobbling down the street; he has something to complain about." This attitude demeans everyone, for there is always someone who is "worse off than you."

As Viktor Frankl, himself a survivor of the death camps, articulates in *Man's Search for Meaning*, each person has a certain level of "hardiness," the word he used to describe one's capacity for existential pain. When suffering pushes one beyond that threshold, they lose their dignity and spirit. No one can say for someone else where that threshold lies or that because one did not suffer as much as someone else, that they did not really suffer.

I know my father suffered from witnessing Nordhausen. I saw it in his sad eyes, his inability to hug me, to say "I love you." I felt it before I had words with which to express my perceptions. I imagine the children of E. Gaillard might use similar words and feelings to describe him.

This enduring suffering was the ultimate evil of the Nazis, not their ideology or its pathetic present-day remnants. The trauma of its victims, cultured to perfection in their camp system, became the resilient virus, continuing to claim victims long after the vanquishing of the Nazis. It spread into French, Russian, Polish, British, Belgian, Italian, Romanian, and Hungarian homes, then crossed the Atlantic to infect new generations in tidy ranch houses with perfect picket fences on suburban cul de sacs.

I remembered my husband's observation: "We're Hitler's victims, also." Those words had felt cruel. But they were true.

While my father had not mentioned Nordhausen to us, he left the photographs in the shoe box along with letters he had received during the war from his sisters, his brothers, and a former girlfriend. The contents of the box are clues to his intention. He wanted us to find them, to see them. To understand. Perhaps, like George Tievsky, he had been caught between not wanting to be alone with the images and wanting to protect us. How could he have not yearned to reveal his pain all those years? But how does a father tell such a story, describe such scenes? I could not imagine revealing such an abyss to my children, my future's hope. My father had told my brothers and me as best as he was able. He had revealed his wound to the extent he was able.

The next morning, after the officials at the Nordhausen train station retrieved my suitcase in exchange for twenty Euros, I left on a train for Weimar and my next destination, Buchenwald, so I could see the site of the camp Nat Futterman had liberated and Kay Nee had witnessed. My afternoon there would intensify my already raw compassion for Mr. Futterman's and Ms. Nee's response to their memories, especially when I entered Buchenwald's crematorium which made Mittelbau-Dora's seem minor league in comparison.

As I sat on the train and watched groomed fields and picturesque towns pass by, the discoveries at the camp memorial and cemetery began to emerge in coherent thoughts. The devastation I had felt the evening before as I lay on the cemetery's damp grass was not new.

I had felt such desolation whenever I watched a movie about the Holocaust, whenever I read, even if for the sixth or eighth time, a book on the Holocaust. The stories of families forcibly separated, of mothers unwittingly parted forever from their children and of parents sending their children off with strangers always wrenched my body. I had been wrenched, in fact, from my mother—and never saw her again. Never knowing what happened to her, where she went, whether she was alive or dead. Instead of an extended family to provide context or consolation, silence and melancholy embraced me. I had my own laminated photograph: the moment I was led away from her. The silence mutated into a plastic coating that thickened month after month, to protect me from the even-worse fate of losing my father by demanding to know about her.

The mind divided the photograph within from the external world, erecting a curtain to remove the trauma from constant view, to allow myself the possibility of at least some chance of small happiness. My father could never take a firm step to happiness, as his curtain veiled the boundary between solid ground and an abyss. I will never know if he ever tried to take the step toward lifting his curtain and looking his trauma in its face.

The French officer, E. Gaillard, showed me that to recover from my loss, I had to remove the curtain and fall into what lay behind it. My grief at the cemetery had shown me a bottom did exist. I had to accept and mourn that America had not protected me from the tentacles of the Final Solution or the centuries of pogroms that preceded it. As repulsive as the image of a victim seemed, I could no longer deny that I was one. But now I knew I could look back and survive.

Perth Amboy

The memory has no words, only the insistence of a pain that has turned into fury.

—Susan Griffin, *A Chorus of Stones*

Main street of Perth Amboy, 1950

My flight from Germany landed at Newark International Airport and, having a few days left before David's summer camp ended, I headed to the Jersey Shore to visit my stepmother. After a couple of days of catching up, I borrowed her car and drove to Perth Amboy. I parked the car at my father's former office and imagined him still examining patients inside the now less-than-sparkling building. Then I drove to the cemetery and sat next to his grave so I could talk to him and tell him what I had learned, how I grieved for him. I pulled the rock that I had brought from Nordhausen out of my pocket and placed it on top of his headstone. As I walked to the car, I decided to drive to Water Street to see the house where I had lived with my mother.

When I was a child, the year-round colors of Perth Amboy were those of Halloween: orange and black. A glass globe of ash sat over the town, the fallout from the smokestacks that separated Perth Amboy from the New Jersey Turnpike. Oil refineries licked the air day and night with orange flames. Sulfurous fumes turned sunsets into spectacular displays of orange, red, and purple. Black trains carried toxic chemicals across trestle bridges, while barges ferried landfill-destined waste up the Arthur Kill.

When my brothers and I learned in #7 School that New Jersey had the shape of a "matronly" woman, we began calling Perth Amboy the "armpit." Many mornings, as we left our house on Market Street, we would pinch our noses closed and yell, "Rotten eggs!"

"Please, dad, please. Can we move away?" I begged on a weekly basis, certain that moving would release us from the sadness. "This is our home," came his stock answer, as mechanical as the accompanying squeeze from his hand. He didn't seem able to imagine living anywhere besides where his parents chose to live, or doctoring anyone besides the Poles, Italians, and Russians who worked for the surrounding oil refineries. His loyalty to the town defied my understanding.

As I now drove down Smith Street, past what had been Hershkowitz Shoes and Fine's Stationery, there were now *bodegas*. Other than the signs on its tired buildings, Perth Amboy seemed suspended in time, the only change being the language, which was now Spanish instead of Yiddish.

On the waterfront, Water Street remained aloof from the surrounding malaise. Its huge Victorian houses, complete with widow's walks and gables and turrets, sat high on the embankment.

Uncle Jake and Aunt Malve had lived in the biggest one—a world apart from my family's former house a mere five doors away. My compassion stretched across the years to my lost father, who chose to move his wife and child so close to the brother who had ordered the other siblings to sever ties with Rube after he married the *shiksa* Clara.

I parked the car. The house's wooden porch behind the bed of ivy seemed too shallow to have accommodated even a four-year-old child, but I remembered sitting on it with a doll in my lap. The door opened, and a man about my age came out and looked at me. I opened the car door and took a deep breath.

"Hi, I'm Leila Levinson. I lived here many years ago."

His words didn't reach me, but his tone sounded suspicious.

I continued, "Would you mind if I looked at the house—briefly?"

His face scrunched up with what... Surprise? Doubt?

"My father was Dr. Levinson, Reuben Levinson," I added hopefully.

"Oh, the doctor who used to be across the street from the hospital?"

"Yes."

"Oh, sure. Fine. Come on in."

Right on the other side of the front door, a staircase led to the second floor. To the right lay the living room and behind it the kitchen, all as I remembered. The arched breakfast nook in the kitchen, where my mother sat with her cigarette and drink, now held the refrigerator and stove.

The man turned and headed back through the living room and led me up the steps. But my legs resisted following him. I forced my body forward, forced my eyes to look into the three bed-rooms—the crystal chandelier no longer hanging in what had been my parents' bedroom. As a toddler I had stood on the bed on my tiptoes to remove the crystal prisms and line them up along the windowsill in my bedroom.

I turned. And found myself facing a door. I knew, with a knowledge that came from my stomach, that a bathroom lay behind it, but before I could turn away, the owner opened the door, my paralyzed tongue not allowing me to yell *No!*

Waves crashed into my ears. Blood poured into my eyes. Red, red. Spinning. Blood. Everywhere on the tiled floor, on the white walls, on the sinks, on my mother, her hands, her face, her clothes, screaming, *Get out! Get out!*

I turned and rushed down the stairs and out of the house. Out into the air, into the car, heart galloping, chest heaving, pressing my back against the seat, my eyes squeezing shut, but still red lay everywhere. "Get out get out get out!" Even under my bed, my ears covered, her screams pierced the walls.

And then the world went black.

That four-year-old saw what no child could understand: her mother dissolving into her own blood. The separation in the police station had not been my Nordhausen. My laminated memory of being taken from my mother had divided my present from the devastating moment when I saw her die. When I left her behind in the station, she had already been dead for months.

When I regained the ability to see the trees and road outside the car, I drove back to my stepmother's apartment at the Shore. That evening, I told her about what I had remembered during my visit to my old home, and she provided the information I had missed for forty-eight years. "Once, when your parents were still married, I ran into your mother and said something about what a nice man your father was, and she said, 'Nice! He wouldn't even come home when I had a miscarriage. I hemorrhaged terribly, and all he did was call an ambulance.'"

That my mother told this to an acquaintance reveals how far

gone their marriage was, her bitterness distorting the facts. I imagined that to save critical minutes, my father had sent an ambulance and waited for her at the hospital, prudence his trained response. But in the chaos that must have ensued, what had happened to me? Had I been overlooked, hiding under the bed? Did either parent have a moment to remember me?

Perhaps what most terrified me was that neither of them could protect me. No one explained what I had witnessed. No one reassured me afterwards, created a safe place for me in which to recover.

The context my stepmother provided for my traumatic memory did not alter the memory's power. In *Memory Perceived*, Robert Kraft presents the observation that even if Holocaust survivors interpret memories with new information, "the visual memories are experienced fully, retaining the status of perceived reality at the time of the event."

That I had completely repressed this event until standing again before the bathroom showed that, just like Holocaust survivors, my memory had split into two. I had split off part of myself to keep my terror behind that bathroom door.

I called Burke and told him where he could find my mother's death certificate in my desk. It listed the name of the cemetery where she was buried: Mount Olivet, some twelve miles from Perth Amboy. After wandering through rows of graves, I found the headstone. Clara Gaddensky Levinson, February 3, 1917 – October 31, 1973.

Forty-seven years after the day we went shopping for white sneakers, I stood next to my mother again. I expected I would cry, but no tears emerged. Perhaps understanding, forgiving, and weeping for my father was one thing, but an entirely different process was necessary before I could understand, forgive, and weep for my mother...and myself. The child who had hidden under her bed and covered her ears while blood gushed from her mother in the next room was stubborn. She had been strong for a long time. She had seen her mother disintegrate; and yet kept herself intact, functioning, acceptable. How could she stop being strong now?

Clara's grave

Boelcke Barracks

For years now I have come to conclusions without my father's
help, discovering on my own what I know, what I don't know.

—Li-Young Lee, "Arise, Go Down"

Boelcke Barracks, April 11, 1945 *(Reuben Levinson collection)*

My attempt to understand my father's role in my family's sad
history as a way to release myself from that history had only
ensnared me more tightly. My situation reminded me of a secret
door hidden in a bookcase: If you pull out the right book, the
door swings open. But rather than just seeing in, I fell in, the door
swinging shut behind me.

235

I had hoped to learn that my parents had been kind, intelligent, handsome people who suffered from the war in general and my father's witnessing Nordhausen in particular. While there was strong support for making that case, the truth seemed more complex and elusive. Perhaps the historical experiences and genetics of their families predisposed my parents to having fragile psyches. The shock of Nordhausen irreparably broke my father, and his resulting depression and melancholy may have tripped my mother over her fragile boundary of sanity. Both their family histories support this theory.

My mother's grave lies next to her brother's. In 1949, at the age of thirty-six, he committed suicide. And the more my paternal cousins and I have shared what we know about our shared grandfather, with his cat-o'-nine tails and tyrannical nature, the more evident it has become that he had a serious mood disorder. One of his daughters never showed a moment of kindness to anyone, especially her own children. Another vacillated on a daily basis between being a sweet, helpless caregiver and an abusive raging bully. "I never knew which mother I was coming home to after school," her daughter told me.

It seems my parents had a few good years after my father returned from Europe. (Though he did not get in touch with my mother for over two months after his return. She found out he had returned when her mailman told her, "Have you heard? Rube Levinson is finally back from the war." Perhaps he had misgivings about his elopement. Perhaps he was insecure about his mental health.) My brother Robert, who is seven years older than I, has good memories of his early childhood years, and happiness is evident in the first few reels of home movies that we also found in our father's basement. A beaming, handsome father runs towards his laughing toddler, scoops him up in his arms and perches him on his hands as if showing him his future kingdom. I did not recognize the face beaming with delight.

Sometime between their reunion and twelve years later, something snapped within my parents. Something went terribly wrong, right before or shortly after I was born.

I had a possible storyline for why. I had a beginning, middle, and end that, on their own, seemed complete, but which, when I tried to join them, left gaping holes. The whole story hid within those gaps, causing me to remember a rabbi's comments during a Torah study I once attended: Not all words of the Torah are written in it, because the Torah is like an accordion. The written story, the words Jews read every Shabbat, are the outer folds like those you see when the accordion is closed up. But learning the Torah requires opening it up and discovering the space between the lines, interpreting what exists within that space, because only there can we find the Torah's full story.

One example is when Abraham takes Isaac up to Mount Moriah to sacrifice him. The Torah does not mention anything about Sarah's reaction to this test of Abraham's faith. The next we hear of Sarah is many pages later, when she dies. Perhaps Abraham and Isaac did not tell her of the day's events. Perhaps Sarah met only a silent son and husband whose trauma and melancholy dissolved her heart.

Or perhaps they did tell her, and she turned to salt.

I needed to decipher the space between the lines of my family's history.

If for no reason other than habit, I continued to read the books and magazines I had bought at the Mittelbau-Dora Memorial bookstore. One morning, after Burke and the boys left for school and work, I sat with my tea and a British magazine *After the Battle*. The issue showed a man astride a huge rocket engine; the cover title read "Nordhausen: Sinking of the Blucher." I flipped through the pages. Toward the back, the

Boelcke Barracks, April 11, 1945

words "Boelcke Barracks" jumped out at me—the puzzling name I had noticed on the cemetery memorial for Mittelbau-Dora's victims. Here the name appeared under a photograph that looked just like the one of my father's, of the endless rows of bodies lying in the courtyard of Mittelbau-Dora. To the left of the bodies the photograph showed the bombed barracks I could find no trace of at the camp memorial.

According to the magazine article, a few weeks before the camp's liberation, the Nazis took all but 700 of its inmates and locked them in a warehouse located down in the town itself. The Nazis called this warehouse "Boelcke Barracks," which, in early April, the Allies hit during an aerial attack on the town. Four days later, on April 11, 1945, GIs entered the town of Nordhausen where they discovered Boelcke Barracks and the victims inside. Those not killed had spent those four days in unimaginable agony, mangled bodies strewn among a chaos of straw, severed limbs and torsos, and excrement.

My father did not treat survivors of Mittelbau-Dora. He tried to keep alive the living dead of Boelcke Barracks.

This was where he took the gruesome photographs. This was where he spent two weeks before suffering a nervous breakdown. This is the place the Signal Corps documented on film, catalogued all these years in the United States National Archives under "Liberation of Nordhausen."

It would have been devastating enough for GIs to open the doors of Boelcke Barracks and find starving prisoners dying an excruciatingly slow death. But the Allies' misdirected bombing turned the warehouse into utter ghastliness, creating a tomb that would claim the liberators' spirits as well as most of the prisoners' lives.

The GIs ordered the townspeople, who could not protest their ignorance quickly or loudly enough, to dig the graves on the hill next to the town's cemetery. This location was chosen because the only way to move the bodies was on stretchers, and the townspeople only had to walk across the street to bury the dead. When I had stood in the cemetery, Boelcke Barracks sat a mere two hundred feet away. It still stands, the shell having been rebuilt into a factory where only a small plaque at the entrance reveals the building's history.

The horror that Nazi soullessness and American miscalculation wreaked on Boelcke Barracks would have ripped anyone from his bearings even before seeing the ovens in the camp itself. Whatever personal barriers the GIs erected at that moment permitted their functioning through the rest of the war and prevented them from plummeting into a nightmare that undefended souls could not possibly withstand. Most soldiers left Boelcke Barracks after a few hours, but my father, the doctor, spent two weeks there trying to

Nordhausen citizens carrying bodies from the barracks to the cemetery

save whatever life remained in those with a pulse. Death and failure were his companions.

Nowhere does the Mittelbau-Dora Camp Memorial mention Boelcke Barracks. Even the movie the museum shows, which includes images of the GIs removing bodies from the bombed warehouse, does not mention the name that only appears at the cemetery memorial. As I did not remember reading about these barracks in any of the books on the camps' liberation, I returned to Robert Abzug's *Inside the Vicious Heart,* the first history of the GIs' liberation of the camps. To my surprise, I found the book does refer to Boelcke Barracks: "Another location, closer to the town itself, became a human dumping ground for Dora's laborers." Though the book does not mention the American bombing that intensified the barracks' ghastliness, a close reading reveals this was where the GIs discovered the thousands of bodies. In my earlier reading, I had missed this fact, perhaps because without additional explanation, the word "barracks" sounded like a part of the main camp itself.

My trip proved essential to assembling the pieces of the puzzle. I had to walk the steps I did to understand what the GIs discovered. I had to see the location of the camp, sort through the

Starving prisoners at Boelke Barracks, April 1945 *(Getty Images)*

various names, and walk the distance to town. I had to walk again and find the cemetery, see the name, read the magazine, and notice the photograph that looked just like one of my father's.

The history of Mittelbau-Dora is multilayered and obscure. Perhaps we can never comprehend it. Perhaps we should wish such comprehension to be impossible. With every answer or discovery, another mystery presents itself. The photographs conceal as much as they show. Truth has layers, and at Mittelbau-Dora, the darkest ones lie at the bottom.

I had assumed a great deal when looking at my father's photographs. As an amateur photographer, I forgot to question what lay outside the frame. Yet, even in all my ignorance, in a way I could not have imagined, the photographs led me to Boelcke Barracks. The photographs caused me to ask about the graves. They led me to the cemetery, where I saw the name Boelcke Barracks written on the memorial wall. They echoed in the British magazine's photograph.

My father's blurred photographs revealed the existence of a mystery and a passage to truth, even if on their face they did not show the truth itself. Even if that passage did not lead me to the truth.

Then I understood: I had to write the words to fill the spaces between the lines. I had to create my own truth.

The Paperweight

That bridge leads to the shore of Reversal
Where everything is just the opposite and the word 'is'
Unveils a meaning we hardly envisioned.

—Czeslaw Milosz, "On Prayer"

Leila, age seven, Adirondack Mountains

Mittelbau-Dora/Nordhausen revealed a truth: I can look back and survive.

I went up to my bedroom and opened up a photo album that my father had assembled throughout my childhood, the years after my mother left. I looked at several photos of myself. There I was as a four-year-old sitting on the sand, by myself, my father nearby, reading the newspaper, his eyes anchored to the page.

There I was as a six-year-old standing in the blue shorts and white middy blouse of my summer camp uniform, the Adirondack Mountains behind me, my mouth open as if I am trying to yell, my eyes creased with confusion or frustration or irritation, my arms straight down at my side, the hands curved as if trying to hold on. In another a lake stretched behind me and I was standing again with my arms at my side, my hair tucked into a swimming cap, my body in a bathing suit, my face dropped, deflated with a pout. The same pout I saw on all the rest, stretching from

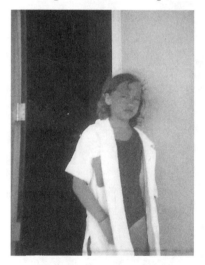

age six to sixteen, the same unhappy child. Pouting.

"I hope your face freezes like that," Doris had said to me over and over again.

My anger had been too vast to own, its unpredictable power so awesome and taboo, it loomed atomic.

After a lifetime of denial, as I looked through an entire album and saw how visible my misery had been, my fury at my father broke through. Fury for his refusing to explain what had happened when my mother miscarried, for never mentioning the day in the police station, for acting as if that awful day had never happened, as if I had never had a mother. For never seeing the unhappiness of the child before him. For so successfully getting me to be the good daughter who had no problems, no distasteful emotions, no disappointments.

The fury felt like a magician's scarf trick, one scarf leading to another to another, an endless coil emerging from within me. How had my soul contained all this rage? It had banished every other emotion, especially grief and happiness.

Leila, age six, and Alan, age ten, Adirondacks Mountains

Fury. Of course. Here, too, I resembled the liberators. "Then you get angry," Nat Futterman said. "The anger was so intense." Those who did not go into shock upon seeing the camps wanted immediate vengeance. Many GIs handed over the remaining guards to the survivors who tore them apart limb by limb. Others killed the guards themselves, as one man had done with his garrote, the memory haunting him sixty-two years later. I thought of Johnny Marino who, for years after liberating Landsberg, knew nothing but hate for the Nazis. *That hate imprisoned me.*

Neither rage nor shock allow grieving. If unacknowledged, anger becomes nuclear, capable of incinerating loved ones and isolating ourselves. So what option is there other than denying the anger and numbing ourselves? But I had learned: Denying fury does not exile it. Fury is endlessly patient. It will find the opportunity. I thought of my father's completely irrational outbursts breaking through whenever fatigue or associations allowed. That was his denied rage. What had seemed indifference—that was his

From the left, my stepmother, Shirley Levinson, my father and myself,
two weeks before my father died, February 1988

numbness, his depression.

Calvin Massey had the extraordinary fortune of opening himself to compassion upon seeing camp survivors, the only viable
response. He had avoided urges for vengeance or paralysis and
had chosen the only action capable of engaging his spirit. The
compassion he expressed to the survivors—his hugs—became the
defining moment of his life, opening him to his grief as well as
providing him with a past he could claim.

But rage will not make room for compassion and grief until we
acknowledge the anger completely, as Johnny Marino did.   He

had to summon the excruciating honesty of owning his rage rather than projecting it and all its darkness onto an apparent or surrogate enemy.

I can now see my truth: My father landed on Utah Beach hours after the first wave of troops, tending to the wounded and dying on the cliffs above the beach and throughout the many skirmishes that followed—St. Lo, Aachen, the brutal siege at Bastogne. And just when he thought it was all but over, that the worst had passed, he walked through the gates of Boelcke Barracks.

After two weeks of treating survivors with inadequate supplies of plasma, penicillin, and bandages, he had a mental breakdown. What that term describes is anything but precise. Panic attacks? Depression that made getting out of bed impossible? Inchoate babbling? Delirium and tremors? Loss of connection with reality?

Who could spend two weeks within the bombed confines of those barracks and not have their psyches crack?

What strikes me most sharply is the juxtaposition of the father I knew—his persona stalwart, indomitable, unmovable—with that of a man with a wounded psyche. To me, to the entire Perth Amboy community, my father embodied reliability, consistency, substance. He was formidable. Like his silence.

What choices did a liberator have in a society that promoted the toughing-it-out approach, that used the word "mad" as an equivalent to being mentally unstable, as equivalent to being violent? On April 3, 1945, eight days before my father saw Nordhausen, he wrote his sister on Nazi stationery ("to me writing paper is writing paper, and this will give you a chance to burn up the swastika"), "I am deep in the heart of the Rhineland, and it is very pretty country—very green and clean, the houses and farms very well-kept. It is difficult to comprehend why people with many virtues should have gone beserk and raving mad."

Deep in Germany

Quadrath, den 3. April 45

Der Ortsgruppenleiter
der Ortsgruppe Quadrath

To Mildred, Herman + Ralphie —

How do you like this fancy Nazi paper? Anyway to me writing paper is writing paper and this will give you a chance to burn up the swastika — I got your package with the salami and mustard + chicken + Coronet Magazine. Thanks very much. Also got your letter of Mar. 19 — telling me about Max being at Camp Kilmer — and now probably over here. I hope that this war finishes before he gets here!

I am deep in the heart of the Rhineland and it is very pretty country — very green and clean; and the homes and farms are very well kept too. It is difficult to comprehend why people with so many virtues should have gone berserk and raving mad. Lots of Russian and french slave laborers around here, and they are a pitiful lot. Just as bad as what you read about. People in wartimes (where man is very forget) become animal-like. Sights one will never forget.

I sent you some Worth's perfume and lipstick from Belgium. Share it with Shirley.

Otherwise nothing much new. Heard from alfie — son. Not much new — all tired of war as I am —

The key aspects of withstanding combat stress—unit cohesion, mutual support and affection—did not function after witnessing the camps. *We couldn't talk about it. I just wanted to get away.* Disconnection was immediate. The horror was too enormous for even platoon connection to withstand it. *You expect people to be blown up; you always have a chance to defend yourself in battle. But what we saw...it violated every principle we know.*

Then, when they returned home just a couple of months afterwards, where support and compassion could have made a significant difference to integrating the memories, the veterans encountered a public only interested in looking to the rosy future. As Kay Nee's mother told her, "That's all behind you. Forget about it, don't even talk about it." Such advice was mild in comparison to the outright hostility some veterans like Al Hirsch received when they talked about what they had seen in the camps. Bitterness and anger reinforced the shield around the heart.

But even if society had recognized the liberators' PTSD, another aspect of the 1950s pushed veterans away from seeking help. Penny Coleman's *Flashback* reveals how the Veterans Administration treated psychiatric casualties of World War II. By the late 1940s the expense of treating the high number of veterans suffering mental anguish had become enormous. Sixty percent of the 123,000 patients in or waiting for admission to the VA hospitals were psychiatric. A neurology professor at George Washington University, Walter Freeman, came up with a "cure": the ice-pick lobotomy that severed the prefrontal lobe from the rest of the brain. While this was primarily used on "hysterical" women, it became the treatment of choice for psychiatric cases in the VA hospitals, as it cost a mere $250, compared to the over $35,000 a year for being in a hospital. Approximately 50,000 veterans underwent this procedure until 1952, when Thorazine was introduced.

Even if a veteran had pushed past all the obstacles to seeking help, who would have risked such treatment? Who would not have chosen to push away his memories, deny his nightmares, accept the depression and melancholy?

So my father and countless others resorted to silence. Silence could hold the psyche together.

I remembered a story one of my father's brothers once told me. When the brothers were first starting out in their careers in medicine and law, though they had no money, they wanted to represent to the community their capability. They decided to do this by driving Cadillacs, which, while putting them into hock, indicated to the community that these brothers were successful, and if they were successful, they were the ones to hire.

My father used the same strategy for his mental health. The more fragile he felt inside, the more determined he became to show solidity, perhaps thinking that if he feigned mental health, mental health would follow. In convincing everyone else, he would find his way to peace.

Silence, only silence, could keep the balloon that contained all the images, all the smells, all the sounds, far under the surface. But the more silent he became, the more pressure pushed against the sides of the balloon. What energy he must have exerted to push down that balloon, so determined to rise up, if he let his guard down in the slightest.

A person holding back their own demons is the least likely person to help keep another person from collapsing. He was unable to help my mother. Or to recognize my trauma, to take in the effect of my mother's cries as the policeman led me down the station steps, to see my pain and loss and descent into depression, my need to grieve when he could not begin to admit his own.

If the balloon had surfaced, it would have exploded, destroying all he had managed to create, all that made hope for happiness possible.

Photograph taken of my father in a German studio, most probably
after "R&R" at Cannes

And wasn't that the true value, the redemptive purpose—hope for new life?

It wasn't that my father didn't love me.

It was that he did.

I went up to my closet, pulled over a step-stool, and retrieved from a high shelf the shoe box and paperweight. I placed in an archival album my father's photographs and then placed the album, the letter from my mother, and the paperweight inside the trunk with my father's army officer's jacket. I didn't want the decision about what to do with the trunk to be mine alone, but for my sons to help me decide, I would need to explain why I was including the paperweight, and that prospect discomforted me.

How different was I from my father after all?

That evening at dinner, my sons heard about the long-term costs of war to a family. How my father's witnessing battle after battle, only to then come upon Boelcke Barracks, wounded his soul, a concept that brought no puzzled looks to my sons' faces, as though they already held the knowledge that the soul suffered wounds. I told them that my father's wounds had made it difficult for him to give me what I needed and wanted, and that I had expressed my anger by giving him something I had stolen.

"But why such a pretty thing?" David asked. "Why didn't you draw an ugly picture?"

"I can't say for sure. I don't think I knew how angry I was. Because he was my only parent, and I didn't want to lose him, and sometimes we fear that our anger will cause people not to love us."

"You don't like it when I'm angry," David reminded me.

"I'm sorry if I haven't been understanding enough." I squeezed his hand, tears flowing down my cheeks. "Maybe your or Ray's or Dad's anger brings back all those uncomfortable feelings I had as a child," I tried to explain, "when I couldn't know for sure what made a parent go away and never come back. But I hope you and Ray know that Dad and I will always be with you."

They nodded their heads.

"So," I said, taking a deep breath, "I think the paperweight belongs in the trunk, because it represents how forgiveness ends trauma and anger. My prayer is that what I've learned will keep those photos from rippling through your lives."

My sons looked down at their plates, their mouths closed. I realized I was asking them for the ending. That while the responsibility for not letting the photos ripple any further depended on me alone, ultimately, the story's ending depends on all four of us.

One day, as I was hanging out with Ray in our den, listening to music he had composed, he asked if I had figured out where to put the photos and paperweight.

"No, not really. They're in an archival box in my closet."

"Well," he said slowly, "maybe you could put the box on the bookcase in here." He stretched out his long, skinny body on the couch. "That way we'll know where they are. When we want to decide."

Ray's formal name is Raphael, and as Burke reminds me, the first Raphael, the Archangel of Knowledge, was "healed by God."

May the world come to know God's healing.

Father is a wonderful man.
He helps us every day.
Some are Docters, some are Lawyers,
some are Teachers, some are Carpenters.
We think of our great-grand fathers and
grand fathers.
My father is a wonderful father,
gives us things we want.
On fathers day we give him things
he wants.
I love him and he loves me.
He give us clothes and food and things
we need.
So on fathers Day we give him our
love.

By Leila
Levinson

P. S. have a good and
merry Fathers Day.

Epilogue

You will love again the stranger who was your self.
Give wine. Give bread. Give back your heart
to itself, to the stranger who has loved you
all your life.

—Derek Walcott, "Love after Love"

My father walks alongside me now. He accompanies me as the sky accompanies me, as the ground holds me. I close my eyes and smell him, hear his voice saying my name, see his shoulders lift as he tucks the tips of his fingers behind his pants waistband, his eyes lighting up.

He is not the father I knew when he lived. He has traveled with me, reclaiming his *neshamah t'hora,* his pure soul.

We grieve together at funerals, but then we part, our grief isolating us from our neighbors, who, even if they wanted to, could not share our pain. For everyone else, life goes on. As W. H. Auden observes in his poem, "Musee des Beaux Arts:" "...everything turns away/Quite leisurely from the disaster." This is most true for veterans who know a suffering only other veterans and victims of war can know. And among veterans and victims, those who have witnessed atrocity become an even more isolated group. "Coming here every fall keeps me from being alone with my memories," Carold Bland told me about his attendance at veterans' reunions.

The rest of the world moves on, forgetting, if it ever recognized at all, that war ravages soldiers' hearts. There is no occasion to mourn what the veterans have lost. After a war ends, soldiers come home to parades, if they are lucky, as the World War II veterans were, or to derision, as the Vietnam veterans did. Or to increasing compassion, as is the case today for the veterans of Operation Enduring Freedom/Operation Iraqi Freedom (OEF/OIF), although they are still without adequate resources to help heal their hearts and re-integrate them into society.

Without the chance to mourn their losses, veterans risk becoming stuck in their anger or numbness. They lock deep within themselves the terrifying images so as not to harm the people they love. But the images do not fade. Time only laminates them.

Did I ever change back?

The image of President Kennedy's coffin on the wagon pulled by a riderless horse floats before me, the endless sidewalks of people stretched along the coffin's route, the mourners' faces contorted with grief. The country wept.

What would it mean for veterans if instead of victory parades we collectively acknowledged what the war took from them? What if we mourned for those who come back with their eyes open as we do those who return in coffins? What if we acknowledged the full cost of war to them and to ourselves?

Acknowledgements

Opening my father's trunk set me on a journey I could not have traveled alone. My husband Burke and my sons Ray and David have been my indispensable companions. They not only supported me in every possible way but physically accompanied me, their love and enthusiasm sustaining me. They are my blessings and proof that life is a blessing.

The veterans themselves have taught me new meanings for generosity and humility. They opened their homes and hearts to me. Their kindness and goodness, their quiet courage and pain and love have changed me. May my words be worthy of their gifts of time and emotion.

I cannot imagine how I could have created a manuscript without the help of my writers' groups. The responses of Esther Mortiz, Saundra Goldman, and Geoff Rips to my very first pages gave me the confidence and critical perspective to keep going. Then the feedback from Esther, again, this time with Andrea Abel and Kit Belgum, persuaded me to persevere. I can't recommend writers' groups enough.

I am grateful to Robert Abzug for his thoughtful responses to my initial ideas for this book and his encouragement along the way. My gratitude goes to the Ella Lyman Cabot Trust whose grant made my travels possible. I also thank The Wellspring House, a writers' retreat in Ashfield, Massachusetts, which provided an invaluable environment and community that got me through a critical juncture in writing my first draft. Allison Supancic of the University of Texas Hogg Foundation is one of my personal heroes for her commitment to helping artists find sustaining resources.

I thank my students at St. Edward's University in Austin, Texas. They were my first audience, and their interest in and receptivity to painful topics inspired me. I especially want to thank Matt Campbell who scanned every single one of my father's hundreds of photographs for me and whose interest in World War II reassures me that the next generation will carry the memories of survivors and liberators forward. And my colleague and friend, Amy Adams, whose encouragement and friendship has sustained me.

I had the good fortune of meeting Flint Whitlock when I moved to Denver. He not only became a magnanimous colleague willing to share his time, resources, and talent, but also introduced me to Nan Wisherd of Cable Publishing. Nan is what every author dreams of: a publisher who is in the business for love of good books and their authors. Through her I have had the great fortune of working with Dean Lamanna as my editor and seeing the book I have always imagined come into being.

I am grateful beyond words to this wonderful community of people.

Bibliography

Abzug, Robert. *Inside the Vicious Heart*. London: Oxford University Press, 1983.

_____. *GIs Remember: Liberating the Concentration Camps*. Washington, D.C.: National Museum of American Jewish History, 1994.

Ames, Ernest C. *Liberation of the Nordhausen and Dora-Mittelbau Concentration Camps: World War II, First Army, Seventh Corps, 104th Infantry Division, 238th Engineer Combat Battalion and Others*. Sacramento: E.C. James, 1995.

Apel, Dora. *Memory Effects: The Holocaust and the Art of Secondary Witnessing*. New Brunswick, NJ: Rutgers University Press, 2002.

Ast, Theresa Lynn. "Confronting the Holocaust: American Soldiers who Liberated the Concentration Camps." Ph.D. Thesis. Emory University, 2000.

Bauer, Yehuda. *Rethinking the Holocaust*. New Haven: Yale University Press, 2000.

Bissell, Tom. *The Father of All Things: A Marine, His Son, and the Legacy of Vietnam*. New York: Vintage Books, 2007.

Bradley, James. *Flags of Our Fathers*. New York: Bantam, 2000.

Bussell, Norman. *My Private War: Liberated Body, Captive Mind: A POW's Story of Survival*. New York: Pegasus Books, 2008.

Coleman, Penny. *Flashback: Posttraumatic Stress Disorder, Suicide, and the Lessons of War*. Boston: Beacon Press, 2007.

Chamberlain, Brewster and Marcia Feldman, eds. *The Liberation of the Nazi Concentration Camps*. Washington, D.C.: United States Holocaust Memorial Council, 1987.

Childers, Thomas. *Soldier from the War Returning: The Greatest Generation's Troubled Homecoming from World War II*. Boston: Houghton, Mifflin, Harcourt, 2009.

Colosimo, Richard. "Coleslaw," 89th Div. Rolling W.

Danieli, Yael. *Treating Survivors and Children of Survivors of the Nazi Holocaust.* Levittown, PA: Brunner/Mazel, 1988.

Dann, Sam. *Dachau 29 April 1945: The Rainbow Liberation Memoirs.* Lubbock, Texas: Texas Tech University Press, 1998.

Delbo, Charlotte. Translated by Rosette C. Lamont. *Auschwitz and After.* Yale University Press, 1995.

_____. Translated by Rosette C. Lamont. *Days and Memory.* Marlboro, VT: The Marlboro Press, 1990.

Dicks, Shirley. *From Vietnam to Hell: Interviews with Victims of Post-Traumatic Stress Disorder.* Jefferson, N.C.: McFarland and Co., 1990.

Dwork, Deborah. *Children with a Star: Jewish Youth in Nazi Europe.* New Haven: Yale University Press, 1991.

Eliach, Yaffa, and Brana Gurewitsch, eds. *The Liberators: Eyewitness Accounts of the Liberation of the Concentration Camps: Oral History Testimonies of American Liberators from the Archives of the Center for Holocaust Studies.* Brooklyn: Center for Holocaust Studies, 1981.

Epstein, Helen. *Children of the Holocaust.* New York: Penguin, 1988.

Figley, Charles. *Mapping Trauma and Its Wake: Autobiographic Essays by Pioneer Trauma Scholars.* Routledge Psychosocial Stress Series, 2005.

Frankl, Victor. *Man's Search for Meaning.* New York: Buccaneer Books, 1993.

Fred R. Crawford Witness to the Holocaust Project Files (database online); SAGE available from http://sage.llibrary.emory.edu/collec-tion-0609.html.

Griffin, Susan. *Chorus of Stones.* Garden City: Doubleday, 1992.

Grossman, Lt. Col. David. *On Killing: The Psychological Cost of Learning to Kill in War and Society.* Boston: Little, Brown, and Co., 1995.

Hartman, Geoffrey. *Holocaust Remembrance: The Shapes of Memory.* Oxford, England: Blackwell, 1994.

Hecht, Anthony. *Collected Later Poems.* New York: Knopf, 2005.

_____. *Collected Earlier Poems.* New York, Knopf, 1992.

_____. *The Darkness and the Light.* New York, Knopf, 2001.

Herder, Harry. "Liberation of Buchenwald," www.remember.org/witness/herder.html

Herman, Judith. *Trauma and Recovery: The Aftermath of Violence—from Domestic Abuse to Political Terror.* New York: Basic Books, 1997.

Hoffman, Eva. *After Such Knowledge: Where Memory of the Holocaust Ends and History Begins.* New York: PublicAffairs, 2004.

Homer. *Iliad.* Translated by Robert Fitzgerald. Garden City: Doubleday, 1974.

Hyett, Barbara Helfgott. *In Evidence: Poems of the Liberation of Nazi Concentration Camps.* Pittsburgh: University of Pittsburgh Press, 1986.

jewishgen.org.ForgottenCamps/Witnesses.

Johnson, Paul. *A History of the Jews.* New York: Harper Perennial, 1988.

Kraft, Robert. *Memory Perceived: Recalling the Holocaust.* Abingdon, England: Greenwood Publishing Group, 2002.

Levine, Peter. *Waking the Tiger: Healing Trauma : The Innate Capacity to Transform Overwhelming Experiences.* Berkeley: North Atlantic Books, 1997.

Lifton, Robert Jay. *Home From the War: Vietnam Vets, Neither Victims nor Executioners.* NY: Simon & Schuster, 1973.

_____. *The Nazi Doctors: Medical Killing and the Psychology of Genocide.* New York: Basic Books, 2000.

Matsakis, Aphrodite. *Back from the Front: Combat Trauma, Love, and the Family.* Baltimore: Sidran Press, 2007.

_____. *Vietnam Wives: Facing the Challenges of Life with Veterans Suffering Post-Traumatic Stress.* Baltimore: Sidran, 1996.

Melander, Billy. "The Hell Hole at Nordhausen." Personal journal, 1976.

Michaels, Anne. *Fugitive Pieces.* New York: Vintage Books, 1996.

"Mittelabu-Dora Concentration Camp, Nordhausen, Germany" www.104infdiv.org/CONCAMP.HTM.

O'Brien, Tim. *The Things They Carried*. New York: Broadway Books, 1998.

Owen, Wilfrid. *The Collected Poems of Wilfrid Owen*. Ed. C.D. Lewis. New York: New Direcctions, 1963.

Pilcer, Sonia. *The Holocaust Kid*. Concord, CA: Delta, 2002.

Rosenbaum, Thane. *Secondhand Smoke*. New York: St. Martin's Griffin, 2000.

Rothblum, Esther D. and Ellen Cole, eds. *A Woman's Recovery from the Trauma of War*. (1986).

Rothschild, Babette. *The Body Remembers: The Psychophysiology of Trauma and Trauma Treatment*. New York: W.W. Norton & Co, 2000.

Salinger, J.D. *Nine Stories*. New York: Back Bay Books, 2001.

Sebald, W.G. Translated by Michael Hulse. *Austerlitz*. New York: Random House, 2001.

_____. Translated by Andrea Bell. *Natural History of Destruction*. New York: The Modern Library, 2004.

_____. Translated by Andrea Bell. *Vertigo*. New York: New Directions Publishing, 2000.

Shay, Jonathan. *Odysseus in America: Combat Trauma and the Trials of Homecoming*. New York: Scribner, 2002.

_____. *Achilles in Vietnam: Combat Trauma and the Undoing of Character*. New York: Simon and Schuster, 1995.

Silko, Leslie Marmon. *Ceremony*. New York: Viking Penguin, 1987.

Sontag, Susan. *In America: A Novel*. New York: Picador, 2001.

_____. *On Photography*. New York: Farrar, Straus, and Giroux, 1977.

_____. *Regarding the Pain of Others*. New York: Picador, 2004.

Sorel, Nancy. *The Women Who Wrote the War*. NY: Harper Paperbacks, 2000.

Sophocles. "Antigone." Translated by Paul Roche. In *The Complete Plays*, New York: Signet Classics, 2001.

Spiegelman, Art. *Maus I: A Survivor's Tale: My Father Bleeds History*. New York: Pantheon Books, 1986.

_____. *Maus II: A Survivor's Tale: And Here My Troubles Began*. New York: Pantheon Books, 1991.

Tick, Edward. *War and the Soul*. Wheaton, IL: Quest Books, 2005.

Van der Kolk, Bessel. *Traumatic Stress: The Effects of Overwhelming Experience on Mind, Body, and Society*. The Guilford Press, 2006.

Walcott, Derek. *Collected Poems, 1948-1984*. New York: Farrar, Straus and Giroux, 1987.

Wiesel, Elie. *Night*. New York: Hill and Wang, 2006.

Wilson, John P., Zev Harel and Boaz Kahana, eds. *Human Adaptation to Extreme Stress: From the Holocaust to Vietnam*. New York: Springer, 1988.

U.S. ARMY DIVISIONS RECOGNIZED AS LIBERATING UNITS BY THE UNITED STATES HOLOCAUST MEMORIAL MUSEUM AND THE CENTER OF MILITARY HISTORY

INFANTRY DIVISONS

1st Infantry Division -	Falkenau an der Eger (Flossenbürg subcamp)
2nd Infantry Division -	Leipzig-Schönefeld (Buchenwald subcamp) and Spergau (labor education camp)
4th Infantry Division -	Dachau subcamp
8th Infantry Division -	Wöbbelin (Neuengamme subcamp)
26th Infantry Division -	Gusen (Mauthausen subcamp)
29th Infantry Division -	Dinslaken (civilian labor camp)
36th Infantry Division -	Kaufering camps (Dachau subcamps)
42nd Infantry Division -	Dachau
45th Infantry Division -	Dachau
63rd Infantry Division -	Kaufering camps (Dachau subcamps)
65th Infantry Division -	Flossenbürg subcamp
69th Infantry Division -	Leipzig-Thekla (Buchenwald subcamp)
71st Infantry Division -	Gunskirchen (Mauthausen subcamp)
80th Infantry Division -	Buchenwald Ebensee (Mauthausen subcamp)
83rd Infantry Division -	Langenstein (Buchenwald subcamp)
84th Infantry Division -	Ahlem (Neuengamme subcamp) and Salzwedel (Neuengamme subcamp)
86th Infantry Division -	Attendorn (civilian labor camp)
89th Infantry Division -	Ohrdruf (Buchenwald subcamp)
90th Infantry Division -	Flossenbürg

95th Infantry Division -   Werl (prison and civilian labor camp)

99th Infantry Division -   Dachau subcamps

103rd Infantry Division -   Aufering subcamp

104th Infantry Division -   Mittelbau-Dora (Nordhausen)

ARMORED DIVISIONS

3rd Armored Division -   Mittelbau-Dora (Nordhausen)

4th Armored Division -   Ohrdruf (Buchenwald subcamp)

6th Armored Division -   Buchenwald

8th Armored Division -   Halberstadt-Zwieberge (Buchenwald subcamp)

9th Armored Division -   Falkenau an der Eger (Flossenbürg subcamp)

10th Armored Division -   Dachau subcamp

11th Armored Division -   Usen (Mauthausen subcamp) and Mauthausen

12th Armored Division -   Dachau subcamp

14th Armored Division -   Dachau subcamps

20th Armored Division -   Dachau

AIRBORNE DIVISIONS

82nd Airborne Division -   Wöbbelin (Neuengamme subcamp)

101st Airborne Division -   Dachau subcamp

Index

Notes:

Notes:

Notes:

True Stories
of
Answered Prayer

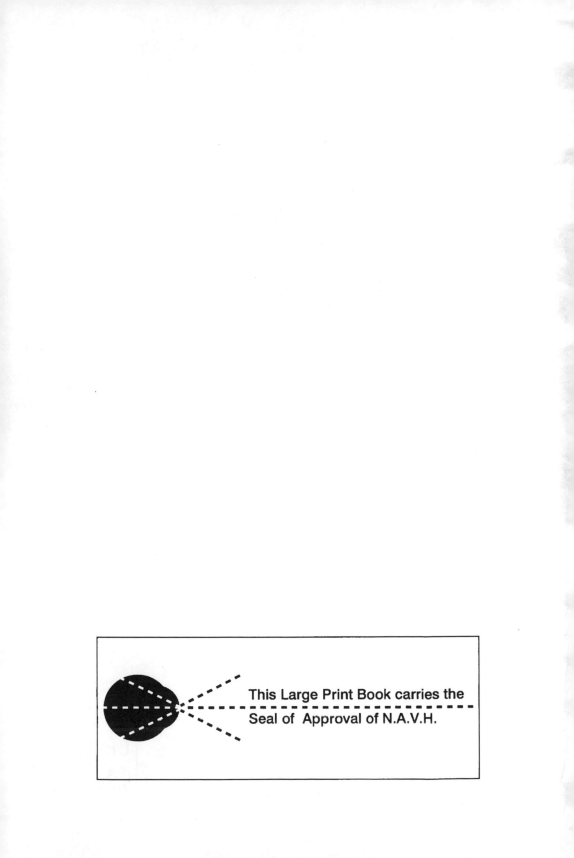

True Stories

of

Answered Prayer

‹❦›

Mike Nappa

G.K. Hall & Co. • Thorndike, Maine

Published in 2000 by arrangement with Tyndale House Publishers, Inc.

G.K. Hall Large Print Inspirational Series.

The text of this Large Print edition is unabridged.
Other aspects of the book may vary from the original edition.

Set in 16 pt. Plantin by Elena Picard.

Printed in the United States on permanent paper.

Library of Congress Catalog Card Number: 00-90284
ISBN 0-7838-9017-6 (lg. print : hc : alk. paper)

For Amy, my partner in prayer and in life.
You, my dear, are my answer to prayer.
I love you!
M. N.

"The beauty of prayer is that anyone can pray.
You don't have to be a certain age,
you don't have to have wealth,
you don't have to have a certain talent
— all you have to have is a stubborn faith
and a willingness to intercede."

MAX LUCADO, *Walking with the Savior*

Contents

Acknowledgments

I would like to gratefully acknowledge a few important people. First, Meg Diehl, Tynedale's former acquisitions editor, whose passion for this book overcame my initial dedision not to write it.

Next, Lee Maynard, who graciously allowed me to reprint his touching story of answered prayer word for word in this book. Thank you, Lee, for your kindness to me, a stranger.

Also, I can't write a book on prayer without acknowledging the one woman who showed me the power of prayer through her own life: my mother, Dr. Zahea Nappa. It is she who has prayed for me since before I was born. It was her prayers that helped me through a less-than-perfect childhood and turbulent teen years and her prayers that continue to strengthen my family and me today. I am grateful beyond words for the power of her prayers in my life.

Last, but certainly not least, I wish to acknowledge Jesus Christ, my Lord, my Savior, my highest reason for living. If I had not met him nearly two decades ago, I truly would have nothing to write about. Ever. The words of the old hymn proclaim:

What a privilege to carry everything to God in prayer!

Introduction

"There is hardly any human activity — including getting up in the morning, exercising, working, driving, eating, having sex, watching TV, reading, talking to people, and going to bed at night — that someone doesn't associate with prayer," says religious researcher Jim Castelli.[1]

Take one look at your life, and you know he's right. Take a look at American life in general, and you see it even more clearly.

Consider:

• Nine out of ten Americans say they pray. Seventy-five percent of Americans report praying *every day.*[2]

• *Life* magazine reported that 98 percent of Americans pray for their families, 92 percent pray for forgiveness. And one of every four Americans even prays for seemingly inconsequential things like victory in a sports event.[3]

• When we pray, nearly half of us do it for about five minutes or less, but 28 percent of us put in an hour or more.[4]

[1]Jim Castelli, "Prayer," *USA Weekend,* 23–25 December 1994.
[2]Ibid.
[3]"Why We Pray," *Life* (March 1994): 58.
[4]Ibid, 60.

• The result of all this prayer? More than 200 million Americans (95 percent) report having experienced answers to prayer.[5]

In spite of this, our prevailing attitude toward prayer is summed up in words like the ones these teenagers wrote on the message boards on America Online.[6]

"I believe in God, but I don't think God answers every prayer. One in ten thousand maybe."

"Any thoughts on prayer? Yeah. It's dumb."

"I'm curious what makes people [pray]. It seems pointless to me."

This book is for those teenagers — and for everyone else who has ever felt abandoned by God, unsure of prayer, and ready to give up hope. When you feel discouraged, let the stories in this book remind you not only that there is a God but also that he is constantly at work in the lives of people like you and me — even when we can't see it, don't feel it, and won't believe it.

All the events recorded in this book are true instances I've collected through interviews, casual conversations, email queries, written surveys, and personal experience. In some cases names have been changed or deliberately omitted to protect the privacy of the individuals involved.

But there's one name that is always the same: the name of Jesus Christ, the one to whom each

[5]Ibid, 62.
[6]Mike Nappa, "When God Seems Silent," *Group's Real Life Bible Curriculum* (1995): 6.

prayer recorded in this book was first directed. Now, as you begin reading about the answered prayers of others, may Jesus meet you within each page and remind you that God never abandons those who seek him (see Psalm 9:10).

Mike Nappa, 1998

1

A Prayer for the Shepherd

Andrae Crouch needed his sleep. It takes a lot of time and energy to be a gospel music singer, pastor of a church, and leader of a street outreach program in urban Los Angeles. And with the recent discovery of three cancerous tumors in his body, Pastor Crouch needed to do all he could do to keep his body healthy.

He was so weary he was tempted not to answer the phone when it woke him up at three-thirty in the morning. He was sleeping in the office/apartment attached to Christ Memorial Church, where he pastored, and he wanted to go back to sleep. Still, the call had come in on his private, unlisted line, so he reluctantly reached for the receiver.

"Hello?" he said.

A woman's voice, heavy with a Spanish accent, responded, "Is this the Memorial Church?"

"Yes."

The voice on the phone was firm. "I am to pray for the shepherd."

Andrae was wide awake now. As pastor of Christ Memorial, he was often called the shepherd of his church.

17

Without hesitation, the woman began to pray, "Father, in the name of Jesus, I pray for the infirmity of this shepherd, and I curse it. I curse it at the root, and it is gone in the name of Jesus."

Then she hung up.

Pastor Crouch lay awake a few moments, wondering how the woman had gotten his phone number, how she knew he had an infirmity, and why she'd called to pray in the wee hours of the morning. He finally returned to sleep.

Two days later Andrae reported to the doctor's office for a checkup. The doctor wanted to assess how quickly the cancer was growing and to begin making recommendations for treatment.

After searching for the tumors for about ten minutes, the doctor put a hand on his hip. "Maybe you can find them, Pastor Crouch, because I don't feel anything."

Andrae pointed and said, "Well, they're here, remember? The big one's right . . . right . . ." Suddenly his eyes filled with tears.

All three of the tumors were gone.

2

Walking Distance

"Dear Jesus . . ." Four-year-old Tony started his bedtime prayer in the same fashion he always did, continuing through the customary list of relatives and his dog (named after a Disney character). "Help my mom, my dad, me and Aladdin, Jody and Erik, Jill and Annette, Grandma and Grandpa all to sleep well."

But this night, instead of ending the prayer as he normally would, Tony added an extra line: "Please help Aunt Jody and Uncle Erik move to a house within walking distance of ours. Amen."

The trouble was that Tony lived in Colorado, while Jody and Erik lived in southern California. Jody had been working as a freelance writer for a publishing company in Colorado, and it was possible the company might need a new editor in the coming months.

Tony continued to pray. Each night before bed, he diligently asked Jesus to arrange for Jody and Erik to move "within walking distance" of his home.

Over the course of the next few months, that editorial job did open up. After a lengthy inter-

19

view process, Jody was chosen to fill the position. Erik and Jody were moving to Tony's town!

But where would they live? Tony never wavered. He kept on praying his special prayer. When Erik got a job in a nearby city and considered moving a twenty-minute car drive to the north, Tony prayed. When Erik and Jody decided to move to an outlying area about fifteen minutes to the west, Tony prayed. When they found a rental a block away, Tony thought his prayer had been answered — but the house was rented to someone else.

Shortly thereafter, the house next to the rental went up for sale. It was well kept, just the right size, close to a small park in a quiet neighborhood, near Jody's work, and within driving distance of Erik's. Best of all, it was within walking distance of Tony's house. Everyone was thrilled . . . until they found out the house had been sold the day before Jody and Erik made an offer. It seemed like Tony would have to settle for having his favorite aunt and uncle live within driving distance.

Then one day Jody and Erik got a call. The original buyer of the house by the park had backed out, and the homeowner had kept Jody and Erik's number "just in case." The owner wanted to know if the couple still liked the house.

A few weeks later Tony himself was in charge of carrying the couch cushions when Jody and Erik moved into that special house — "within walking distance."

3

High and Dry in Budapest

In 1988 Eastern Europe was ruled by the Communist Soviet Union. John and Katherine Wilhelm felt sure God was leading them behind the Iron Curtain to share with others the news of Jesus Christ and his resurrection.

After months of study and outreach in the Soviet Union, John and Katherine were traveling by train to Budapest, Hungary. There, they were to meet a missionary, who would care for them and see them on the way to their next destination of Vienna, Austria.

The train lurched into the station at 7:00 A.M., Budapest time. After thirty-three hours of travel, John and Katherine were looking forward to resting and bathing at the home of the missionaries scheduled to meet them. They gathered their luggage and made their way to the crowded platform. They spotted a bench, sat down, and waited for their Hungarian contacts to pick them up.

After an hour, no one had come. John tried to call the missionaries. No answer. He tried to call the office in Germany that had coordinated their trip. Again, no answer. John went back to the bench and waited with Katherine.

They waited a long time.

Five hours later they were still stranded on the bench in a crowded train station, thousands of miles from home, unable to speak the language, and thereby unable to communicate their need to anyone but God. They whispered several prayers to the one who understands all languages and asked for help and guidance out of Budapest.

John and Katherine tried calling the office in Germany again. Finally, Katherine was able to get through. She was told there had been a mix-up. The missionaries who were to meet them had traveled to America for a brief furlough. John and Katherine would have to make their way to Vienna on their own.

Near tears, Katherine hung up the phone and walked back to where John was waiting. Overcome with hopelessness, she sighed aloud, "Lord, what are we going to do?"

Suddenly, an elderly man in front of her turned and said clearly, "You speak English."

Katherine was stunned, then overjoyed. "*You* speak English!"

"Yes, I used to live here in Hungary, but many years ago I moved to New Zealand. I'm here visiting friends." He paused. "Now, what is your trouble?"

Although it was a risk to tell a stranger her missionary goals in a Communist country, Katherine said a quick prayer and then explained her predicament.

The man nodded. "I will help you."

For the next hour he helped John and Katherine make the necessary arrangements. First, they needed a place to stay. After checking around, they found that the cheapest available hotel room cost $100 — more than they had. A few moments later they were standing in line at the post office, and the man struck up a conversation with the woman behind him. All but the man seemed surprised to find out she had a spare bedroom she was willing to let them use for the night for only a ten-dollar fee — she agreed to transport them from the train station and back and to make dinner and breakfast for them as well!

Next, the man brought Katherine to the currency-exchange building. Ignoring hour-long lines, the man strode up to the counter without protest from anyone. He helped Katherine exchange her money so she could buy train tickets for the trip to Vienna the next morning.

When all the details were covered and the man was certain John and Katherine had been taken care of, he shook John's hand and looked him straight in the eye. "God bless you."

John was so surprised to hear him speak of God in public, he turned to tell Katherine. When he turned back a half second later, the man was gone.

4

The Answer's in the Can

What do you do when you're the oldest of four children, when there's barely any food in your family's cupboard, and when your church is having a canned-food drive to help needy families on Thanksgiving?

Thirteen-year-old Anne wasn't sure, but she knew she had to do something.

According to her Sunday school teacher, each child was to bring one nonperishable item to the morning church service that week. Those items would be gathered into baskets and given that evening to poorer families in the community for Thanksgiving dinner. Anne looked in the cupboard and found two cans of vegetables, a box of macaroni, and a bag of rice — four nonperishable items, one for each child in her family.

But giving those items to the canned-food drive left nothing for Anne's family. After pausing for a brief prayer, Anne felt that God was directing her to help those needy families by giving the food. With a deep sigh, she gathered the items in the cupboard and distributed them to her siblings. When they put the nonperishable goods in the collection at church, Anne prayed again that God would use their gifts and provide for her family as well.

After church Anne and her family played away the Sunday with games, television, football, and books. That afternoon the doorbell rang. Standing at the door were representatives from her church; in their arms they held baskets overflowing with food for the holiday.

Anne's family had been chosen to receive the gifts her church had donated to the canned-food drive — including the four items her family had given. That Thanksgiving their cupboard was full.

5

Cameron Dante

"Cameron Dante was a pop star in England," says Andy Hawthorne, leader of the popular Christian dance band from Britain called The World Wide Message Tribe.

"He had four top ten hits," Andy continues, "[and] he's an amazing dancer. He was the U.K. break-dancing champion and third in the world championships and . . . an amazing rapper — just a great communicator. Trouble was, he was off his face on drugs most of the time."

When Cameron decided to record an album at the studio used by The World Wide Message Tribe, Andy and his bandmates decided it was time to pray. For the next six months the band prayed for Cameron each day.

They prayed that God would change his heart and lead him out of the jungle of drugs and clubs and parties that went along with the lifestyle of a pop superstar. They prayed Cameron would one day meet and be changed by Jesus Christ.

While Cameron was recording his album, The World Wide Message Tribe's producer had an opportunity to tell Cameron about what faith in Christ meant. Cameron hesitated to make a decision at that point, but he agreed to come to a church service where the band was scheduled to play.

Andy chuckles. "He came to one [church service]. The first one he came to, he gave his life to Christ."

Cameron was transformed almost immediately; he burned with zeal for God and the Bible. Then he did what seemed to be the natural thing to do. He went home and told his live-in girlfriend all about it. She became angry. Like Cameron, she loved the party scene, even performing regularly as a cage dancer in a nightclub. She didn't like that Cameron had gotten so caught up in religion, but she couldn't help noticing a difference in him. It wasn't long before she wanted that difference too. Cameron's girlfriend became a Christian.

Nine months after his conversion, Cameron Dante left his mainstream music career and joined The World Wide Message Tribe as a vocalist. Eighteen months after he became a Christian, Cameron and his girlfriend married. Andy Hawthorne preached at the wedding, and the band performed at the reception.

"It's probably the most exciting thing I've ever seen, those two," says Andy. "Praying for somebody who's about as far away from God as you can imagine. And then to see that process of God working in their life, them being set on fire [with a] hunger for the Bible and prayer and then see *them* start winning people. It's fantastic."

6

A Christmas Wish

The sleepy town of Odyssey is a magical place. Children in this fictional city are constantly treated to a world of wonder, excitement, and adventure There's Whit's End, a soda shop and discovery emporium that's often the center of action in the town. There's buried treasure, a spy ring, churches, politicians, greedy merchants, and unsuspecting children. But no matter what's going on, Jesus is the hero constantly working in the lives of his children.

When Phil Lollar co-created this wonderful world more than a decade ago for Focus on the Family, he could not have imagined that the *Adventures in Odyssey* radio program would grow to become a family tradition. In addition to novels and animated videos, *Adventures in Odyssey* has been translated into fifteen languages and has aired on radio.

But thirty-four years earlier, on Christmas Eve in 1964, the writer/producer/actor who launched Odyssey was just a five-year-old child who missed his daddy.

Little Phil and his family were living in Klamath Falls, Oregon, at the time, staying with

29

the boy's grandparents. For many years Phil's father had suffered from asthma, and 1964 was especially bad. His father had to go south to a hospital in San Francisco for treatment. For the first time in Phil's life, Christmas would come and go without his father being there.

The family celebrated the holiday as best they could. They sang carols, ate Christmas dinner, played, and happily anticipated opening their presents. Still, for one young kindergartner, it just wasn't the same. How could it be Christmas while Daddy lay wheezing in a hospital bed many miles away?

In a bit of holiday kindness, Phil's mother allowed him and his older brother to sleep under the dining-room table on Christmas Eve. When they awoke, it would be Christmas; they would be close to the tree.

Phil got comfortable under the table and waited for sleep to come. As he closed his eyes, he prayed to himself, *Lord, all I want for Christmas is my Daddy*. Heavyhearted in spite of the holiday, he drifted off to sleep.

The night was still black when Phil felt his mother gently shaking him awake. Was it Christmas Day already? No, it was only midnight. Why was his mother insisting he wake up?

Sleepily rubbing his eyes, Phil followed Mom to his parents' bedroom. There, sitting up in bed, was Daddy. The hospital had released him so he could come home in time to spend Christmas Day with his family. Phil felt an inexpressible joy.

Daddy was home!

Phil still thinks fondly of that 1964 Christmas. "I knew from that moment on — no doubt in my mind — that God answers prayer."

7

Misery Loves Company

Andy Chrisman was miserable. There's no other way to describe it. He was out-and-out miserable.

The year was 1987, and Andy was sitting in his apartment feeling certain that the whole world wanted him unhappy. He was attending college, trying to make his way through the career maze that confronted him, but he wasn't enjoying it. His grades were good, but he felt discontented, discouraged, and disillusioned. His whole life at that point seemed meaningless, just a daily collection of useless activities.

In short, he was a miserable wreck.

Since misery loves company, Andy didn't bear his sorrow alone. He cried out to God, begging the Lord to reveal his will to him. Should he stay in college, work toward a degree, prepare for a career, and save money for his future? Should he skip out of college and pursue his dream of being a Christian singer? Should he ignore those ideas and be a janitor, fulfilling God's will by serving others in an often-unappreciated position?

Andy didn't know what to do, but he knew he wanted God to be involved — no matter what.

He sat in his room, praying, imploring his Creator, "God, use me. Whatever you want me to do, I'll do. Just use me" After Andy's prayer time was over, nothing had really changed. At least he had been able to share his misery with One who cared and who could help.

The next day Andy waited for a word from God to let him know that God had heard his prayer. Nothing happened. The second day came and went without a whisper.

The third day Andy's phone rang. On the other end was the leader of the Christian music ensemble Truth. "Andy, there's an opening in Truth, and we want you to come audition for the group. If you pass the audition, we'd like you to join us for our road tour. Will you come try out?"

Andy enthusiastically agreed. He joined Truth and toured with them. A few years later, in 1989, he and three other guys started the vocal group 4Him. The band members have performed worldwide in their ministry. 4Him has recorded more than six albums. Ten of their songs have been number-one hit songs on Christian radio; they have won three Dove Awards. The group members of 4Him speak unapologetically about faith and experience.

"Just use me," Andy Chrisman prayed in 1987. God answered that prayer with a phone call, using that little spark to launch a music ministry. Andy says with confidence, "I believe so much in prayer. I believe in specific prayer. . . . My wife and I practice it as much as we can!"

8

Hole in the Sky

Don Weber loved to fly. Nothing else in the world could bring the peace and beauty of winging through the clouds, of literally touching the sky. Don enjoyed many opportunities to fly because of his job as a missionary aviator to the jungle tribes of the Amazon basin.

Don regularly flew his single-engine plane across the Amazonian expanse, noting landmarks and rivers that would guide him safely through the uncharted jungle. He didn't fly those routes alone. Don was the pilot, but he trusted God to be the navigator leading him safely to his destination and back home to his family.

One gray day, Don walked up the runway to his plane and surveyed the sky. The clouds were turning black; the wind whipped at his clothes. If he flew now, he might make it home to his wife and children ahead of the oncoming storm.

Strapping himself into the cockpit, Don revved the engine, taxied down the airstrip, and zoomed into space. Keeping an eye on the snaking brown river below, Don carefully pointed his plane in the right direction and settled in for the journey home.

The flight went well at first — a little bumpy but navigable. Then, with frightening speed, the threatening rain exploded into a full-scale jungle monsoon. Don's plane bounced and groaned, straining against the wind and rain that buffeted everything in sight. Menacing clouds billowed and rolled, surrounding the missionary and blocking his view of the ground below.

With visibility gone, Don knew he had to get to safety immediately, or he would never make it home. His only hope was to return to the airstrip he'd just left. Banking his plane through the monsoon, Don turned to go back — and was greeted by massive, impenetrable cloud cover. There was no way out. Effectively blinded by the storm, he braced for the worst and prayed.

"This is it, Lord My life is in your hands" Don readied himself for the crash landing that would probably kill him.

He gazed through the cockpit window, awaiting death. Then, slowly but unmistakably, he noticed a change in the storm. Like heavy blankets being tossed aside, the clouds ahead began piling up and shifting. Directly in front of him, as if in response to an unheard command, the billows rolled away; a bright hole appeared in the sky — a path of visibility through the storm.

Watching the miracle unfold around him, Don shot forward into the opening, thinking that this must have been how the Israelites felt when God parted the Red Sea to allow them to pass. The path in the air stayed open, a quiet spot surrounded by the storm. Before long Don spotted the airstrip and made his way to a safe landing.

As the plane's wheels whined to a stop on the runway, Don heaved a sigh of relief and turned to view his miracle once more. He saw the opening suddenly collapse, overtaken by the torrential rain and wind.

God, the Great Navigator, had made a way where there was no way. Don was safely on the ground. God had answered Don's prayer, leaving the aviator to worship and wonder at the power of his mighty Savior.

9

On a Mission of Prayer

Denise Hildreth had her own problems. She was sitting in the hospital lobby crying because one of her family members was near death. All Denise could do was sit, wait, cry, and pray.

Looking around the lobby, Denise noticed another family. Like her, they were expressing sorrow. Denise wondered what had caused their tears. As she got up to leave the lobby area, she felt compelled to stop before the exit. Hesitating for a moment, she thought to herself, *I'm going to see what they need. Maybe I can offer a prayer or something.*

Denise walked over to the sorrowful family and inquired about their situation. The mother had heart failure, and she was in that hospital hovering between life and death. The family had lost hope. They were beside themselves trying to prepare for the great loss of this loved one.

Denise quickly realized there was little she could do to change the situation, but she determined to do *something.* "I do believe in prayer, and I do believe in Christ. All I can do is pray for you."

The family members all bowed their heads

39

while Denise prayed a simple prayer, asking Jesus to heal and restore to this family the mother they were afraid of losing. Then Denise walked out of the room and, she thought, out of that family's life.

Later that week Denise was at the hospital to visit her family member, who was recovering quickly. As she made her way down the hall, she spied a group of people who looked familiar. Yes, it was the family she had stopped to pray with a few days earlier!

Something was different this time. Instead of frowning, they were smiling. Instead of crying, they were laughing. Instead of grieving, they were chatting freely.

When that family saw Denise, they stopped to fill her in. After Denise's prayer, their mother had unexpectedly begun improving. In fact, she was doing so well, the doctors thought she could return home in the next few days! God was answering Denise's prayer, working a miraculous healing inside the mother's heart.

Denise smiled. Yes, she still had problems, but pausing to pray for that family *had* made a difference. The news lightened Denise's own burdens.

Denise told her husband about the outcome of her prayer, and the two of them sat down to write a song about the experience. The name of the song is "To Be a Christian." You can hear Denise's husband, Jonathan Pierce, sing about it on his 1997 album, *Mission*.

10

Addition and Subtraction

The numbers just didn't add up. Craig Keener sighed and pushed aside the page that held his budget for the next year. No matter what he did, Craig couldn't figure out a way for his income to match the expected expenses. Fresh out of school, unemployed, and needing a large amount of money soon, he wasn't sure what to do next.

Craig was not a man without resources. He had sketched a scholarly study of the New Testament, resulting in some eighty thousand note cards detailing the historical context of nearly every passage of Scripture from Matthew to Revelation.

Craig had hoped that a Christian publisher would be interested in having him write a contemporary commentary on the New Testament. Unfortunately, his efforts remained fruitless. Even if someone wanted to buy his commentary, there was little hope they would pay him enough to live on during the year he would write it!

Craig had recently completed a seminary degree. Surely that was worth something — but what? Perhaps he could find a pastoral job somewhere. Maybe he could be a teacher at a Bible school.

Craig sighed again. His eyes kept coming back to that figure at the bottom of the page, the amount of money he'd need to make it through the next year. It seemed impossible. But he knew Someone who specialized in doing the impossible: God.

Before Craig Keener went to bed that night in 1990, he spent some time in prayer with God. Talking about the subject of his budget, Craig pointed out that he didn't know how or where to earn the money he needed to cover his upcoming expenses. He pleaded with God to help him find a way. He did his best to turn the whole matter over to God and went to bed trusting that somehow, someway, God would provide.

The next morning came as normal. The sun rose. The alarm went off. Craig greeted the day and waited for a miracle. This day, the miracle would come in the form of a phone call.

On the other end of the line was an editor at the Christian publishing house InterVarsity Press. Craig could hardly believe his ears. They wanted him to write a commentary He felt like holding his breath as they outlined the terms. They came to the part about the royalty advance they'd pay Craig while he worked on the book.

The editor named a figure.

Craig felt like shouting. The figure the editor named was *exactly* the same number he had written on his budget and had prayed about the night before. God had answered his prayer in dramatic fashion.

Dr. Craig S. Keener wrote his book, published in 1993 as *The IVP Bible Background Commentary: New Testament.* Going verse by verse through the New Testament, Craig shared his knowledge on the historical background surrounding the Bible. Thus, he created an invaluable resource for Christians who wish to understand a bit more of what they read in the Scriptures.

11

Little Red Geo

"My fellow bandmates and friends tell me that my life is just a long list of miracles," laughs Erik Sundin, lead singer for the Christian reggae band Temple Yard. "God just provides and provides and provides. It's just amazing."

Before starting Temple Yard in 1998, Erik was the lead singer of the pioneer Christian reggae group Christafari. Until Christafari, most people assumed that the Jamaican drug culture and Rastafari religion associated with reggae preempted Christian music of the same style. Christafari not only made it possible but also excelled at it. Call that miracle number one.

Miracle number two was the group's immediate acceptance both in Christian circles and in reggae circles. The band played all the major Christian festivals and toured with the high-profile mainstream event Reggae Sunsplash. They charted top ten hits in *Billboard Magazine*, performed at the 1996 Summer Olympics, and played at the 1997 Presidential Inaugural Ball in Washington, D.C.

But for Erik Sundin those miracles pale in comparison to the personal miracles he's experienced. Despite the success of Christafari, Erik had to work part-time as a delivery driver in Nashville, Tennessee, in 1996. One night, Erik loaded his car with sumptuous goodies and headed for the address on his delivery slip. Rain poured from the sky, filling the streets of Music City with little rivers running through traffic. Turning a corner, Erik unexpectedly hit a current in the pavement, and his car started to hydroplane.

He had a sickening feeling when his car began "surfing." He steered and nothing happened. He pounded on the breaks, yet his car didn't slow. All Erik could do was watch helplessly as his vehicle, skidding at about thirty miles per hour, careened into a brick wall.

The auto was completely totaled, with all four wheels bent under the chassis and the engine crushed. Thankfully, Eric walked away from the accident unharmed. Call that miracle number three.

Not only was Erik's car lost, but the wreck had jeopardized his job. After all, how can a guy make deliveries without a car? Erik prayed for another miracle. He and his wife prayed together, asking God to provide a new means of transportation in spite of their low funds. Erik recruited friends to pray for him, including Matt O'Conner, a staff member at Erik's church.

Family and friends prayed for three days, and on the third day Erik got a phone call while away from his home. It was Matt. "God has answered your prayers, man. I'll see you when you get to your house."

When Erik arrived, he found a red 1990 Geo Storm parked in the driveway. With a smile on his face, Matt announced to Erik, "This is yours."

An anonymous person in the church felt God leading him to give away this car, but he didn't know anybody who needed one. The man approached Matt O'Conner to see if he knew anyone in need of reliable transportation — and Matt immediately told him about Erik. When the car was delivered to Erik's door, prayers of all three men were miraculously answered.

Erik Sundin remains grateful for the way God responded to his prayer by providing a little red Geo Storm. "I still have it," he reports with pride. "Still running!"

12

Through the Uprights

Coming out of college in 1993, kicker Todd Peterson was thrilled to be drafted in the seventh round by the New York Giants — most kickers aren't drafted at all!

Todd couldn't wait to fulfill his dream of being a professional football player. Then, before the season began, the thrill turned to disappointment. The Giants cut Todd from their roster, opting to go with veteran David Treadwell instead.

Todd still had opportunities to try out with other NFL teams: Washington, Miami, New England, Arizona, Pittsburgh, Cincinnati. One by one, those teams all said the same thing: "Thanks, but no thanks." Todd earned tryouts with over a dozen teams. Nobody took him.

"Basically, all those teams were saying, 'We're not willing to take a chance on you right now. You need to get into a game.' And I kept thinking to myself, *How do you get into a game unless somebody takes a chance on you?*"

Frustrated, Todd went to the place he knew he'd always be accepted — straight to Jesus. "Finally, I just got on my knees one day and was like, 'God, what's going on here? If you want me to play pro football, then *you've* got to open the doors. If you don't want me to play, then take the desire out of my heart.' "

Todd didn't hear anything from God right away, but he did start getting encouragement from teams. "Teams continued to tell me, 'You're going to be good. You're going to be good.' So I finally said, 'Lord, I'm going to trust that the sign you're giving me is that you want me to keep plugging away at this. . . . I'm going to trust that you want me doing it.' And that's what my approach was."

In May 1994 that faith and perseverance seemed to pay off. The Atlanta Falcons signed this up-and-coming field-goal specialist to their team! . . . And cut him just days before the opening game. Todd could hardly bear his disappointment. The 1994 season started, but Todd was still grounded in the bleachers, watching the action from afar. Then, unexpectedly, he got another chance to prove what he could do in the NFL.

In October of that year, Arizona Cardinals kicker Greg Davis went down with an injury. Arizona needed someone to fill Davis's spot for a few weeks. Remembering his solid tryout months before, the Cardinals turned to Todd.

On October 16, 1994, Todd played in his first NFL game against the Washington Redskins, a team that had passed him up earlier. Todd went out ready to make the 'Skins sorry they'd let him go . . . and promptly missed a field goal that could have given the Cardinals enough points to win the game.

Still, at the end of regulation, the score was tied at sixteen. With 4:56 minutes left in the overtime period, the Cardinals coach called on Todd once more, now asking him to win the game.

Todd said a quick prayer and tried not to let the pressure get to him. *Kick the game-winning field goal and be a hero, or miss it and walk out of the NFL forever.* The ball was hiked and set. Todd went through his routine. . . . And this time he booted the football through the uprights for the win. On the strength of his performance as a substitute kicker for the Cardinals, the Seattle Seahawks signed Todd Peterson to a multiyear contract starting with the 1995 season. He was a full-time pro at last.

With the Seahawks, Todd set several team records, including most points scored in a season. He was chosen as the AFC Special Teams Player of the Week. Through all the honors, the wins and losses, and the pressures and temptations of life in the NFL, Todd remains focused on what really matters: his relationship with Jesus.

"God has been gracious to me. God gave me the talent, and he's blessed me. He's been gracious to allow me to use that talent to glorify him." He shakes his head in wonder. "That has been an amazing thing for me."

13

Nine Hundred Thousand Shillings

Nine hundred thousand shillings is how much home currency Tony Ombogo of Kenya, Africa, needed to pay for his first year of school at a Christian college in the United States. Because of his status as an international student, he had to have all that money in hand before the U.S. would issue his visa.

Assuming Tony worked seven days a week and saved every bit from his twenty-seven-shilling-a-day job as a telephone technician, Tony figured it would be ninety-one years before he could start his freshman year.

To compound the problem, financial aid monies were unavailable for Tony. He explains, "As an international student, I cannot receive any assistance for my first year. I do not even receive federal aid when I'm in school."

Tony prayed for God's help, asking him to somehow provide the money he needed to pursue his dream of becoming a medical missionary. Despite fervent prayer, Tony was ready to give up. It looked like his dream would die.

Looking back on that time in his life, Tony reflects, "I didn't think it would happen."

But God had a different idea, and it came in the form of Tony's dad.

Tony's father was determined to make it possible for Tony to pursue his dream at Emmanuel College in Franklin Springs, Georgia. "My first year, I think my dad made that happen," Tony says proudly. His dad talked to friends, colleagues, and anyone else who would listen. He called about 150 relatives and family friends, inviting them to come to a special reunion/fundraiser for Tony.

On the appointed day, around seventy people showed up. Tony reports, "Everybody [brought] as much as they could and dropped it in a bucket. At the end of the day, we collected about five hundred thousand Kenya shillings."

Slowly but surely, the Ombogo family saw money trickling in. On the day the fall semester began at Emmanuel, Tony had the tuition money! He had scraped together funds to cover room and board, and he even held his travel visa in hand. . . .

But he was 144,000 shillings short of the amount needed to purchase a plane ticket to America. While he languished at home in Africa, classes started without him.

God then revealed that he has a sense of humor. Tony was traveling to a *Christian* college, but a *Hindu* businessman responded to a request by Tony's father and agreed to provide the needed plane ticket.

Tony arrived at Emmanuel College two weeks

into the semester, quickly enrolled in classes, and worked his way through to completion of a solid college career.

Tony muses about his experience, "If I'd looked at the money and decided, 'OK. I can't do this,' I'd still be in Kenya, and I wouldn't have had the opportunity that I've had here. Just take that first step with what you have [and] allow God to direct toward your next step. Let your need be known to those who can help . . . and you will do it."

14

A Phantom's Prayer

If you own a copy of *The Phantom of the Opera* (The Complete Original London Cast Recording), then you know who Michael Crawford is. If you have witnessed the musical on stage in either London or New York, you've probably seen firsthand the power and grace this English actor brings to the role of the Phantom.

If you follow the life of the stage even more closely, then you know Michael has earned a number of accolades, including a Tony Award, a Drama Desk Award, the Dramalogue and Los Angeles Critics Awards, and the Olivier Award for Best Actor in a Musical.

Perhaps you didn't know that years before the world of theatre, music, and film, Michael Crawford was a lonely twenty-one-year-old sitting in a church, mourning the loss of his recently deceased mother.

The days of her death and burial had been especially hard on Michael. The woman who had spent the last two decades looking after him, caring for him, loving him, laughing with him, and crying with him was no more. It was almost too much for Michael to bear.

He found himself back in the church where his mother had often taken him. A sorrowful prayer formed inside him. In the silence of eternity, the young man poured out his grief into the lap of his loving Savior. He didn't expect Jesus to raise his mother from the dead. He really didn't know what to expect. He only knew that he needed to pray.

There was no miracle of resurrection that day, but there was a miracle taking place. While he was praying in the church, Michael felt the comfort of the Holy Spirit washing through him. A sense of peacefulness and understanding replaced the sorrow that had filled his heart. A seed of regeneration, watered by his tears and brought to life by God, had been planted in Michael's heart.

There's a reason for things happening in life, Michael thought to himself. *From this point on I will take what I've been taught by my mother and go on with my life and do good with it.*

Michael felt God speaking to him and felt that his mother would have wanted this. So gathering his courage, he walked out of that church to face the world with confidence found only in God.

15

Ain't it Grand?

Kelly Nelon Thompson, a southern gospel performer, has recorded over twenty albums and six videos. Many of her songs have been number one on the charts. She has appeared on television; she has performed in sold-out concert halls; she has won three Grammy Awards and many Dove Awards; she has won a Gospel Voice Award, a New York Film Festival Bronze Award, and numerous Singing News Fan Awards. She also performs on cruises, at amusement parks, and in local churches. But Kelly's style is simple. One such tribute is her rendition of "I Have Decided to Follow Jesus," sung in Navajo. Her songs have the capacity to soften any heart — young, old, fragile, hardened.

But on January 22, 1997, Kelly Nelon Thompson wasn't caring about her credits. As a mom, she was desperately worried about her newborn baby.

She had carried the child during the recording of a new album with her family, The Nelons. She had felt the child kick and move inside her. She and her husband, Jerry, awaited the day they would welcome their baby into the world. The day finally came on January 20, 1997. Two days later doctors discovered a hole in the child's lung, resulting in oxygen-deficient blood. The little life hung in the balance as the baby was placed in intensive care.

Kelly was distraught, filled with emotion and fear. She turned to the only one she knew could help her: Jesus. As she was praying for her child to recover, Kelly thought of a dear family friend and fellow gospel singer, Vestal Goodman. Kelly wished she could spill her heart to Vestal's listening ear; she wished Vestal could be there to pray for the new life God had brought into her family. But Vestal could be anywhere on a gospel tour.

Kelly continued praying and waiting to see how God would respond. Unexpectedly, the phone rang. On the other end was Vestal Goodman, calling to chat with Kelly.

Until the phone call, Vestal had had no idea that Kelly's baby had complications. She simply felt impressed by God to check on her friend, calling around until she'd tracked down Kelly's phone number. Then Vestal prayed for the baby, for Kelly, and for the family.

Two hours later doctors reported a miraculous change in the baby's condition. The hole in the lung was closing itself! By the next day, January 23, the lung was completely healed. With joy, Kelly and Jerry thanked God for healing their child.

16

Alphabet Dreams?

Janice Thatcher woke up with a start. The night was still dark, but she was wide awake.

DCE. DCE. DCE.

Those three letters kept running through her mind as if planted there by some subconscious force. She lay in bed for a few moments, thinking *DCE? What is that?*

Janice rolled over and tried to get back to sleep, but she still felt troubled by her thoughts. Too many decisions were weighing on her mind. Among the weighty decisions was where to attend college next year. Having just completed a two-year program at a junior college in the San Diego area, Janice was at a crossroad. It was time to choose the four-year university where she would complete her degree — and time to decide what that degree's focus would be. Shouldn't a junior in college know by now what she wanted to do with her life?

Janice wasn't sure. She sighed and rolled over again. *DCE. DCE. DCE.* The letters continued to echo in her mind.

Janice had been praying for weeks now, asking God's direction to help her know which major and career to pursue. Honestly, all she wanted to do was serve the Lord in the way he wanted. But what did he want? Janice didn't know, so she prayed each day for God to reveal his will to her.

The frustrated college student started to drift off to sleep once more, then suddenly her eyes flew open.

DCE! she thought.

Wasn't that somewhere on the bulletin board at church? Yes, it was. It was on the flier about Christ College in Irvine, California — a place about an hour north of Janice's San Diego area home. DCE, of course! It stood for "Director of Christian Education." In many Christian denominations, the DCE was the person in charge of the educational ministry of a local church.

Could the director of Christian education be God's direction for me?

With possibilities meandering through her head, Janice dropped off to sleep. The next morning, she sent a letter to Christ College, requesting information about their director of Christian education program. When the proper materials arrived a few weeks later, she knew she had the answer she'd been praying for.

Janice Thatcher enrolled in Christ College and earned her bachelor's degree in the DCE program. Janice shared what she was learning and practicing in her own church and as an intern in the magazine department at the church resources company, Group Publishing. Before long, Janice became the editor of Group Publishing's *Junior High Ministry* magazine, using her college training to empower thousands of DCEs across the nation in their ministries to America's young people.

17

The Goats Head Club

Matt, Charlie, Steve, and Dan prayed silently as they approached the door of the San Francisco nightclub. They were scheduled to perform there that night but had second thoughts when they saw the bouncer standing at the door wearing a T-shirt that proclaimed, "666 is my favorite number."

The four guys in Jars of Clay (Dan Haseltine, Steve Mason, Charlie Lowell, and Matt Odmark) had been praying for an opportunity to use their music to reach out to unbelievers. They had pleaded with God — both individually and collectively — to let them be "bridge builders" and "ground softeners" who prepare the way for Christ to come into people's lives. When they received the invitation to play at the city's party spot by the bay, they had accepted. And now, despite reservations, they were determined to go through with their performance of Jesus-focused songs in the San Francisco hangout.

About an hour before midnight, they walked inside the nightclub and saw a big goat's head — a symbol of Satan worship — prominently displayed above the stage. They laugh about it now, but at the time they weren't sure how to react. Dan says, "We were all pretty naive to the club scene. We didn't know *what* to expect. . . . [The goat's head] showed us that this is *not* a place Christians frequent! I think we were all really scared about how people were going to react to what we were doing and things we were singing."

The guys began their set. Just then, a fight broke out in the back of the bar. Trying to calm their shaking nerves, the four young men continued singing, praying for God's Spirit to take over and bring peace to the room. They sang, and stone-faced drinkers stared back up at them — or simply ignored them altogether. They performed hit tunes like "Love Song for a Savior" and "Flood."

Almost imperceptibly, a hush began to fall over the nightclub. Trickling through the strings, keyboards, and lyrics, the message of the music started penetrating the hearts of those who had previously ignored it. God was present, moving quietly in the club, answering the silent prayers of the band members who had asked to be vehicles of his love to this lost world.

"By the end of the set," Dan says, "the transformation that took place from the beginning of the show to the end of the show was so obvious . . . just to watch the faces turn from very stone cold, to transparent. It was intense that night."

Steve adds, "We were so afraid, and there were so many variables involved. It was obvious this was one of those places where God wanted us to trust him. . . . We were kind of ill at ease because we knew we were right there where the Word and the world were colliding, and we were watching it happen."

The band reports that new prayers passed their lips — prayers of praise and deeper commitment. "OK, God," Steve remembers praying. "We know this is what you want us to do. You've worked here and shown us that if we're obedient to this calling then you have work to do in these people's lives."

18

Indiana Prayers

"Heather's desperately ill."

Sandi Stonehill audibly choked back her tears on the phone line. Christian musician Randy Stonehill sank into the hotel-room bed, stunned.

It was November 1982. The man known to his fans as "Uncle Rand" was on the last leg of a concert tour that finished up in Indiana. As was his custom before a concert, he called his wife in Seal Beach, California.

When he called, she gave him the news: Their eight-month-old daughter, Heather, was ill. The physicians had extracted a vial of spinal fluid, and instead of being clear like healthy fluid, it was milky and white. The doctors diagnosed Heather with spinal meningitis.

Sandi continued relating the news to Randy. "They said she could die. If she doesn't die — if she survives it — she could still come out of the experience with retardation or deafness, or muscular problems — any number of things. So we're in bad shape here." She broke off.

The couple ended their conversation. Devastated and in shock, Randy sat on the edge of the bed. A thousand thoughts flooded his mind. He prayed, earnestly seeking God's healing hand. Randy caught himself trying to strike a bargain. "God, if you'll heal Heather, then I'll . . ." But he realized that God didn't need anything Randy had to offer — and that God actually cared about Heather more than he did.

"I realized there was nothing I could do, which is a very helpless, vulnerable feeling," Randy reports today. "But then I realized that God was God, and what I needed to do was trust grace."

Trembling, Randy picked up the phone and called his wife back. "Please don't be angry at me. I think God is telling me to stay and — I don't know how I'm going to get through the show tonight 'cause I'm sort of in shock — but I think I'm supposed to stay and have the audience pray for Heather."

Sandi did not respond angrily, as Randy had expected. "I think you're right. Stay and do the show tonight and call me. And do the show tomorrow night and call me."

There was silence on the line as Sandi composed herself. "There's nothing you can do if you're here. You could sit at her bedside and pray or you can pray in Indiana. God's going to hear you either way. God's going to do what he's going to do."

Though he felt his heart had been ripped out, Randy went onstage that night and performed. During the concert, he paused and enlisted the audience in prayer for his baby daughter. He repeated the request the next night. When Randy entered the plane to go home that third day, all he knew was that Heather wasn't getting better; but she wasn't getting worse.

When Sandi picked up her husband at the airport, her eyes were red but dry. "Doctors don't know what's going on, but Heather's recovering — rapidly!"

Noting Heather's health improvement, the doctors took another sample of spinal fluid. This time the fluid was clearing up! The meningitis was leaving. The puzzled doctors returned to the original milky fluid they'd removed from Heather's spine three days prior. Much to their surprise, the fluid in that vial was miraculously clearing up too — at the same rate that Heather was recovering. As the fluid in the vial progressed, so did Heather. In a short time the vial was clear — and Heather was healed. God had answered those Indiana prayers to the most minute detail.

Sixteen years later, Randy — now the father of a teenager — reports there have been no aftereffects of the disease whatsoever. He still tears up when relating the story of how God healed both his daughter and a vial of fluid, commenting with a grateful smile, "This is how romantic God is."

19

A Meeting with God

John Croyle almost didn't stop by that day in 1988, but he was in Pensacola and decided to visit his friend anyway.

John spent most of his time at the Big Oak Ranch in Gadsden, Alabama. He and his wife, Tee, had started the place more than two decades ago to provide homes for orphaned and abused children. At Big Oak Ranch, the Croyles have ministered to over thirteen hundred children who have grown up there. The Croyles have been answers to the prayers of others.

But this day John had a prayer of his own. He had located a piece of property that was perfect for the new girls' ranch he was hoping to build, but it cost forty thousand dollars — which was forty thousand dollars more than Big Oak Ranch could spare. John felt strongly that God was leading him to buy this land, so he made it a matter of prayer. He outlined the need to God, then asked him to provide the means to purchase the property.

On his business trip to Pensacola, John visited his friend, a man who was a successful and busy attorney. Little did John know that God was about to arrange an important meeting through that visit.

John entered the friend's office and greeted him warmly. The lawyer returned the greeting, then asked curiously, "What are you working on now?"

"Well, I'm trying to put together a girls' ranch. There's one piece of property that's going to cost us forty thousand dollars. . . ."

Before he could finish, the phone rang. On the other end of the line was the lawyer's partner. "What are you doing?"

Smiling at John, the lawyer in the office answered, "Well, I'm sitting here talking with John Croyle about this girls' ranch he's wanting to build and this piece of property."

"What's he want?" the partner asked.

"Forty thousand dollars."

Without hesitating, the partner said, "You do half; I'll do half."

When John's friend immediately agreed, John realized that his prayer had been answered affirmatively.

Ninety seconds later John Croyle walked out of the lawyer's office with forty thousand dollars to buy that piece of property. He would build that girls' ranch after all!

Looking back on that experience, John still marvels at God's timing. God had put it in John's mind to visit the friend and then convened a phone meeting with the two lawyers right on the spot.

"That's big-boy stuff!" John comments today, adding, "There's no such thing as a little miracle. They're all big."

20

Interview with a Killer

It was probably when the killer sat down in front of him at that Florida prison that Bill first thought, *What in the world am I doing here?* Swallowing his discomfort, Bill proceeded with the interview. He had to. It was an answer to a prayer he had prayed years before.

As a collegian at the University of Washington, Bill had taken a course in writing. The Cs and Ds he earned on assignments in that class soon convinced him he was not cut out for that line of work.

Twenty years old at the time, Bill approached God with a prayer: "Lord, I'll do anything for you that you want me to. Except write, of course."

Following God's leading, Bill changed his major to stage directing and earned a degree from the university. He traveled to Italy, adding filmmaking to his studies, and completed his coursework at the Italian State Institute of Cinema in Rome. Bill attacked the avenues of stage and screen with a passion. Returning to the United States, he acted and directed, using his gifts and talents on a variety of stage and film productions.

Then one day a publisher approached Bill and

asked him to write a book. He thought about turning it down — after all, he had made poor grades on many of his college papers. But the prayer he prayed as a twenty-year-old still echoed in his heart: *Lord, I'll do anything for you that you want me to. . . .* Maybe it was time for Bill to drop the *except* from that prayer. Did God want him to write? Bill accepted the opportunity.

More than forty books and two dozen screenplays later, Bill Myers is still writing. He's received over forty national and international awards for his work. He authored and cocreated the video series McGee & Me! Each of these videos has sold over 2 million copies. Related book sales total 450,000 copies. Additionally, he's sold over a million copies of other Christian books for children and youth. He is the author of Christian thriller novels for adults like *Threshold* and *Blood of Heaven*.

It was his research for *Blood of Heaven* that brought him face-to-face with a convicted murderer in the Florida prison. The premise of the book was a game of "What if . . ." that explored the changes a hardened criminal might experience if he received a sample of Christ's DNA. Bill felt it would be important to research his novel to the fullest extent — which meant visits to genetic labs as well as prisons.

Bill was determined to be present for that interview with a killer. He had to. It was one of many answers to a prayer he had constantly prayed.

21

God at the Grammys?

If you watched the 1996 Grammy Awards, you remember that a highlight of the show was when Christian singer CeCe Winans performed a gospel segment with mainstream singer Whitney Houston. A standing ovation erupted at the end of that portion of the show, with Christians and non-Christians alike touched by the Spirit of God through the performance. But CeCe Winans originally wasn't even scheduled to perform. The show's organizers had decided against including a gospel segment.

However, CeCe didn't believe them. During her prayer time, she felt God strongly encouraging her to pray for her performance at the Grammys. She knew she wasn't scheduled to sing but prayed to that end anyway. "It's almost like God put it in my spirit [that] it was going to happen before it happened. And I just began to pray on it and ask the Lord to magnify or to let it be an explosion. Let it be something that people will remember and will remember him in."

Then she waited — but not for long. She chuckles. "All of a sudden, things just started happening. God started working in the minds and the hearts of men. And Whitney called me, and she said, 'CeCe, they're only going to do a gospel singing if I'm a part of a gospel segment.' I was like, 'Oh, really?' And right then I knew God had started working."

The two singers began planning for the newly installed gospel segment of the show. They would start off with the duet they had recorded, "Count on Me," but then what? CeCe made it a matter of prayer once more and felt God was leading her to sing "I Surrender All." But that was a mellow song, a plain old hymn from days gone by. Would the director go for that one?

With a twinkle in her eye, CeCe reports that soon after, "The musical director called and said, 'CeCe, what do you want to do? I was thinking about "I Surrender All." ' And I said, 'Yeah, that would be good.' So it's like all through that whole planning thing, I was just like, 'God, you are tripping me out!' "

In a matter of days, the show had gone from no-gospel-segment-and-no-CeCe Winans to straight-up-gospel-with-CeCe Winans and Whitney Houston!

When it came time to perform, CeCe gratefully remembers, "Before we went on, I prayed. I was like, 'Lord, I'm not here for myself. It's not about me. It's all about you. You anoint this thing.' And the power that came in that place was just incredible!"

22

The Grinning Pastor

Max grinned in his office at the little Florida church where he was an associate pastor. He was really enjoying himself.

He paused for a moment, then typed out the next sentence for his column in the church bulletin. Creating this column was part of his pastoral responsibilities at the Central Church of Christ in Miami, Florida. He knew this would only go out to the people in his church, but he gave it his all anyway. That wasn't difficult to do, for he really enjoyed putting together those short pieces for the congregation.

The congregation enjoyed the pieces too. "You should try to get these published!" many exclaimed each week when a new bulletin came out. Max would smile, shake his head and say, "Well, maybe . . . and maybe not!"

After two years at Central Church, Max was approved to pursue his dream of being a missionary to South America. With warm farewells from his congregation, he packed his things and moved to Brazil to spread the good news of Jesus there.

He arrived in Rio de Janeiro, Brazil. He immediately plunged into a crash course in Portuguese, doing the best he could to learn the new language so he could communicate with those in the mission field. Still, in the back of his mind he heard the words of the Miami church about his articles in the bulletin: "You should try to get these published!"

A seed had been planted, and Max began to pray, asking God to help him decide whether or not to pursue publication of his weekly musings. Although his days were filled with studying Portuguese verbs and nouns and dialect, his evenings were almost always free. During those evenings in Brazil, he pulled out his past columns and worked to compile them into a coherent manuscript.

Max continued to pray through the writing; then he sent out his new manuscript to a publisher. He waited weeks for an answer. When the letter came, it was a rejection notice. The publisher wasn't interested in what Max had to offer.

Could this be God's answer? Max wondered. He thought about giving up, but deep inside he felt God urging him to send the book to another publisher. So he did. . . .

And got another rejection letter.

Max sent his manuscript to fourteen Christian publishers and received fourteen different rejection letters. The fifteenth publisher on Max's list was Tyndale House Publishers in Illinois. He mailed his book one last time. . . .

And this time Max Lucado's first book was accepted. Published with the title *On the Anvil*, it began his professional writing career.

Since then, Max Lucado has written *No Wonder They Call Him the Savior, In the Grip of Grace, When God Whispers Your Name*, and *Just Like Jesus*, among other books. His books have sold over 5 million copies. His lyrical writing style has earned him several awards, including two Gold Medallion Christian Book of the Year Awards. During the 1990s his books were often among the best-sellers. He has much to offer to twentieth- and twenty-first century Christians.

Max chuckles when remembering his start as a writer. "*[On the Anvil]* is actually the only book I've ever done with Tyndale. But it was the first one, and I've always been thankful to the Tyndale people for publishing it."

23

College Confusion

Junior college student Jim Gray was out-and-out confused. He was hardly able to make sense of anything. An overwhelming amount of financial-aid paperwork was the source of his dilemma.

"It seemed like every other day in the mail I was receiving something that I had to sign for some kind of loan or whatnot. And with all the different loans and grants and scholarships that are available, it's really confusing."

Although he was bewildered by the financial-aid process, he felt certain about one thing: God was leading him to transfer out of junior college and continue his studies at Anderson University in Anderson, Indiana.

"I'd planned on transferring to Syracuse University . . . and that all changed. Through prayer and conversation with God, I got the calling to go into youth ministry; Anderson kept popping up. I felt that if God really wanted me to go there, he was going to provide for me."

Though confused, Jim determined to tackle the maze of forms and applications before him. He enlisted the help of independent financial-aid counselor C. K. Dykstra. "There was a lot of frustration," Jim remembers, "knowing that money was there somewhere but not knowing how to get to it through all the red tape and stuff. [C. K. Dykstra] helped me get through that."

Dykstra not only helped Jim fill out the forms line by line, but he also gave sound advice to help Jim make paying for school a priority.

Jim laughs when he recalls one conversation with Dykstra. " 'Don't be spending!' he said to me. 'Now's not the time to blow the money you're making. You need to save your money.' That's something I had a hard time with. [But now] I really wish I would have saved more money!"

Dykstra also encouraged Jim to be willing to work to help pay his own way — even if it meant scrubbing dorm toilets and cleaning classroom desks through the college work-study program. Jim worked as a janitor through college, earning the nickname "Janitor Jim" from his classmates.

With financial-aid forms out of the way, Jim knew he had to make the biggest investment he could toward school — an investment in prayer.

"I prayed that if God wanted me [here] that he would make it possible."

Jim also recruited several youth leaders at his church to pray specifically for his school finances because "the financial part of it was the only thing that was going to hold me back." The youth leaders held occasional prayer meetings in their homes, asking God to provide money for

Jim's schooling.

Jim's investments paid off when he sat down in the Financial Aid Office of Anderson University to go over his aid package. He found that the aid was enough.

Reflecting on that meeting, Jim smiles. "When I saw that financial-aid package, I was ecstatic about it. That was an answer to prayer."

24

Redeeming Prayer

Rob Anderson held the letter in his hand and smiled. He read it again, then folded it up and put it in a safe place. He had to keep this one. It was an answer to prayer.

Rob remembered the day when he started praying his prayer. A successful game designer who had helped create Scattergories and Catch the Mouse, Rob turned an eye toward the games that were being created for teenagers. What he found were dark fantasy/adventure games: Dungeons and Dragons; Magic: The Gathering; and Vampire: The Eternal Struggle.

That was when the prayer began to form in his heart. "Lord, help me to create a morally positive alternative to these games. Help me to create a game for teenagers that will draw them closer to you."

Making that his constant prayer, Rob set to work. Adopting the trading card method of Magic: The Gathering, he designed a fantasy/adventure game for teenagers based on biblical themes.

Carefully crafting the game, Rob decided that the quest would be to win lost souls. The "heroes" would be godly men and women found in the pages of the Bible. The "villains" would reflect real-life characters whose prototypes are mentioned in Scripture. To help them win lost souls, players would be armed with Bible-based "enhancement" cards, and even a few "miraculous" power cards. Because each player could choose the cards that go into his or her own deck, no two decks would be exactly the same.

With the craft finished, Rob hired the finest artists available to create illustrations for the cards. He called his new game Redemption and released it in the summer of 1995. A year and a half later, a quarter million decks of the game had been sold. Redemption tournaments cropped up in schools, and in some areas youth groups were playing Redemption every week. The Redemption worldwide championship takes place each year.

But what really made it all worthwhile for Rob was the letter. It was the first letter he'd received from a fan of the game, a young man who was then a sophomore in college.

This teenager had been raised in a Christian home but had abandoned his faith while away at school. He had also become involved in playing several unhealthy, role-playing fantasy games. Along the way, someone introduced him to Redemption. God began convicting him with the gospel message of the game and the Scriptures found on each card. Before long, he had thrown out the dark fantasy games and recommitted his life to Jesus. He wrote Rob Anderson to tell him about it.

"I think that will stand out in my mind above anything else," Anderson says today. "Now, I've gotten other letters since then from kids who have gotten out of the dark and horrific games, and they've started reading their Bibles or walking closer with the Lord. But I think the first one that I got was probably the most memorable. It was so exciting!"

25

More like a Whisper

To be honest, Joyce Martin McCollough was ready to leave. As one-third of the award-winning southern gospel trio the Martins, Joyce had gathered with her siblings at their record company's office building to preview new songs in hopes of finding a few for their new album.

Looking back on that day of listening to songs in Phil Johnson's office, big sister Joyce admits, "We were not really in the best of moods. And we were not really agreeing about song selection and all that."

Eventually Phil said, "I have one more song to play you." He cued up a song written by Scott Krippayne and Steve Siler called "More Like a Whisper."

Judy Martin Hess, the "little sis," wasn't listening all that closely either. She and Joyce almost let this song pass by. Then she noticed Jonathan, the brother in the middle of the two girls, weeping quietly as he listened. Judy and Joyce immediately tuned in to the song.

The lyrics of the chorus rang out, "When questions rain down like thunder, sometimes the answer is more like a whisper. . . ."

With tears rolling down his face as the song ended, Jonathan said, "That makes me think about Taylor."

Taylor Martin, Jonathan's son and the nephew of Joyce and Judy, was born as a twin with his brother, Michael, on New Year's Eve, 1995. Jonathan and his wife, Melinda, were thrilled to welcome the boys into the world. But they were worried since the twins weren't expected until March 1996.

Born two-and-a-half months premature, both babies struggled at birth, and doctors weren't sure either would survive. Family and friends prayed, and somehow the boys gained strength and were allowed to go home healthy. No one knew anything was still wrong with Taylor until just over a year later, February 1997.

Michael had begun sitting up and crawling and doing all the things babies do, but Taylor still was not progressing in his development. Tests revealed that Taylor had brain damage — the crippling disease cerebral palsy.

Jonathan and Melinda, along with their extended families and friends, immediately began praying for healing, asking God to restore health to this child. In concert after concert across the country, Jonathan shared about his sons and requested prayer for Taylor. Deep inside Jonathan hoped for a miracle of the mountain-moving kind. He wanted his child to be completely transformed by the healing power of God.

But sometimes miracles don't come in that

shape and size. Sometimes they're more like a whisper.

When Taylor was around eighteen months old, he did something doctors weren't sure he'd ever do. He began to speak.

Yes, he still had cerebral palsy. Yes, he was still unable to walk. Yes, he still had difficulty moving his lower body and his arms. But he did begin to speak.

Jonathan states, "He says, 'Dada,' and 'Mama,' and 'Papa.' But he also says the name of Jesus, which is for us a very, very special thing."

If Taylor is able to speak, then it's possible he will walk and grow and eventually be able to live a normal life, despite his disability. Taylor's voice became a whispered answer to Jonathan's prayer, a breath of hope.

Jonathan explains, "God didn't just heal Taylor, but through Taylor improving and starting to speak, it was that little one-and-a-half-year-old voice speaking 'Daddy' and saying 'Jesus' and saying 'I love you,' confirmed in my heart that 'Hey! This is your answer. This is God saying everything's going to be all right.'"

Back in the record company's office, Judy said to Phil Johnson, "We've got to listen to that one again." Phil cued up the tape of "More Like a Whisper" once more. When the song ended this time, there wasn't a dry eye in the room.

"More Like a Whisper" made the album. You can hear it on the Martins' CD, *Dream Big*. If you're a fan of the Martins, you'll notice something special about this song on the album. The trio opted not to sing it in their trademarked three-part harmony style. Jonathan sings it solo, telling the world that sometimes God's answer to prayer is more like a whisper.

26

Stage Fright!

By the time she was seventeen years old, Nikki Leonti had already released her debut album, *Shelter Me* — a CD that immediately rode up the charts to a slot in *CCM Update*'s top-five Christian albums and earned a place in the top twelve on the *Billboard* charts. She has also toured the nation singing her lively brand of pop music.

When Nikki confidently takes the stage for a show, she fears little when it comes to singing. She loves to sing — it comes easily. But when it comes to *talking*, Nikki's confidence fades a little. Performing for an audience comes more naturally than sharing about her life in front of them.

"I had a problem talking when I sang or did a concert. I always knew what I wanted and needed to say to people, but I had a fear that they would think I sounded juvenile. I also wanted the courage to talk about past circumstances, such as [when] my six-year-old brother died of cancer. . . . I wanted to share about that, but I never knew how to word it."

For concert after concert, Nikki would sail through her songs with ease, then stumble over her words when it came time to speak. She knew something had to be done.

Nikki turned to the one who created her mouth, who blessed her with the talent to sing. She prayed, asking Jesus to give her courage to share and wisdom to speak the words that others needed to hear. She felt certain that in each audience there might be at least one person who would be helped by hearing how Jesus had brought her through trials and hard times in her life. She prayed for God to help her overcome her stage fright and for God to use her words to minister to those who came to hear her sing.

During March 1998, Nikki stood onstage. She did not know that a hurting young man was sitting in the audience that day. The man's brother was fighting a losing battle against cancer. The man felt helpless and discouraged knowing that his brother would soon die, but he didn't know what to do about it.

Neither Nikki nor the young man could have guessed that they shared this experience. But in between songs, Nikki felt God's strength flowing through her as she shared a bit of her testimony with the audience. She spoke of the despair she felt when her brother passed away and of how Christ had brought her through that time.

The young man sat deep in thought, realizing he was not alone. After the concert, he sought Nikki out and shared his experience with her. The two young people prayed together, thanked God that he had brought them to this place at this time, and asked God for strength and healing in the days to come.

Afterward Nikki thought about how things might have been different if God hadn't answered her prayer or given her the courage to speak about her life. That young man might have walked away never knowing that Jesus could carry him through times of trouble.

Today Nikki rejoices that God continues to answer her prayer for courage. She rarely struggles with stage fright anymore. "Now I share [my] testimony at every concert. And at least one person in the audience will be going through the same thing. I've learned now to open up and share what the Lord is leading me to say."

27

Eleven Angry Commissioners

It was like a scene from the movie *Twelve Angry Men*. In that classic film, Henry Fonda plays the part of a juror who stands alone in his conviction that a defendant is not guilty.

This time, however, there were only eleven decision makers in the room. They had been assigned to the Attorney General's Commission on Pornography. The year was 1986, and the commission had just voted ten to one in favor of releasing a report that did *not* classify pornography as harmful to individuals, families, and society at large.

Dr. James Dobson, founder of the Christian organization Focus on the Family, had cast the sole dissenting vote. The commission had spent the past year and a half studying and debating the effects of pornography on the nation. At the end of the process, only Dr. Dobson believed in pornography's detrimental effects on people.

The commission was about to come to a close. The final week was upon them; everyone looked forward to walking out of their Washington, D.C., meeting room and stepping back into their everyday lives. Then came Wednesday's vote.

Dr. Dobson voted to classify pornography as harmful in the commission's report. The ten other members voted against him.

Thousands of miles away, at the Focus on the Family offices then located in southern California, Dr. Dobson's staff received news of the vote's outcome. Only two days remained before the commission was to dismiss. What could they do to help?

Noontime at Focus headquarters was an unusual sight. Three hundred employees streamed into the organization's parking lot, choosing to give up their lunchtime for corporate prayer. They asked God to allow the truth about pornography to be revealed through the commission. They prayed that Dr. Dobson might be firm in his stance against pornography. They asked for a miracle to occur in the hearts and minds of the members of the commission. When the lunch hour was over, the staff returned to their work, not knowing if their prayers had made a difference.

Thursday morning in Washington, D.C., the attorney general's Commission on Pornography assembled as planned. Unexpectedly, one of Dr. Dobson's opponents asked to speak. Although he had previously demonstrated a liberal approach to pornography, he stunned everyone by telling them he had changed his mind. Now, he saw pornography as a complex moral issue instead of a slight educational one. He proceeded to give an impassioned speech in favor of Dr.

Dobson's position, completely reversing his view — and his vote — from the prior day.

Several of the commissioners nodded their heads. They, too, changed their vote as the discussion continued into Friday — the last day of the commission. The final report issued by these commissioners stated very clearly that pornography is both immoral and dangerous.

Reflecting on that tenuous, yet rewarding, week, Dr. Dobson had only one explanation. "The entire situation changed in a matter of two days. Why? Because three hundred people were fasting and praying."

28

Finding God on the Reservation

Between 9:00 P.M. and 10:00 P.M. on September 19, 1997, forty-one-year-old Rich Mullins was tragically killed in an automobile accident. The man who had written the songs "Awesome God" and "Creed" (which is a musical recitation of the Apostles' Creed) no longer lived on earth.

The Christian community mourned, remembering the uniqueness of Rich's life and musical vision. For some years Rich had been a schoolteacher on a Navajo reservation in New Mexico, where he taught music to the junior highers. His decision to invest his life in Native American children came as an answer to prayer.

During a trip to Asia several years before his death, Rich was able to view Christianity from the perspective of a completely different culture. The result was life-changing for him. "I got to go to Asia for the summer. It was a great opportunity for me to see Christianity from a non-twentieth-century, American slant. What that did for me was confirm the truth of the essence of Christianity, and it challenged my opinions about peripheral issues."

When Rich returned to the U.S., the idea of

living out his faith in a different culture appealed to him. But family and financial constraints prevented him from returning to Asia. He prayed, asking God for the opportunity to live, work, and reach out to others in the context of a different culture. He prayed for God's direction and asked that God show him how and where to go. Rich desperately wanted to follow God in the matter.

After a time the answer became clear, and he didn't have to travel far to see it. He found different cultures right in the heart of the U.S. "Here in this country we have some two hundred cultures that are *not* white-Anglo-Saxon-Protestant-twentieth-century-evangelical-Christian."

Certain he was following God's direction, he went back to school, earned a degree in music education, then moved to the Navajo reservation in New Mexico to live, teach, and make music within the Navajo culture. "I came here [to the Navajo reservation] hoping to once again include in my vision the slant that these people have."

29

Right Off the College

"A musician's nightmare . . . So horribly uncomfortable. So naked." The voice on the phone winces audibly. The Christian artist Eli remembers struggling as a musician.

On the night before Thanksgiving, Eli found himself prepping for a show at a Penn State University coffee shop called "Right Off the College." Fresh off a few dates at big venues with large crowds, Eli was ready. . . .

Until show time, when he realized the audience that evening would be a paltry seven people.

"You stand in front of a hundred people, you can do no wrong," Eli comments. "It's easy to stand in front of a thousand people because you can smile and they go, 'Yeah!' You sit down and they go, 'Yeah!' But when you get in front of [seven] people like that . . . you'd better have something to say."

Eli felt like leaving, but instead, he decided to pray. Silently he asked God to bless the concert and to be present in the music and the message. Inside he wrestled with nervousness, but he knew God had arranged the situation. Perhaps one of those seven kids really needed to hear what Eli had to share. Maybe it would somehow encourage one person to draw closer to Christ.

Eli prayed that God would use him that night, no matter how few people showed up. Then Eli did what he does best: "We sang songs, and I ministered to them." He shared his faith and how Jesus had rescued him from an addiction to alcohol and drugs, making him a new creature inside and out.

After the concert most of the students went their separate ways to prepare for the Thanksgiving holiday. One student hesitated, however, and made his way up to the artist.

"Man," he said, "I just became a Christian thirty days ago. I've been clean [sober] for thirty days. Thank you so much."

The words of Eli's testimony and the lyrics of his songs had reached out and touched this one student, encouraging a new Christian to pursue a deeper relationship with Christ. The student and the artist lingered during the cold November evening, warming the night with conversation and prayer together. If more people had been in the audience, it's possible the young man might have skipped the chance to chat with Eli. Or perhaps, if he hadn't found a seat, he might have left the show altogether. Two years later Eli smiles when he remembers that encounter.

30

Mom's Little Project

Karyn looked up and down the aisle again, then shook her head and picked up a book. A mother of both a preschooler and a toddler, all she wanted was a Bible storybook to read to her children. But since she was also a trained teacher with a specialty in early childhood, she knew what was — and wasn't — appropriate for young minds.

She returned the book to the shelf. That one wouldn't work — too babyish for her preschooler. Skimming the shelves at the Christian bookstore, she reached for another story Bible and quickly put it down again. The pictures were cute, but the text was way over a little child's head.

Karyn sighed. She hadn't expected it to be this difficult to find a resource for sharing the Bible with her kids. She took one last look at the books that lined the store's shelves. She made a decision and left empty-handed. At this point, no story Bible was a better choice than a poorly done one.

At home, Karyn regaled her two sons with other stories from a set of books she'd ordered through the mail. These books also came with read-along tapes, and her children loved them! The delightful stories reached her kids right where they were, capturing the boys' imagination while teaching a life lesson.

Why not have Bible stories produced in a set like this? Karyn thought in frustration. She wanted to give up but instead pursued her thoughts and turned to God for help.

God, please give me guidance and help me make this dream a reality, she prayed as an idea brewed in her head. That prayer became a constant plea from Karyn during the months that followed, and she began a task many Bible publishers had ignored.

Opening her own adult Bible and recruiting her husband, Ralph, to help with development, Karyn started "translating" stories of the Scripture into language appropriate for — and entertaining to — preschoolers. Before long, the work took on a life of its own as Karyn carefully scripted each scene, even adding her own illustrations to help visualize the text.

"In the beginning the earth was empty. Darkness covered everything. But God was there, and He had a plan . . . ," began Karyn's retelling of the creation story from Genesis.

Slowly but surely Karyn worked, eventually "translating" ninety-five stories from the Bible for children. She quickly had two avid fans in her sons. They thought hearing Mom's new stories was great! Before long, she had another fan, a friend who offered to market the stories for her. At that point, she recruited another friend, Dennas Davis, to illustrate her stories.

Together, Karyn Henley and Dennas Davis put together a series of sixteen paperback Bible storybooks and tapes for kids that they called Dovetales. Those little books were later compiled into one hardcover book just the right size for little hands and renamed *The Beginner's Bible*.

Since that time, Karyn Henley's book has sold over 3 million copies and has been translated into seventeen different languages. The story Bible has inspired CDs, other books, puzzles, and games for children. You may even have a copy of Karyn's book in your child's library!

Reflecting on the time she spent writing *The Beginner's Bible*, Karyn recalls feeling dependent on God for help and direction. "I was always seeking God and yielding the project to him for inspiration and skill. After all, it's his original work!"

31

Let it Rain ... Please?

If you enjoy a good medical thriller, chances are you've already discovered Harry Lee Kraus Jr. A physician by trade, he works as a Christian novelist on the side. His fiction titles include *Fated Genes* and *Stainless Steel Hearts*.

But in 1968 Harry played soccer during recess as a boisterous fourth-grader. He ran, kicked, skidded, blocked, shouted, and generally enjoyed himself out on the school's playground.

Then, after an unexpected collision, Harry got up limping. The pain in his leg told him he must have taken a hard knock. He hobbled to the sidelines for the rest of recess; when the bell rang, he joined his buddies as they all made their way back to the classroom.

The pain in his leg worsened as the day went on. If he had been a doctor back then, he would've quickly diagnosed the problem: a fractured tibia. But Harry was still too young to know he'd broken his leg. He just knew that it hurt badly.

After school, the pain from the injury was so great he couldn't put any weight on his foot. He was unable to walk. Although the school's staff neglected to call Harry's parents to inform them of the accident, a teacher was kind enough to help him climb carefully into the school bus for the daily ride home.

There Harry sat, a fourth-grader with a broken leg, waiting for the bus to take him to his assigned stop. Feeling the pain, he quickly realized he would not be able to walk the quarter mile from the bus stop to his home. Worried and hurting, Harry thought to pray.

He knew that if it was raining, his mother would drive to pick him up so he would not have to walk home in the wet weather. That's what he prayed for. "God, please send rain so my mother will pick me up." He waited nervously as the bus rumbled through the streets toward his assigned stop.

He checked the sky. It was a clear afternoon, but he kept praying.

Suddenly, out of nowhere, a dark cloud emerged and poured rain all over the city! Until that moment, there had been no indication of a storm.

The bus arrived at Harry's stop, and Harry saw his mother waiting patiently in the car. Gratefully, Harry hobbled down the steps into his mother's car. His mother took him to a doctor, who treated the broken leg, giving relief to the suffering boy.

Harry remembers that sudden cloudburst that prompted his mother to be in just the right spot at just the right time. "I knew God had answered my prayer then. And I believe it now."

32

A Ten-Dollar Bag of Dog Food

"Phil, we're out of dog food."

Lisa Vischer hated having to tell her husband that.

It was 1993 and he was working so hard, praying so hard to make his vision a reality. All he wanted to do was tell stories that would improve kids' lives. He wanted to create an animated series that would use vegetables to teach Judeo-Christian values. Phil possessed creative talent. Phil and his buddy, Mike Nawrocki, were already making high-quality products for children.

The only problem was, nobody wanted them.

Phil had approached several Christian publishers with his idea, explaining his vision, showing samples and mock-ups. None of the publishers expressed an interest in his products.

So Phil became his own producer. Taking part-time commercial work to support his family, he plunged into the grinding legwork needed to bring to life his big idea. In fact, he even named his fledgling company that — Big Idea Productions.

Phil contacted just about everyone he knew for start-up capital. His parents took out a second mortgage on their house and gave the money to Big Idea. His sister invested her toddler's college money in the company. Friends from the Vischers' Bible-study group pulled their retirement funds from the bank and loaned them to Phil. The support was overwhelming. In July of 1993, Phil and Mike gratefully set up shop in a small storefront on the north side of Chicago and started producing their first animated video for kids.

Then, unexpectedly, Phil's commercial work ended. Phil and Mike were still producing the video series, and without other projects on the side, Phil had no way to provide for his family — for his wife, two-year-old daughter, and, of course, the family dog.

Phil prayed long and desperately. He asked God for guidance. He pleaded with God to provide for his family while he finished the Big Idea production.

Little by little the family's money trickled away right up until the night Phil discovered they were down to their last ten dollars. That was it. The extent of their monetary holdings was a single ten-dollar bill tucked away in Phil's wallet.

And the dog was out of food, which cost exactly ten dollars.

Reluctantly, Phil handed the bill to his wife and sent Lisa to the store for more dog food. Phil Vischer was officially broke.

Alone and bewildered, Phil wrestled with God in prayer. *Maybe this crazy idea wasn't God's will after all,* he thought. *Maybe it's time to give up.*

He prayed for a while. Then, to distract himself, he thumbed through the day's mail that lay on the table in front of him. Mixed in the pile was a plain-looking envelope with no return address. Curious, Phil opened the letter and read this anonymous note: "God laid it on my heart that you might need this."

Attached was a cashier's check for four hundred dollars.

Phil recalls, "It couldn't have been any clearer if God himself had walked into our apartment and said, 'I'm right here with you. Just keep going.' The battle I was fighting for the hearts and minds of our kids was his, not mine. I have never doubted it since."

Phil Vischer and Mike Nawrocki went on to complete their first video — and more. They called that first video *Where's God When I'm S-scared* and named their series Veggie Tales. To date, VeggieTales has sold over 3 million copies; Big Idea Productions employs around fifty people full time.

And that first video? Recently, it was the number two kids' video in the entire United States, outselling every Barney video, every Rugrats video, every Arthur video, and others snapped up daily in our nation.

Not bad for a guy who could barely afford to buy a bag of dog food, but easy for a God who knew just how — and when — to answer Phil Vischer's prayer.

33

Five-Year-Old Headaches

"Daddy, my head hurts!"

Eddie Elguera's heart went out to his five-year-old son, but try as he might, this caring Dad couldn't seem to bring relief to his child's ailment.

True, Eddie could do many things. For starters, he'd been a two-time national skateboarding champion, performing wonders on his board. Now retired from skating, Eddie worked different kinds of wonders, sharing Christ with teenagers as a youth pastor in southern California.

But when his middle son started having recurring headaches in 1992, Eddie was at a loss. Nothing he could do would bring relief for long. He and his wife took the boy to the doctor, but the physician couldn't find the problem either.

"Maybe it's his sinuses," the medical expert suggested. But none of their treatments made the headaches go away.

Eddie checked his son into Loma Linda Hospital. They were going to run tests and find out what the problem was. The hospital staff did CT-scans and physical examinations, running a full battery of tests on the child. But in the end, the doctors came up empty-handed. They couldn't find anything that would cause the massive headaches the poor boy endured.

Through it all, Eddie and his wife prayed. They pleaded with God to bring relief to their son. They asked the Great Physician to locate the problem and heal it. They knew that when the medical world was at a loss, God was just getting started.

The kindergartner checked out of the hospital no different than when he went in. Eddie brought his boy home and, knowing there was nothing doctors could do to help, prayed all the more fervently for God to intervene. After all, God was a Father too, and he knew what it felt like to have a child who was hurting.

At first nothing seemed to change. The headaches came and went as usual. Then one day Eddie noticed that his son had stopped complaining of pain in his head. No, he wasn't hiding the pain — he just wasn't feeling it anymore. As abruptly as the headaches came, they seemed to disappear.

Eddie waited for the headaches to return, through the end of 1992 and into the beginning of 1993. When 1994 rolled around, Eddie's son still hadn't had another headache. At last check, more than five years later, the child remained headache-free.

Eddie testifies to God's goodness. "We just

prayed and believed and went to my pastor at the church. And just prayed and believed. We just know that God healed him. The headaches went away."

34

Funny Business

Jonathan Slocumb had a problem. A Christian who was also a gifted young comedian, he was praying for a way to break into the comedy circuit.

When Jonathan heard about the Redd Foxx Comedy Search, he thought perhaps that was the answer to his prayer. He decided to enter — and was determined to win.

That was his problem. All the other prominent comedians he knew seemed to get their laughs by lacing their monologues with cursing and obscenity. A self-proclaimed "skinny church boy," Jonathan was not fluent in the language of profanity and was unsure of what to do.

His desire to fit in and win overruled his conscience. "I had never done this before," he recalls, "but I wrote my material out and asked one of my best friends to read it and then write in some curse words where he thought it should be appropriate. So he did, and then I memorized it [for the contest]."

The strategy seemed to work, as Jonathan kept passing the qualifying rounds. In the end Jonathan Slocumb won, tying for first place with another comic. But for Jonathan it was a hollow victory.

God was answering Jonathan's prayer but in a way Jonathan hadn't expected. He was allowing Jonathan to experience the emptiness that comes with success outside of God's will. He was challenging him to live up to a higher standard in his career goals — the God standard.

"I've never been so uncomfortable in my whole life," Jonathan admits. "In fact, I felt like a member of the KKK standing up at the NAACP with his robe on!"

Even as he was posing for his championship picture with Redd Foxx, the Holy Spirit was working on Jonathan's heart. "I said right then, 'I'll never do this again.' "

"I knew I was doing wrong, but I thought, *I'll just do it*. But after I won it, I said, 'I believe I can do this without [cursing]. In fact, I know it. . . .' And that was it. Been going straight up ever since."

Over twelve years later Jonathan's prayer for success and God's humbling response keep him busy. Taking his material from the "holy humor" found inside church walls, Jonathan Slocumb's clean comedy has won an audience of both Christians and non-Christians.

He's performed acts on television spots as different as the Christian talk show *The 700 Club* and HBO's gutter-dwelling *Def Comedy Jam*. He's shared the stage with well-known artists like The Winans, Take 6, Kirk Franklin, Aretha

Franklin, Natalie Cole, and Toni Braxton, and counts among his fans the heavyweight champion boxer Evander Holyfield and the comedy heavyweight Sinbad.

Jonathan has no plans for slowing down. Because of that, prayer still plays a big part in this comedian's life. "I've learned that you can communicate with God all through the course of the day. I mean, as much as you want to or, sometimes, as little as you want to, knowing that he got the message the first time. So . . . I'm in constant communication with the Lord. I don't think that I can move without him!"

35

God Calling?

Gina Brown already had one man in her life, but she was praying for another. Being a single parent was not an easy job.

Married as a teenager, Gina had her first child at the age of nineteen. A beautiful little boy, she named him Corey. Unfortunately, Gina's marriage deteriorated, quickly becoming an abusive — and dangerous — situation. As such, the marriage ended in divorce before Gina's twenty-second birthday.

Newly divorced and struggling to survive, Gina tried to carve out a new life for herself and her son. Whenever Corey laughed, gave Gina a hug, or brightened up a room just by entering it, Gina knew it was worth it all — all the heartache, all the hard times, everything. Gina would pause to pray and thank God for this precious gift.

Still, as much as she enjoyed life with Corey, she couldn't deny the longing within her to be loved and treasured by a husband. She wanted a godly man who would put Christ first in his life and who wouldn't get messed up on drugs and become violent. She wanted someone to enter her life to be both a godly husband and a Christ-like daddy for Corey.

Gina made that her constant prayer, asking God to bring just the right man into her world. She prayed God would bring that man at just the right time and that he would be all she hoped for.

But, of course, men like that don't come calling every day . . . or do they?

Ellejandro Patrick sat with his headset on and prepared for the next call. It was the 1995 holiday season, and Ellejandro was looking for a way to make a little extra money to spend on Christmas gifts. When he heard about the job at the telemarketing firm, he applied for it and got it. Now he was cold-calling person after person, hoping they wouldn't hang up in his face, wishing that this time the person on the other end would actually buy his product. The next person on his list was someone named Gina Brown. . . .

Gina contemplated not answering the phone that day. After all, chances were good it would be just another one of those phone salesmen trying to get her to buy something she didn't want or need. But she answered it anyway. On the other end of the line, Ellejandro started his pitch. Gina knew she ought to hang up, but there was something about the salesman's voice that captured her attention.

The two started talking. Before long, they forgot the sales call and were chatting about more important things — each other! They ended the call, but Ellejandro knew he had to call Gina Brown back again, this time outside of work.

So he did. Gina and Ellejandro quickly became over-the-phone friends, getting to know each other a little better after each conversation. The two decided to meet face-to-face sometime. When they met, they hit it off so well, they started dating regularly. In Ellejandro, Gina found a man who was all she'd prayed for, a man who was a committed Christian and a good person.

"We met each other, and we just clicked and everything was fine," Gina laughs now. "We continued to go out, and the next thing you know, he asked me to marry him! I had been praying that God would bring someone like him into my life."

36

Her Name Was Grace

"Grace Miller, RN" her name badge said. She was a nurse, a woman in her midfifties with short, curly hair who worked at the Boca Raton, Florida, medical clinic where Jodi Jantomaso went for health care. Though the two had never really met, Grace always greeted Jodi with a warm smile and a wave whenever Jodi came into the office.

But that spring Friday in 1988 Jodi didn't notice whether or not Grace was on duty. She had another thing on her mind — her 2:00 P.M. abortion appointment that afternoon. She had arrived at the clinic at 10:00 A.M. for the preliminary blood work and preparations. Now she sat in the waiting room, feeling helpless and afraid.

She hadn't intended for things to work out this way. Twenty-seven years old, Jodi had already been through a painful divorce and had — until recently — been very much in love with a man named Michael. They'd met at the posh resort in Boca Raton where Jodi worked managing the spa and fitness facility. Young, fit, and attractive, she'd quickly caught Michael's eye at the spa. He was handsome as well as wealthy and fun to be around. It wasn't long before they were dating. Soon Jodi moved in with Michael so they could be together more.

"Spiritually, I was at a low point," Jodi admits now. Turning her back on what she knew God wanted, she chose to pursue happiness in the form of her lover, Michael. Together they talked of marriage, children, and living happily ever after.

While Michael was away on a business trip, Jodi found out she was pregnant. She was so excited about telling him the good news! He would return on February 14, 1988, so Jodi planned a special Valentine's surprise to reveal to him that he would be a father.

When he walked in the door on Valentine's Day, he seemed distracted, or tired, or both. Jodi was nearly bursting with excitement. She handed him a gift, a baby's rattle she'd wrapped to clue him in to the pregnancy.

"He opened the rattle, looked at me, and said . . . nothing. I said, 'We're having a baby!' He got up from the table, looked at me, and said, 'Well, things have changed now.'"

And then he dropped the bomb. While on his business trip, he had decided to leave Jodi for another woman — his attorney, Maria. He spoke to Jodi as if the matter were settled. "You'll need to do something about this. Soon."

The next days and weeks were a blur. Jodi found herself sitting in a doctor's office, nervous, numb, and alone, waiting for an abortion. *Oh, God, what am I supposed to do now?* she had cried time and again during the recent days. But God wasn't listening. Or so it seemed.

Before the actual abortion, the doctor wanted to do a preparatory ultrasound. She turned on the equipment and began looking at a fuzzy black image — the inside of Jodi's womb. Suddenly, desperately, Jodi wanted to see what the doctor was seeing. She asked to look at the ultrasound monitor's screen. At first the doctor refused, but when Jodi insisted, the doctor repositioned the screen to allow her a brief glimpse.

Jodi gazed at the near-incomprehensible picture and saw something blinking in the X-ray-like blackness. "What's that?"

"The heartbeat," the doctor replied matter-of-factly.

Jodi was stunned. Tears immediately sprang from her eyes. "I'd been so naive about everything!" she says. "This wasn't just a fetus; it was a live baby!" With that knowledge came a new resolve. Jodi instantly got up from the table, canceled her appointment, got dressed, and went outside, where she sat on the sidewalk, crying.

Oh, God, what am I supposed to do now? she silently sobbed again.

Then Jodi felt someone standing next to her. She looked up and saw the name badge: "Grace Miller, RN."

The kind nurse put a hand on the young

woman's shoulder and spoke. "Jodi, you've made the right choice," she said. "God is going to bless you *and* your baby, and use you more than you could imagine. He'll always provide for you both."

The nurse's words were like a breath of fresh air, and Jodi clung to them, desperate for the hope they offered. Grateful for the encouragement, Jodi thanked the nurse, dried her eyes, and drove home.

Michael was enraged. He tried everything to get Jodi to change her mind, even offering her an envelope containing twenty thousand dollars in cash if Jodi would abort the child. Remembering Grace's words, she refused.

September 29, 1988, Jodi Jantomaso gave birth to a beautiful baby girl, Joelle Aleece. Returning to her Christian roots, Jodi became involved in church again, and when Joelle was only two years old, she joined her mother in singing and performing for their delighted congregation.

Several years after that, Jodi met and fell in love with a Christian musician, Eric Jaqua. They married, and now all three — Jodi, Eric, and Joelle — are involved in speaking and performing for churches and charities nationwide. Inspired by "Grace Miller, RN," they also invest their time in ministering to women who, like Jodi, have found themselves in a crisis pregnancy situation.

The story doesn't end there, though. In 1995, Jodi and Joelle went back to that medical clinic in Boca Raton, hoping to find Grace Miller and thank her in person for helping Jodi to choose life.

But Grace Miller wasn't there. A look at the payroll records from 1988 revealed that *no* Grace Miller had worked at the clinic. Unbelieving, Jodi asked to speak with her former doctor at the facility. Thankfully, the doctor remembered Jodi and came out to greet her.

Jodi explained the situation. To her surprise, the doctor shook her head and said, "There's never been anyone by the name of Grace who's ever worked here."

Then Jodi realized that God was listening when she cried to him for help so many years before. In response, he'd sent an angel of comfort — one appropriately named Grace — to bring hope and courage to Jodi for a few brief, critical moments. And by doing that, he had saved both a child and a mother at the same time.

"Grace left such an impression on me," Jodi says today. "She touched me by her kindness and words — words from God for me. They're never forgotten."

37

A Father's Prayer

John Elefante believes in prayer. The former lead singer of the group Kansas has seen its power time and again. The invitation for him to even join Kansas was an answer to a prayer twenty-five hundred people had prayed at a massive Bible study. John was a new Christian then, trying to decide how his faith would impact his career as a musician.

Quite frankly, John didn't even pray when he bought the shoes. He just wanted comfortable, nice-looking shoes to wear, so he bought a pair of Doc Martens. He had no idea those shoes would one day trigger an answer to something he and his wife, Michelle, were praying about: children.

John and Michelle felt they were ready for parenthood. "We were trying to have kids and had a few problems, so we were casually talking about other options." They were also praying that God would help them know which direction he wanted them to go in regard to children. The couple was really in no hurry, though, and was satisfied to pray and talk and wait on the Lord for direction.

In 1993 John performed at a Harvest Crusade

in California. Backstage after the show, he noticed a woman he did not know walking directly toward him. John paused to talk, assuming she was a fan who might want an autograph or something.

The woman startled John. "You would be the perfect father for a baby to be born in about five weeks!" An earnest discussion ensued about adopting this child.

John and Michelle were nervous going through the whole adoption process. They prayed for God's will to be done, filled out the paperwork, and paid the appropriate preliminary fees. It came time for the birth parents to make a choice. They interviewed John and Michelle and twenty other couples wanting to adopt the child!

Next came the waiting. The Elefantes could do nothing while the birth parents discussed their options. The news came: John and Michelle were chosen as adoptive parents for a beautiful baby girl they called Sammy.

Little did John know that the answer to his prayer was actually triggered by his shopping habits. "When they asked the natural father why he chose us, he said because he liked my shoes. I would have wanted a better answer, but God chooses the foolish things of the world. In the Old Testament, it was a donkey, in the nineties — Doc Martens."

A few years later the Elefantes adopted a little brother for Sammy, naming him Daniel. After experiencing the way God brought these children into his life, John is grateful that God answers prayer. "God wanted these children in our lives and he made it happen. I wouldn't trade them for *anything*. If God came to me right now and said, 'I'll trade you for two biological children,' I'd say, 'Nope. I've got them.' "

38

Late-Night Television

Jim Smith lay awake on the bed, cursing the darkness and pleading with God to erase it at 1:30 A.M. that warm summer night. It seemed like his life had been filled with darkness lately, no matter what time it was.

Jim had been a Christian since high school, active in church and a leader among his peers. During those days, Jim and his best friend, Nicholas, had been inseparable. They had both vowed to take the world for Christ. But, as often happens, Jim and Nick grew up and went their separate ways. Nick married and moved to another state. Jim married also and settled near where he'd grown up. The two friends kept in touch, mostly just trading Christmas cards each year.

As the years rolled on, Jim wavered in his belief — at times on fire for God, at other times allowing the cares of this world to overshadow his commitment to Jesus. That was what had brought him to this point. Several months prior, he'd realized the damage done by ignoring his relationship with Jesus, so he recommitted himself to Christ and pledged to be the man God wanted him to be.

The only problem was that he'd effectively led his family in straying from God, too, and they weren't quite as ready to return as he was. His wife, Candy, an accomplished medical professional, had allowed her career, her friends, and even her husband to distract her from her own commitment to God. Now she was enjoying her unhealthy lifestyle and was unwilling to change.

The friction in Jim and Candy's marriage mounted to the point where the couple even considered divorce. Jim moved to an apartment nearby and spent nights going back and forth from the couple's home to his lonely apartment.

On this night when Jim was visiting the family, he and Candy had a fight. They'd already made plans for him to stay the night, so in frustration Jim went to bed while Candy stayed up a while longer to watch some late-night TV.

It was 1:30 in the morning, and Jim was praying, begging God to heal his marriage and to give him courage to face another day. Broken, he just didn't know what to do. He was exhausted, but sleep wouldn't come. Angry and hurt, Jim felt totally alone.

At 1:45 A.M., Jim looked up to see Candy standing in the doorway, a surprised look on her face. "Nicky is on television — right now!"

Jim bounded out of bed and into the living room. True, there was his old buddy Nick, a guest on the Christian talk show *The 700 Club*. For some reason, the TV station was airing a rerun of the show to fill its early morning programming. Nicky was talking about a book he'd written, an encouragement for families to draw closer to God and each other.

"As soon as I heard Nick's voice," Jim reports now, "the Spirit of God just came over me like a wave. I experienced God's presence in a way I haven't felt him in years. I felt him telling me, 'If you just get through this [current difficulty], you'll see how mightily I'm going to bless you.'"

Jim and Candy's problems didn't disappear the next morning; they are still working through some of their difficulties. With tears in his eyes, Jim says, "Seeing Nicky right at that moment was an answer to prayer. *That* was my miracle."

39

Changing Times

By all rights, Terri Blackstock should have been happy with her career. Writing romance novels under two pseudonyms, she had established herself as a favorite — and sold more than 3 million books in the process.

But something wasn't right, and Terri knew it. Writing romantic fiction in the mainstream market required her to include a strong sexual undercurrent in her books. The mainstream market also welcomed profanity. As a Christian, Terri felt increasingly uncomfortable about writing that kind of fiction.

Still, the money was good, and she was gifted at writing. Perhaps God didn't mind *too* much. . . .

The struggle within her became too great. She hated the thought that something she wrote might become a stumbling block for another Christian. After much prayer and thought, Terri made a decision. She would never again write anything that didn't glorify God. If that meant the end of her writing career, so be it.

Her decision posed two problems. She was already under contract to write more romance novels for her publisher. "I knew that under my new commitment to God, I could not write the books I had agreed to write. But I had been paid for them and had lived on that money. I didn't have it to pay back!"

Terri immediately made that a matter of prayer. Although she didn't know how to work out the details honorably, she knew that God could find a way. So she prayed, asking the Lord to help her keep the new commitment she'd made to him.

Then mustering her courage, she informed her publisher of the decision to stop writing mainstream romance. She asked if she might be able to buy back the outstanding contracts, thereby releasing her of the obligation to write books she no longer felt comfortable writing. Her publisher begrudgingly acquiesced but did not understand Terri's perspective. The publisher agreed to allow Terri to buy her way out of the contracts.

Then came the real surprise. When the publisher tallied the amount of royalty money still owed to Terri for previous books, it was more than she needed to buy her way out of the contracts! Even after deducting enough to pay for the cancelled contracts, they still owed her money.

Terri gratefully thanked God for his provision, but there was still another problem — a more personal one: Terri's agent. This woman had been Terri's ardent supporter — and friend — for over a decade. This friend depended on

Terri's work to contribute to both their incomes. Though she knew she must, Terri hated the thought of hurting her friend by discontinuing their work relationship.

So she prayed again, fervently asking Jesus for help and guidance on when and how to break the news to her agent. God affirmatively answered that prayer. Terri's agent unexpectedly called one day to say she'd decided to leave the business and that Terri should find a new agent!

Terri reports, "This woman had been an agent for most of her adult life and was completely focused on it. I would never have imagined that she would give it up for anything. God knew better."

Breaking her ties with mainstream romance publishing, Terri set about writing more wholesome fare for Christians. Within a few years she had become a favorite for her Newporte 911 series. The suspenseful Newport 911 series exhibits her new vision. Terri aims to honor God in her writing.

She testifies, "When I go through trials, I often try to remember all the ways that God answered my prayers a few years ago. It reminds me that he is in control, that he's listening, that he loves me."

40

Back to School?

"I knew I was going to finish high school, and I was going to go to college," says Susan Lee. "I wanted to so badly, but I just didn't see how I was going to do it. Where was the money going to come from?"

As a twenty-one-year-old sophomore at Christian Heritage College in San Diego, Susan Lee was older than her peers — and older than her years. When she was fifteen, she had become an adult, staying in San Diego while the rest of her family moved to Los Angeles. Over the next three years she'd worked her way through high school, earning good grades and money for living expenses.

Upon graduation, attending a Christian college seemed financially unfeasible. Susan struggled to pay her regular bills and winced over college tuition and books. She took classes at a junior college and finally dropped out of school altogether.

It was during that time that she felt God prompting her not to give up on college just yet. "I prayed, 'Lord, I need you to make a huge change in my life' because I'd gotten to a point where I was so directionless. I didn't know what was going to happen to my life."

Over the next few weeks, Susan became reacquainted with old friends from her church and made new friends who were attending Christian Heritage College. "All I heard about [from them] was this school!"

She decided to visit the campus. *Just to go in and get information.* Soon it became obvious that she couldn't afford to pay for tuition. Still, she remembered her prayer and decided to apply for admission anyway.

"I made the decision that this was what I was going to do. God had provided for me financially all my life, and I knew he wouldn't stop now. I knew he wasn't going to let me be stranded."

Not long after that decision, Susan got a call from an aunt she had lived with briefly in the past. "Susan, I got some mail for you a couple months ago."

Susan went to pick it up and saw that it was from the state of California. It seems that when she had dropped out of school before, she'd had an application for a state-funded Cal Grant pending. Now, two years later, they wanted to know if she still wanted the money — which was enough to cover more than half of her expenses at Christian Heritage!

From that point on, Susan became a regular visitor at the Financial Aid Office of Christian Heritage College. She was determined to find a way to pay for this school. "I was persistent.

They saw me in that office every day. They were all saying, 'Susan's here. Oh, dear.' But they were very good." In the end, they were able to piece together enough financial aid for Susan to return to school.

41

Trouble with Tics

It was the early 1990s, and Michael W. Smith and his wife, Debbie, were worried.

Their eight-year-old son, Ryan, who was otherwise healthy and active, had recurring facial tics. The tics had started suddenly when Ryan was seven and had continued into his eighth year. Without warning, his face would start twitching, sometimes becoming so violent that he would actually fall to the floor.

One doctor diagnosed Ryan's problem as Tourette's syndrome. A counselor suggested that emotional problems triggered the tics. Neither of these diagnoses matched with what Michael and Debbie saw in their son from day to day.

The Smiths did not know the cause of Ryan's problem and were unsure how to treat it. Since modern medicine could offer no help, they decided to treat the tics with prayer instead of pills. Michael and Debbie began praying for Ryan together and individually. They asked the Great Healer to help their son and to heal whatever was causing the tics.

At first they saw no change. Months passed, and Ryan had not improved. Then one day after prayer together, Michael and Debbie felt an overwhelming sense of peace, comfort, and confidence that God had indeed heard their prayers.

Recalling that moment, Michael says, "I remember at one point Deb and I just praying and just getting up and going, 'You know what? He's going to be OK. He's going to be OK. I think God really heard us.'"

Ryan continued having difficulty. His face would twitch and twitch, and no relief seemed to be in sight. But after that prayer, the Smiths were unphased by the continued problem. "It didn't go away immediately," says Michael, "but we just stood our ground [and said], 'Hey, you know what? God's in control. He's going to be OK.' I just never had a doubt."

So they waited. One month. Two months. Ryan still battled the twitching. Three months. Four months. Then suddenly, at five months, Ryan was healed!

During the period when the tics continued, Michael thought, *Oh, maybe he's not OK. . . .* Then he'd say to himself, *Hey We've committed him to the Lord and we believe God's healed him.*

Michael says, "Before Ryan's ninth birthday, he had a few more tics. And three, four, five months later — boom! Gone! History!"

42

Warts and All

Sometimes it seemed to Marty Nagy that he and his brother were cursed. No matter what they tried, neither could rid himself of recurring warts. For Marty, the warts appeared primarily on his right hand, and nothing could make them go away for long.

Sometimes Marty tried burning the unsightly growths off, repeatedly removing them with the heat of a flame. He tried freezing them until they came off. Still, it seemed that just as he'd get rid of one, another would crop up somewhere on his hand. He couldn't keep up with them.

Then two warts started growing right under his fingernails. The larger they grew, the more they pressed on Marty's nails, and the more painful they became. About the same time, a new rash of warts began to cover his hand. Before long Marty had nearly twenty warts on his hand — and the two under his fingernails were getting more painful each day.

In desperation, Marty turned to his friend, a Catholic priest, for help. Marty asked his friend if he would pray for God to heal the wart-covered hand. Perhaps God would have pity and at least make the two under his nails go away.

Following biblical instructions, the priest carefully anointed each of Marty's warts with oil. Then he prayed to Jesus, the eternal Healer, asking God to intervene. After the prayer, Marty checked his hand. The warts were still there — oily, but there. He thanked the priest and went home.

The next morning Marty awoke and realized that he no longer felt pain under his nails. Glancing at his right hand, he was disappointed because it was still covered with the curse. Then he looked more closely. The two warts under his fingernails were gone! Marty decided to wait and see what would happen.

Within a week all the warts were gone.

That was more than fifteen years ago. Although his brother has continued to have wart problems for more than thirty years, Marty reports, "I've never had a wart since."

43

Sweet Reunion

One look at the three sisters on the stage and you're tempted to think, *These girls have it all.* Watching them perform as the Christian R&B group Out of Eden, it is clear why so many fans have shown up to see the talented women Lisa Bragg, Andrea Kimmey, and Danielle Kimmey.

What isn't so obvious, however, is that these sisters grew up for many years without a dad. As often happens, their parents divorced when the sisters were young, and the girls lost contact with their father for more than ten years.

Yet Lisa, Andrea, and Danielle wanted to renew that relationship — to be a part of their father's life again — even though they knew he eventually remarried and had other children. In the silence of their hearts, each sister prayed that God would somehow bring Dad back into their lives.

When the sisters reached their teenage years, their musical talent sparkled. By 1994 they were signed to a recording contract; they performed worldwide while touring with the Christian group dc Talk. It was then God began to answer their silent prayers.

During the tour, Lisa — the oldest sister — discovered that her father was living in California. With the help of her father's new wife and daughter, Lisa orchestrated a surprise Christmas visit to reintroduce herself to her dad.

Of that happy meeting, Lisa says, "He was crying. . . . It was really awesome." Father and daughter hugged and laughed and spent time getting to know each other once more. Lisa knew she had to share this joy with her sisters. Since she was engaged to be married, she invited her dad to attend her wedding the following September in 1996. "He came to my wedding and gave me away. That's when he and Andrea and Danielle were reunited."

Meeting their dad again was a little nerve-racking at first for Andrea and Danielle. "We met again at Lisa's wedding," Andrea says. "At first I was really nervous and was desperately trying to think of something to say!"

Danielle had much the same experience. "It was pretty weird!" she laughs. "My parents divorced when I was like one or two, and we moved away; so I didn't have any memories of my father."

But it didn't take long for that nervousness to fade. "Now we're making memories," says Danielle, "and the feelings I have are ones of joy, security, and love."

Andrea also feels her dad's love. "After ten years I didn't know what he thought I'd be like, and I didn't want to make a bad impression. But now I see that it doesn't matter to him; I realize he loves me for who I am. . . . I'm so glad that he's in my life."

And it turns out the three sisters weren't the only ones praying for a sweet reunion. Lisa reveals, "It's a blessing [for us] because now we talk and everything. He's there for me; we all know he's there for us.

"It's [also] a blessing for him to see what God has done in our lives, and through that be drawn closer to God. He's always prayed for us to be back together. It was like an answer to his prayer."

44

Cutting the Lifeline

Twenty-nine-year-old Sigmund Brouwer stared at the cover of *National Racquetball*. As an editor for the magazine, he felt that the cover represented his livelihood.

As a bachelor living in Red Deer, Alberta, Canada, Sigmund was able to keep his living expenses low. But the thought of leaving his steady income disquieted him. It was nice to get paid regularly, to buy groceries regularly, and to pay the electric bill regularly.

Still, Sigmund was having that thought again. He was thinking about leaving his career as a magazine editor to pursue what he really wanted to do: write books. And the first book he wanted to write was a mystery for teenagers. He wanted to write a whole series of mysteries for kids. Unfortunately, no publisher had agreed with Sigmund yet. Nobody wanted his books.

Sigmund felt he had to make a decision. He had to choose between a safe career at *National Racquetball* and the risky life of a freelance writer — knowing he was an unproven writer to most publishers. Deep inside, though, he knew the choice had already been made. He had to try to follow his dream; it was now or never. He knew he'd be discontented in his "safe" career at *National Racquetball*.

Summoning his courage, Sigmund resigned from the magazine staff and walked out the door without knowing where he would go from there. He only knew that he wanted to be a writer.

Fortunately, Sigmund didn't have to navigate the world of publishing alone. He turned to his most faithful friend and helper, God. He prayed constantly that first month out, asking God to provide and to lead. Praying for strength and courage to pursue his dream, he asked God to bless his determination to write books that would glorify God.

He wrote letters to publishers, encouraging them to take a chance on this new, young talent in Christian publishing. Two weeks passed without a response.

Sigmund swallowed hard, prayed some more, and kept working. Three weeks passed, then four. Finally, after a month on his own, he got the call he'd been waiting for. Victor Books wanted his youth mystery series!

Victor would publish it under the title The Accidental Detectives. They published ten books in that series — and sold about a quarter of a million copies! Sigmund Brouwer had found his answer to prayer, and it was the start of his writing career.

Since then he's written over two dozen books for youth and adults. Many have reached the best-seller status. He's also started the Young Writer's Institute, an organization dedicated to helping kids age nine to fourteen pursue their own dreams of writing.

Interestingly enough, God used Sigmund's career as a writer to answer another of his prayers — a prayer for a godly wife. When his first adult novel, *Double Helix*, came out, his publisher lined up Christian musician Cindy Morgan to perform a reading from the book with Sigmund at a bookseller's convention. The two hit it off and soon had a budding romance. Less than two years later, they were married and enjoying each other's company.

45

Not Just a Fairy Tale

Terry Noss is the vice president of production for Hollywood's Rich Animation Studios. He is the coproducer of the successful animated feature *The Swan Princess* and its critically acclaimed sequels. You can see a caricature of Terry Noss in *The Swan Princess*.

"Our artists caricatured both coproducers," Noss chuckles. "Freeze-frame at the very end of the movie when [lead character] Derek and [heroine] Odette have just been married and they're coming out the door. We're the footmen! I'm the one with the mustache."

Terry Noss does not keep his Christianity a secret. People know he is working hard to create wholesome, family-friendly feature films for mainstream audiences. Terry cannot be quiet about his whole life being a miracle and an answer to prayer.

He was never an exceptionally healthy child anyway. A tonsillectomy came when he was seven, appendicitis when he was nine. At age eleven, he began to notice aching in his joints. This aching only got worse.

At first doctors thought it was just growing

pains, but the pain became so severe in his knees and ankles that he often felt like collapsing. Terry went in and out of hospitals as he was tested for polio and other illnesses. The doctors were eventually able to diagnose the problem: rheumatic fever.

Having such a critical illness seemed like torture to Terry, just now entering junior high. For the next two years Terry spent most of his life in a hospital bed donated to his family. He was unable to attend school, so private tutors had to come to his home to help him learn what other kids his age were learning in school.

One night when Terry was twelve, his family hosted a Bible study with families from their church. People streamed into the Noss home. Children ran around and played. Laughter was heard throughout the house.

After everyone left, Terry broke down in tears. Seeing and hearing all those healthy children enjoying a normal life pained him. He longed to jump out of his bed and go play with the others, but he couldn't do it. Seeing a glimpse of what he was missing overwhelmed him, and the boy was left sobbing in his parents' arms.

That night Terry pleaded with Jesus, "God, please. Heal me!"

When family friends from the Nosses' church heard about Terry's despair, they requested that Terry's parents bring him to church for prayer. To be sure, members of the church had already been praying for Terry for more than a year, but this time they felt Terry should come to the church for prayer.

The boy's parents agreed, bringing him the next time they went. Following the biblical instructions, they brought Terry before the elders and the deacons of the church, who placed their hands on him and prayed for his healing.

Terry didn't notice change right away. A few days later Terry noticed the pain in his joints lessening. It was still there, but with a marked difference. Could the healing have begun?

Because rheumatic fever can damage the heart, Terry's doctors scheduled a test to check the boy's condition. But even before the tests, Terry could feel the strength returning to his limbs. The chronic pain he'd felt for two years was ebbing away like water from a storm.

The time came for the tests, and the doctors were surprised. Terry's heart tested normal — no damage at all! A few months later Terry was granted permission to return to school. His disease was inexplicably gone!

It's been thirty years since that healing took place, and Terry gratefully reports no more trouble with rheumatic fever or heart problems. The boy is a now a man, investing anew in the lives of children by creating wholesome family entertainment that even a bedridden junior higher would enjoy.

Asked about it today, Terry points to that prayer at the church altar as the turning point in his illness. "It was at that point that the healing really was triggered."

46

Hey, God, Can I Hitch a Ride?

Norm Wakefield sighed as another car whizzed past him on the open freeway. He adjusted his backpack and stuck out his thumb for the next car, hoping to hitch a ride back to Westmont College in Santa Barbara, California. He tried to smile and appear friendly to passing drivers — then couldn't help frowning again as yet another motorist zipped by without a thought.

It was 1961, and twenty-six-year-old Norm realized that hitchhiking wasn't working. He'd been on that road for about forty-five minutes already, waiting, hoping, and praying for a ride. As Norm prayed, he got a strong feeling that this wasn't what God had planned for him this day.

Norm paused and thought about his remarkable summer thus far. As a student at Westmont, he had finished the school year with one hundred dollars still owed on his account. Around that time, he'd also been offered a summer job as assistant director of a camp for teenagers. The problem was that the camp was located in southwestern Virginia — literally a continent away from his school. The camp couldn't pay much

169

for Norm's work. He'd do well just to break even at summer's end.

Several of his friends advised him to stay in California and earn money to pay his school bill. Still, as Norm prayed about the decision, he sensed God leading him to Virginia to spend his summer ministering to teenagers. So he left California, trusting God to provide the one hundred dollars needed to pay off what he owed.

About six weeks into the summer — unknown to Norm — several of his high schoolers took up a collection to pay off his school fees. God had used them to meet Norm's need. As an extra blessing, another person had donated a one-way bus ticket for Norm to visit his brother in New York when the camp ended.

Norm knew that God could be trusted to meet his needs. Right now, though, what Norm needed most was an all-expense-paid ride back to California — and he wasn't going to get it standing out here on this New York freeway.

Gathering up his bags, Norm prayed quietly as he trudged back to his brother's home in Buffalo. He asked Jesus to lead him and to provide the way for him to get back to school. He also confessed to God that even if he did get back to Westmont, he still didn't have the money to pay the upcoming semester's tuition and fees!

When Norm arrived at his brother's house, he explained that he had prayed and felt that God had another way for him to return to school. Just then a neighbor interrupted, "There's an ad in the paper for a company that needs a car to be driven out to California. Maybe you should call."

Norm called. The company had a car that needed to be delivered to a place about ninety miles away from Westmont College. Norm volunteered, then gathered his things once more and headed to the car owner's office. Along the way, he prayed about another detail — gas money! Although Norm now had a car that could take him across the continent, he still didn't have any money to fuel the trip.

Norm stood in the office of the company's manager, receiving instructions for his journey — and still wondering to himself what to do about gas money. As they were talking, the manager's phone rang. On the other end were two men who needed a ride to Los Angeles — and who were willing to pay all the expenses for the trip! Norm silently thanked Jesus for his wonderful provision and quickly agreed to take on these new passengers.

A few days later Norm walked onto the campus of Westmont College, happy to have made it back in time to attend his classes. Then he discovered that while God was answering his prayers for transportation on the East Coast, he had also been busy answering his prayers on the West Coast.

Norm reports, "When I got back to school, I was surprised to find that I had a full-tuition scholarship waiting for me that would pay for the remainder of my schooling!"

He smiles when remembering the way God answered those prayers of a student back in 1961. "You'd better believe there was a lot of prayer and thanks for God's care. It was probably the greatest faith-building experience of my life."

47

Stranded!

It seemed like a perfect beginning for a tragic ending. Two young women, on summer break from college, were stranded along the freeway running through the southern California desert. Only an hour from midnight, Amy Wakefield could almost picture the newspaper headlines: "Coeds Abducted! College Girls Leave for California, Disappear on the Way! Murdered Women Found Only Yards Away from Broken-Down Car!"

Amy shivered involuntarily and turned to her friend and driver. "Exactly where are we, Lori?"

"I'm not sure. I wasn't really paying attention to the signs."

Amy sighed. After spending the school year studying at Arizona College of the Bible in Phoenix, she was headed up to Washington State for a much-needed vacation at Lori's home. Climbing into Lori's Mustang, the two girls had planned to go from Arizona west to California, then north to Washington.

They sat by the side of the road wondering what they should do next. A few moments ago the car had emitted a loud clunk; the engine had quit, leaving Amy and Lori to coast to the side of the freeway. They were stranded and afraid.

The girls had heard enough horror stories about stranded motorists who were robbed or beaten by criminals who pretended they were stopping to help. Still, what other choice did they have but to try to flag someone down for a ride?

Before they did anything else, the girls decided to pray. Sitting in the vehicle in the middle of the night, they asked their Father in heaven to help and protect them in this crisis. Comforted some by the prayer, they got out of the car, raised the hood to signal distress, then returned to their seats, waving a T-shirt flag out the window to try and capture other drivers' attention.

One car flew past, then another. Semitrailer trucks rumbled by without so much as slowing down. The girls wondered if they'd be stuck out there in the desert all night.

Finally, around 11:30 P.M., the highway grew quiet. Amy and Lori sat in the car, waiting. Suddenly a light shone through the passenger window. Amy stifled a scream. A gruff male voice asked, "What's the problem?"

A man was standing outside the car shining a flashlight inside. Apparently he'd stopped his car up the road a bit and walked back. Since it was night and the hood was up, neither Amy nor Lori had seen him approach.

Amy started to respond to the stranger, then noticed a flicker from the flashlight bounce off the man's glasses. She also realized that she recognized the voice!

"Dave? Dave Mielke? Is that you?"

"Well, yes." Then he looked more closely into the car and suddenly relaxed and smiled. "Amy Wakefield! What are you doing out here at this hour?"

Dave had been one of Amy's instructors at Arizona College of the Bible. He was traveling with his wife to California that night when he saw the broken-down Mustang. Having heard his own horror stories about would-be good Samaritans abused by crooks who posed as distressed motorists, he was reluctant to stop and help — especially at this time of night! But as he drove past the car, he felt a strong compulsion to stop. It was as if God himself was ordering Dave to return and help. So, unsure of the outcome, he pulled off the road and trekked about one hundred yards back to where Amy and Lori waited.

The Bible teacher and his wife drove Amy and Lori to the next town, Indio, California. He helped the girls get the Mustang towed to a garage and made sure they were safe in a motel before he left them.

Amy now says of the experience, "Of all the people who could have stopped on the road that night, God sent an angel named Dave Mielke — someone I trusted and who cared about me — as an answer to my prayer. Isn't that cool?"

48

Lost and Found

The security guard standing in front of the bank's glass-enclosed night depository was both polite and firm. "I'm sorry, ma'am. The night deposit is jammed and not accepting any envelopes."

Zahea (pronounced Zuh-HAY-ya) Nappa received the news with a worried frown. It was 1991, and she had traveled by bus and subway from her work in Virginia to her bank in Washington, D.C., to deposit her paycheck. Having just recently moved to Virginia from D.C., she hadn't gotten around to switching banks yet. Thus, every payday she made this trek to the night depository to replenish her checking account.

But not this Friday. With the deposit jammed, how would she deposit her money? The thought of making this trip again tomorrow Monday wasn't a pleasant one. Plus, wasn't her bus coming down the street? She didn't to miss that. . . .

"If you'd like, ma'am," the security guard offered kindly, "I'll take your check inside the bank tomorrow morning when I come to work

He seemed so trustworthy and customer-friendly that Zahea agreed, handing over her endorsed paycheck and deposit slip with grateful thanks. Then she ran to catch the bus home for a restful weekend.

Saturday morning Zahea began to doubt the wisdom of giving her paycheck to a complete stranger. She called the bank just to make sure the friendly guard had deposited it — and was informed that no deposit had been made. The "guard" had been nothing more than a con man, stealing deposits from unsuspecting customers by passing himself off as an employee of the bank!

Zahea felt sick. She felt so foolish that she didn't even report the robbery, determining to try to scrimp her way to the next payday without her money.

Back at work the next week, a coworker named Chuck noticed Zahea skipping lunch and being particularly frugal — something a bit out of character for her. Out of compassion, Chuck asked, "Zahea, are you short of money for some reason?"

Since he was both a Christian and a friend, Zahea confessed her error over the weekend. Chuck responded by suggesting that they pray, right there and then. They asked God to somehow, someway restore the money that had been lost. Encouraged, they both went back to work.

Zahea made it through the next several days, a

bit thinner and a bit wiser for her recent experience. As the weekend approached, she began to make preparations to celebrate the upcoming Easter holiday at her church.

As she left the office to head home, Chuck stopped her at the door. "I have an Easter card for you."

"Thank you, Chuck." Zahea took the envelope and turned once again to leave. Chuck stopped her once more.

"Aren't you going to read your card?" Zahea promptly opened the card to read the sentiment her friend had noted inside.

What she found was the exact amount of money that had been stolen from her Zahea was stunned and surprised. "Is this a loan?"

Chuck shook his head and grinned, explaining that many people had contributed to the restoration of her lost wages — but he refused to reveal their names. Zahea could only assume it was some of her coworkers who cared enough to share from their own paychecks to make up for hers. God had answered the prayer she and Chuck had prayed just days earlier in that same office building. Zahea thanked God for answering her prayer.

"I have often heard that God protects children and fools. God certainly protected this fool, and he restored my lost wages through the charity of others during the Easter season!"

49

Post-Op (Mike's Story)

Something was trying to kill me. I could feel it in my gut.

This was supposed to be a simple operation. Though only thirty-three years old, my gallbladder had become so diseased it resembled an old man's and was causing me great pain, making it impossible for me to eat. The surgeon recommended the standard treatment: remove the gallbladder.

I agreed, eager to be rid of the malfunctioning organ. Two days after Christmas in 1996, I entered the hospital for a routine surgery. The anesthesiologist administered the anesthesia, and I was soon ushered into a dark and dreamless sleep.

Ouch! Something was wrong. I couldn't open my eyes or move a muscle, but I could *feel* someone tearing inside my stomach. The pain was unbearable, but I couldn't scream. Had I awakened before the surgery was over? I managed a weak thought. *Help me, Lord.* . . . Moments later I welcomed the darkness that swirled back into my consciousness.

The next time I awoke I knew the surgery was

over because I opened my eyes and saw myself in the recovery room. The pain in my stomach, where the surgery had been performed, was overwhelming. I groaned and immediately tried to sit up, not caring that the two nurses near me were trying to hold me down. *This isn't supposed to hurt this much!* I thought. *Something is wrong.*

Apparently I was too strong for my two helpers. The nurse in charge quickly sent the other running to get help to hold me down. I was dangerously close to ripping the IV out of my arm and could possibly tear the fresh stitches in my stomach.

I knew I needed to relax, ignore the pain, and lie back down, but I wasn't strong enough to do it myself. I grabbed on to the metal bar of my bed and became aware of the one nurse left behind still trying to calm me down.

"Pray for me," I croaked to her. Then I demanded it. "Somebody pray for me!"

"OK, OK, Just lie —"

"Pray for me!"

"OK." She took a deep breath and placed her hand on my arm. "Heavenly Father . . ."

As soon as she spoke that name, a sense of peace flooded through me, starting at my head and trickling all the way down to my toes. I felt the Holy Spirit saying, "I'm here. No matter what happens, I'm here."

I watched my hand relax its grip on the bar. I still felt pain, but I was in control of my body once more. Slowly, I lay back onto the gurney. The nurse kept praying. To be honest, I don't know what she said, but I watched her lips move as she continued praying for me.

"Read to me," I said. "From the Bible. Read to me." More medical staff arrived and were beginning to surround me.

"Get me a Bible," the nurse commanded. I saw someone pass a book into her open hand. She flipped it open, paging through to find what she wanted. Then she began to read, " 'The Lord is my Shepherd, I shall not want. . . .' "

I closed my eyes. The merciful darkness soon came swirling back into my mind. *Thank you, Lord,* I whispered to myself. Then I slept.

When I woke again later, all was calm. I was sore and weak, but the agonizing pain had been dulled by pain medication. I was in a private room, now. My wife sat next to me, pale faced.

"You had a rough time in there," she said. "I was really afraid for you."

So was I, I thought. *So was I.*

My operation had had complications. While removing my gallbladder, the surgeon had accidentally spilled scores of gallstones inside my body. He had carefully removed each stone, but that added task had apparently triggered unexpected pain for me.

As I write these words, I still feel the effects of that operation, my body never having fully adjusted to the absence of a gallbladder. I am grateful for that nurse — a woman who, at my point of great need, was willing to pray for me — and for my Father, who paused to answer her prayer.

50

My Only Prayer

My fellow writer, Lee Maynard, has told a story of his own experience with prayer so eloquently, I thought it best for him to relate it to you in his own words:

We are hunkered down at the base of a rock overhang, the summit far above us, watching the rain fall softly. We are tired from climbing and running from the rain.

My eleven-year-old grandson, Tristan, is with me. He knows about Martian landings and cyberspace, and just when you think that's all he is — an interesting child of a technological age — he names the Greek gods and tells how the citizens prayed to them.

"Maybe we should pray for a way out of here," I say, watching the rain grow heavier.

"Does prayer really work?" he asks. "Would it really get us out of here?"

I think carefully about what to say next . . . for I am not a prayerful man.

I have had my share of hurts and pains in the wilderness. The stings of scorpions. The snapping of bones. Dehydration so severe my eyes stung. But I never prayed over any of that. I always thought that if I put myself into those places, it was up to me to get out. God probably wasn't interested.

Prayer, I have always thought, was the thing you saved for last. But every time I got to the last, there was no time for praying. And when it was over, all I could do was wonder that I was still alive.

And so I never prayed. Except once.

It was 1978. In the early hours, when the tops of trees were still lost in darkness, I parked my truck and stepped into New Mexico's Gila Wilderness. My plan was to hike to 20 miles in, then join up with a group of nine Outward Bound School students and their instructors, a "patrol." I was the school director, and I was worried about this patrol: three New England preppies, a college freshman, three high school graduates from Dallas, and two South Chicago street kids who had been sentenced to Outward Bound in lieu of jail.

I looked forward to hiking in the Gila. Even after half a lifetime spent outdoors, I couldn't seem to see it enough. But it was midsummer, and the sun's heat poured down relentlessly. At midday I stopped, drank some water, and for the first time noticed the heat in my boots.

The boots were not new. I had worn them for some weeks and thought they were ready for the Gila. I was wrong.

I tried everything for relief: stopped and aired my feet, put on extra socks, quickened my pace, slowed my pace, tightened the laces, applied moleskin. Nothing worked.

I reached camp in the middle of the evening meal, took off my boots and socks, and padded around on the soft forest floor. I inspected my feet and counted eleven blisters, near blisters, and hot spots. Still, I told no one about my problem.

We sat and talked for hours. After two weeks in the wilderness, only one student, a New Englander, seemed disenchanted with the course. He had tried to quit but had been talked out of it by the staff.

In the morning, the New Englander was gone. He had left hours before, thrashing back down the trail I'd come in on. We couldn't just let him go into the unforgiving wilderness. Since I was the extra man, I put on the devil boots and went after him.

I soon realized I wasn't just limping anymore — I was walking as though barefoot on hot glass. As I shuffled and stumbled, I tried to keep my mind above my ankles. Again, nothing worked.

A new sound sucked its way into my consciousness, and I realized it was coming from my boots. I sat on a fallen tree, held my feet out in front of me, and looked at the crimson oozing from the eyelets. If I took the boots off, I would never get them on again.

Eventually the trail came out of the brush and straight into the Gila River, flowing down from the high country through shaded canyons. By the time it got to me, this narrow, shallow river was still icy, and I couldn't wait to feel it against my baking feet. But when the water poured into my boots, the burning sensation was replaced with a thousand stabs that seemed to puncture every blister.

My scream cut through the canyon, and I went face forward into the water. Then I got up and staggered across the river.

Since there was no rational solution to my problem, my mind began to create irrational ones. The answer, obviously, was . . . a horse. If I just had a horse, my feet would no longer be a problem, and I could catch the New Englander.

Like King Richard III, I began to implore, "Give me another horse! Have mercy!" What was the next word? Oh yes. "Jesu."

I knew I had only another hundred paces or so in me, and then I would stop, sit, and wait. I'd probably see no one for days.

The sun was low against my back, and my shadow reached far down the stony trail. I would never get to the end of my shadow. And then I stopped.

The right shoulder of my shadow moved, a bulging darkness down on the trail. A huge mass, motionless now, blocked most of the low sun, an elongated head bobbing up in attention to my presence.

It was a horse. A ghost born of pain.

God, I thought, *the mind is an amazing thing.* It was a beautiful ghost, but I would have to make it go away. So I confronted it directly, dragging myself right up to the horse and grabbing its halter.

It was a real horse.

The animal had a halter and a lead rope but no saddle. Something was going on here that I didn't understand, but I was not going to question it. I gathered up the lead rope and struggled onto the horse's back. "A horse, a horse," I mumbled as it calmly carried me down the trail and into the falling darkness. "Jesu."

The horse walked through the night and did not stop until we got to the trail head, where I found the New Englander sitting on the bumper of my truck. I took off the hated boots, bandaged my feet, and hobbled the horse in a patch of grass. The New Englander and I slept nearby.

At first light two wranglers showed up looking for the horse. They said it had never wandered off before and didn't know why it did this time. They said the horse's name was King.

The rain turns to sleet, and I think maybe Tristan and I will have to sleep out the storm on a mountain where there are no horses. He leans against me, and he is smiling.

"Did you really pray?" he asks. "For a horse?"

"Well . . . I was a little out of it. Mumbling. I'm not sure anything I said would qualify as a prayer."

"I think you did pray," he says. "And you got what you prayed for, and it scared you." As usual, he's gotten to the heart of the matter.

The sleet disappears, and a thick mist suffuses the mountain. But behind the mist is a bright light, glowing first silver, and then gold.

"I did, didn't I?" I admit. "I *did* pray."

We leave the overhang and start down the mountain, the air thick with the nectar of after-storm. It is one of the best days of my life.

Prayer still mystifies me. Maybe I shouldn't save it for last.

Epilogue

I'd be remiss if I ended this book any other way than to allow you an opportunity to add a fifty-first story — *your* prayer story.

Perhaps as you've read through these pages, God's Spirit began speaking to you, calling you, telling you as he told Lee Maynard that prayer is not something to save for a last resort.

Perhaps it's time for you to pray that prayer that God will always answer — the prayer of a sinner asking forgiveness.

The message is simple. All of us — you included — have done wrong. The Bible calls that sin and tells us that the penalty of sin is eternal death. That's the bad news.

The good news is that God sent his Son, Jesus Christ, to pay the penalty of sin. Jesus gave his life, suffering and dying on a cross, to pay that penalty. And then to show that he was more powerful than sin and death, Jesus came back from the dead, resurrected and bringing an offer of eternal life to all who would believe. He offers that life to you.

Listen to how the Bible describes this:

For all have sinned; all fall short of God's glorious standard. (Romans 3:23)

The wages of sin is death, but the free gift

191

of God is eternal life through Christ Jesus our Lord. (Romans 6:23)

For if you confess with your mouth that Jesus is Lord and believe in your heart that God raised him from the dead, you will be saved. For it is by believing in your heart that you are made right with God, and it is by confessing with your mouth that you are saved. As the Scriptures tell us, "Anyone who believes in him will not be disappointed." (Romans 10:9-11)

And so now we are back to you. Would you like to experience the salvation that God offers you? If so, it's only a prayer away.

Open your heart to Jesus right now. Pray to him, and ask him to forgive the failings of your past, to erase the penalty of your sin. Ask him to fill you with his Holy Spirit, to make it possible for you to follow him for the rest of your life — and beyond. Why not do it now?

After you have prayed, please contact a church near you, and let someone know about it. Tell the folks there that you have just given your life to Jesus and would like help to learn more about following him.

And if you think of it, let me know about your prayer, too. I'd love to hear from you. You can email me at

Nappaland@aol.com

I look forward to hearing from you soon.